Back to the Drawing Board

Do not leave anything undone in the attempt to eliminate legalized crime. . . . Every person of good will must feel called to mobilize for this great cause, and must be sustained by the conviction that every step taken in defense of the right to life and in the concrete promotion of it is a step toward peace and civility.

Pope John Paul II, on the fifth anniversary of his encyclical, *Evangelium Vitae* (The Gospel of Life).

Back to the Drawing Board
The Future of the Pro-Life Movement

Edited by Teresa R. Wagner

ST. AUGUSTINE'S PRESS
South Bend, Indiana
2003

Manufactured in the United States of America.

1 2 3 4 5 6   09 08 07 06 05 04 03

Library of Congress Cataloging in Publication Data
    Back to the drawing board: the future of the pro-life
      movement / edited by Teresa R. Wagner.
        p. cm.
    Includes bibliographical references.
    ISBN 1-58731-060-0 (pbk.: alk. paper)
    1. Pro-life movement – United States. 2. Abortion – United
    States. I. Wagner, Teresa R., 1964–
  HQ767.5.U5B32 2003
  363.46'0973 – dc21   2002154986

∞ *The paper used in this publication meets the minimum requirements of the American National Standard for Information Sciences - Permanence of Paper for Printed Materials, ANSI Z39.48-1984.*

TABLE OF CONTENTS

Part III: Politics and the Movement

Part IV: Religion

Part V: The Culture

Part VI: The Future

Acknowledgments

First, I would like to thank all the writers on this project. Obviously this book would not exist without their timely work, their constant cooperation and their ability to put up with me.

I must also thank my many unofficial advisors – that is, family members. I am especially grateful to Mom and Dad, Mark, Joe and Caroline, and Michael, who listened and counseled, and then listened again.

I am indebted to my neighbor, Cherie Harding, who watched the kids on several occasions – sometimes on very short notice – so I could make or take a call. Cherie is the mother of eight and is a shining example to me of how one welcomes children. Thanks also to Diane Mosimann and Dick and Deirdre Pennefather, who helped in similar fashion at critical moments.

Lastly is the immeasurable gratitude to my dear husband, Frank, who gave his time (in such demand by so many) and support for this book from the start, and to our beautiful children, Francis Joseph, John Clifford, and Audrey Maria, who would inspire anyone to be pro-life.

Editor's Preface
Thirty Years After Roe: *What Now?*

It would be both untrue and overly dramatic to say that the pro-life movement has lost. But we are not winning. And the sooner we face it, the sooner we change it.

This does not diminish the importance of the many significant victories along the way. The movement is responsible for countless, common-sense measures that help protect women and children from the abortion tragedy: informed consent requirements for mothers, parental involvement mandates for minors, and statistical reporting laws in some states. Though data on abortion are notoriously sketchy, reported numbers in recent years are also down, and polls have shown a decided shift in public opinion toward protecting the child *in utero* when possible. The movement deserves credit.

Still, thirty years after *Roe v. Wade*, the fundamentals of the "big picture" have not changed. That Supreme Court decision, which effectively legalized abortion for any reason and at any point in pregnancy ("abortion-on-demand"), still stands and continues to authorize the violent destruction of the smallest members of our human family on a massive scale. And recent opinions of that Court stubbornly cling to that ruling.

In the summer of 2000, for example, the U.S. Supreme Court decided *Stenberg v. Carhart*. At issue was a Nebraska law banning a particular abortion method, known legally as "partial-birth abortion." The technique is especially gruesome, even horrific: The abortionist delivers the baby feet first up to the neck, stabs the skull's base, inserts a catheter, suctions out the brain, collapses the head, and delivers an obviously dead baby. That such a practice had even developed demonstrated how inhumane the abortion trade had become.

But the American people are not inhumane, and in a rare showing of consensus, they moved to stop the practice. Within just a few years of the method becoming public, as many as thirty states had acted to outlaw it, many in record time, and at least three (New Jersey, Florida and Alaska) over gubernatorial vetoes. The United States Congress reacted similarly, with several veto-proof votes in the House (but not in the Senate) to ban the procedure.

And then the Supreme Court was tasked with evaluating Nebraska's law. No one should have been surprised that the Court struck it down as unconstitutional, siding with the abortionists, who insisted the procedure was necessary to preserve women's health. For in so doing, the Court mimicked the reasoning and outcomes of almost twenty lower court opinions.

Stenberg is simply the most recent and dramatic example of what is now the tired abortion story in our country: Courts, rather than people, decide our abortion policy and practice, under the pretext that the issue is "constitutional," though all honest and informed people know it is not. Abortion advocates lose in the legislatures, where the will of the people is best expressed and where pro-life laws can be passed. But they take their case to the courts, where judges, groomed in abortion-sympathetic law schools and bar associations, and schooled in *Roe*-based jurisprudence, do their bidding.

This, for thirty years.

But *Stenberg* was new in one respect. Before the summer of 2000, legal abortion concerned *in utero* killing; now, the Supreme Court has extended the abortion license to *ex utero* killing. This can only be classified as a backward step. For this reason, the decision should have prompted serious soul-searching on the part of the country's pro-life leaders. But it never happened.

Until now.

This book is an unprecedented collection of thoughtful and sometimes painfully honest evaluations of our cause. It is an invitation for all concerned to stop, and think critically about our record. We go "back to the drawing board" to understand – not repudiate – this record, and help shape the one to come.

Contributing writers include those who know the movement best: its leaders. They are statesmen, scholars, doctors, lawyers, judges, activists, and mothers. They are Evangelical Christian, Muslim, Atheist, Jewish, and Catholic. They are men and women, young and old, liberal and conservative, Democrat and Republican – and third party. Many are veterans, some are new; but all have labored in the effort, and care about its outcome.

But the book is not for them. It is said that a new generation begins every fifteen years. Therefore, we have seen the start of at least two generations in the thirty years since *Roe*, and the years to come will see, of course, yet more. These generations, themselves spared abortion, must now carry the torch, and fight this fight. This book is for *them*.

They will learn from these pages of the movement's pioneers and foot soldiers. They will understand the movement's history and predicament. They will read tributes and critiques. But most important, they will see a great variety of views – indeed, disagreements – not just about our past, but about future.

And they will need to answer: What now?

Teresa R. Wagner
Fall 2002

Foreword

According to most social scientists and analysts of culture, there should never have been a pro-life movement – never mind a movement persistent and strong enough to keep abortion at the center of our public life. They did not understand that those who signed up with the movement were less enlisting than enlisted, less choosing than chosen.

Has there ever been in the annals of history a movement for which so many have given so much, with no personal stake in the outcome, other than knowing that they did the right thing? If so, I am not aware of it.

This remarkable book is by and about the pioneers of the pro-life movement, and also by and about the successor generations who will, please God, carry the cause through to victory. The pro-life movement of the twentieth century laid the foundations for the pro-life movement of the twenty-first century, and of however many more centuries it takes. Back in the 1960s, when we raised the alarm about what was then called the movement for "liberalized abortion law," we knew that we had signed on for the duration.

Perhaps in ten or twenty years, people will look back in revulsion and disbelief at the decades of unbridled killing legally licensed by *Roe* v. *Wade*. Perhaps it will take much longer than that. Meanwhile, the encroaching storms of the culture of death threaten new horrors in the form of euthanasia, cloning, eugenics, and genetic engineering. It is not alarmist – but rather an indisputably alarming fact that at stake is the very future of what it means to be a human being. Historical developments are too often and too casually described as unprecedented. But this *is* unprecedented.

After thirty years of the regime of *Roe*, it is easy to become discouraged. All those marches, all those mailings, all those articles, all those books, all those pickets, all those counseling sessions, all those rallies, all those arguments over the kitchen table. It is understandable that some say, "Enough already!" While discouragement is understandable, we have not the right and, finally, we have not the reason to despair.

For all that is new and threatening, we know that abortion remains at the heart of the contest for what Pope John Paul II calls the culture of life. We know what our goal is: Every unborn child protected in law and welcomed in life. That goal cannot be achieved fully, for there will always be some abortions, as there will always be adultery, robbery, theft, and rape. But one day, when the regime of *Roe v Wade* is a nightmare past, we will again be a nation constituted by the truth that nobody is a nobody; by the truth that, at the entrance gates and the exit gates of life, and all along the way, no life is expendable. Every human life, destined from eternity for eternity, bears the mark of the Creator and has a claim upon our protection and care.

On January 23, 1973, the media declared that the Supreme Court had "settled" the abortion question. Today, there is no more unsettled question in our public life. That is reason for immeasurable gratitude. At the time, almost every institution of public influence supported the decision of *Roe v Wade*. The predominant powers in the legal and medical professions, the academy, and most of the churches – all declared the matter "settled." The dissenters seemed marginal and hopelessly out of step. According to most social scientists and analysts of culture, there should never have been a pro-life movement – never mind a movement persistent and strong enough to keep abortion at the center of our public life. They did not understand that those who signed up with the movement were less enlisting than enlisted, less choosing than chosen.

And now we are joined by a generation of young people who recognize that this is *the* great human rights cause of our time and theirs. It is for us, but mainly for them, that this book is intended. It is the story of where we have been, what went wrong, and what went right. More importantly, writers who have learned from the hard wisdom of experience lay out the arguments, the analyses, the strategies, and the visions that will carry this cause into the future. The cause of life is irrepressible. It may at times be slowed, but it will never be stopped. It may be dimmed, but it will never be extinguished. And that is because this cause is inseparable from the One of whom it is said, "The light shines in the darkness, and the darkness has not overcome it." The darkness will never overcome it. Never. Never ever.

This century's contest for the culture of life against the culture of death is just beginning. The battles are uncertain. The final outcome is assured.

The Reverend Richard John Neuhaus
Editor in Chief
First Things
New York, New York
October 2002

Introduction

This collection of essays appears thirty years after the U.S. Supreme Court decisions, *Roe v. Wade* and *Doe v. Bolton,* and fulfills the editor's plan of providing a needed opportunity for serious and thoughtful evaluation of the pro-life movement. But it is also an invitation to strategize for the future. These papers – from a variety of activist, pro-life professionals, specialists, religious, and laymen – supply the pro-life movement's ever-present need for factual information, as well as sharply differing opinions on what is to come. No one will fall asleep while reading this book.

If we were dealing with a less-complex endeavor, this Introduction would have been a preview of the chapters to follow. Instead, I prefer to provide a capsule-guide to the pro-life movement to establish some base of understanding for those who have been less immersed in pro-life activity. My perspective is that of one who was there at the conception, birth, growth and maturation of the movement. I have traveled to forty-seven of the fifty states, and have reached the other three by print and electronic means. My perspective is of one who has helped bring together the coalitions that now march under the "pro-life" banner.

*   *   *   *   *

The 1973 U.S. Supreme Court decisions on abortion did not come out of the blue. Margaret Sanger's "Birth Control Movement" had been working in this direction from the 1920s. By the time decisions were handed down in *Roe v. Wade* from Texas and *Doe v.*

Bolton from Georgia, intense legal and legislative activity had been instigated in Alaska, California, Colorado, Florida, Hawaii, Massachusetts, Michigan, New York, North Carolina, Oregon, South Dakota, Virginia, and Washington (listed alphabetically, not by occurrence of incidents). Many who followed the contraception legal battles saw the ominous portent in *Griswold v. Connecticut* in 1965 and *Eisenstadt v. Baird* in 1972 (Commonwealth of Massachusetts), when the U.S. Supreme Court found a "right to privacy" which secured a "right to contraception" and the right of a woman to decide when "to bear or begat a child."

But most were caught off-guard by the cultural and judicial assault on life brought by *Roe* and its subsequent cases. Certainly, the institutions of Church, School, and Home for the most part were unprepared, and did not have the structures in place to make an effective counter-response. Men and women of conscience, whose moral values had been shaped by these institutions, came forward ahead of the institutions themselves, to create the national right-to-life movement whose mission is to defend the right to life of each innocent human being from conception to natural death against abortion, infanticide, and euthanasia.

The situation in my state of Massachusetts is one example. When a resolution was again proposed in 1970 to challenge the American Medical Association's (AMA) founding position against abortion in the House of Delegates – which had just re-confirmed opposition to abortion in 1967 – Dr. Joseph Stanton and Dr. Barbara A. P. Rockett circulated a petition in Massachusetts to arouse physician-opposition to it. (I signed the petition.) The resolution did not condone abortion as such, but it would have accommodated doctors doing abortion under new, loosened state laws who otherwise may have been liable to malpractice actions on ethical violations.1 The AMA capitulation that year gave new ammunition to the abortion-promoters in Massachusetts. To balance the discussion, physicians who had signed the Stanton-Rockett petitions joined with lawyers, nurses, theologians, businessmen, educators, and others to form our first public right-to-life organization, The Value of Life Committee of Massachusetts (VOLCOM). Using the momentum gained from the public response to the AMA action, the abortion-promoters went forward with a non-binding referendum question to repeal the abortion laws of the Commonwealth on the ballots of twenty carefully selected cities and towns. Although ad hoc citizen groups did spring up to fight the question, the abortion-advocates won 55-45 percent. Dr. Stanton and I brought the groups together to form our first citizen-action right-to-life group in our state – Massachusetts Citizens for Life (MCFL). Not winning the referendum did not defeat the group, and the fledgling MCFL decided to incorporate as a permanent organization in the Fall of 1972 and received its certificate of state incorporation ten to fourteen days before the January 22, 1973, U.S. Supreme Court decisions on abortion came down.

Having a structured and working state organization made it possible for Massachusetts to join with other states in founding the National Right to Life Committee (NRLC). When NRLC announced its re-birth as a national citizen-activist organization (different from its origin as an information service of the U.S. Catholic Conference under the auspices of then-Msgr. James McHugh), I had the honor of giving the keynote address that launched it.

The Right-to-Life Movement belongs to no one political party, nor does it hold a monolithic political philosophy. Although often designated as "Conservative," our philosophy of defending the weak against the strong is truly a "Liberal" position. On the national level, pro-lifers fought on both sides of the majority-party aisles. The left wing of the Democratic Party defeated us as we were beginning our political drive in the mid-1970s, and we eventually defeated the Rockefeller wing of the Republican Party to gain control of the Convention-Delegate apparatus which writes the party platforms. We joined the conservative coalitions (although a majority of our grass-roots are neither Conservative nor Republican) because that was the only place we could make coalitions and help elect pro-life President Ronald Reagan in 1980. When a pro-life Republican president sits in the White House, he does so because millions of pro-life Democrats vote to elect him.

The Right-to-Life Movement does not exist to serve the personal ambitions of any given candidate. We work with any qualified pro-life candidate, of any party, who is committed to restoring the legal and constitutional protections to innocent and vulnerable lives that have been stripped away by the U.S. Supreme Court. Political effectiveness depends on numbers, consistency, tenacity, and money. Our best lessons are from our own history: We gained political clout initially by winning elections no one expected us to win. (I will know when we have made the do-or-die political commitment to life when we and our allies have at least one-half as many working federal and state political action committees as our adversaries have.)

The public perception of the Pro-Life Movement since 1981 has been created almost entirely by overt or covert pro-abortion propagandists. A *Los Angeles Times*–commissioned survey in the 1990s found that 85 percent of the major media identify with the pro-abortion position. Barbara R. Nicolosi's essay "Abortion and the Entertainment Industry: The Problem of Selling Half the Story" examines how this plays out in Hollywood.

But an activist who has not read Lawrence Lader's *Breeding Ourselves to Death* or Dr. Bernard Nathanson's *Aborting America* is ill-equipped to bring the pro-life message to the public, whether through movies or through the news. Lader is credited with devising the strategy of portraying the U.S. Catholic Bishops as tyrannical busybodies forcing their views on everyone else, even while most of their parishioners ignored their teaching. Therein lay a contradiction, though he continued to try to characterize opposition to abortion as "Catholic only."

The Right-to-Life Movement does indeed have an impressive presence of Catholics, but biased-media representation simply fails to show those of us who are Methodist or other religions. Our founding numbers include Orthodox Jews and non-observant Jews who describe themselves as "agnostic." In the paper on the Pro-Life Movement and the Jewish Community, Rabbi Daniel Lapin and Adam L. Fuller offer new insights on reasons for attitudes which appear to be contrary to what one would expect of a presumed-to-be-liberal community.

Attempts to deny our numbers notwithstanding, we of the "Pro-Life, Pro-Family Movement" are the largest general movement active in the country today. I am proud to be part of this great movement, and also proud and grateful for the opportunity to write the Introduction for this important book that looks at what has happened in our movement since its beginnings. Every pro-life person in the country should read this book; it should also be read by anyone else who is undecided or uninformed on the life issues.

*   *   *   *   *

As I contemplate our current place in the right-to-life history, I am reminded of a story my mother (a teacher) told me when I was in elementary school. She said it was a tale from India about six blind men and an elephant. I have not yet found a source of the tale in India, but it is attributed to a nineteenth-century American poet, John Godfrey Saxe, as "The Blind Men and the Elephant: A Hindu Fable." All of it is included here:

The Blind Men and the Elephant

It was six men of Indostan
To learning much inclined
Who went to see the Elephant
(Though all of them were blind),
That each by observation
Might satisfy his mind.

The First approached the Elephant,
And happening to fall
Against his broad and sturdy side,
At once began to bawl:
"God bless me! But the Elephant
Is very like a wall!"

The Second, feeling of the tusk,
Cried, "Ho! what have we here
So very round and smooth and sharp?
To me 'tis mighty clear
This wonder of an Elephant
Is very like a spear!"

The Third approached the animal,
And happening to take
The squirming trunk within his hands,
Thus boldly up and spake:
"I see,"quoth he, "the elephant
Is very like a snake!"

The Fourth reached out an eager hand
And felt about the knee
"What most this wondrous beast is like
Is mighty plain" quoth he;
"'Tis clear enough the Elephant
Is very like a tree!"

The Fifth, who chanced to touch the ear,
Said: "E'en the blindest man
Can tell what this resembles most;
Deny the fact who can
This marvel of an Elephant
Is very like a fan!"

The Sixth no sooner had begun
About the beast to grope,
Then, seizing on the swinging tail
That fell within his scope,
"I see,"quoth he, the Elephant
Is very like a rope!"

And so these men of Indostan
Disputed long and loud,
Each in his own opinion
Exceeding stiff and strong,
Though each was partly in the right,
And all were in the wrong!
Moral:

So oft in theologic wars,
The disputants, I ween,
Rail on in utter ignorance

> *Of what each other mean,*
> *And prate about an elephant*
> *Not one of them has seen!*

We, the founding leadership of the Right-to-Life Movement and our successors, are not blind, and we are already acquainted with elephants. We must move on to accomplish our goal of restoring legal protection to innocent and vulnerable lives. Too many are dying in the meanwhile.

Mildred F. Jefferson, M.D.
President, Right to Life Crusade, Inc.
Past President, National Right to Life Committee, Inc.
Former Assistant Clinical Professor of Surgery
Boston University School of Medicine
Boston, Massachusetts
September 30, 2002

Endnote

1   The substitute resolution which was adopted at the 1970 AMA Annual Meeting was considered by many as so much worse that I am including all of it here:

"RESOLVED, that abortion is a medical procedure and should be performed only by a duly licensed physician and surgeon in an accredited hospital acting only after consultation with two other physicians chosen because of their professional competency and in conformance with standards of good medical practice and the Medical Practice Act of his State; and be it further

RESOLVED, that no physician or other professional personnel shall be compelled to perform any act which violates his good medical judgment. Neither physician, hospital, nor hospital personnel shall be required to perform any act violative of personally-held moral principles. In these circumstances, good medical practice requires only that the physician or other professional personnel withdraw from the case so long as the withdrawal is consistent with good medical practice."

Part I

The Legal Arena

Should We Blame the Lawyers?
Charles E. Rice

Can we blame the lawyers for *Roe v. Wade*? Not exactly. A decade prior to *Roe*, one legal and one cultural change made that ruling inevitable. First, the Supreme Court interpreted the First Amendment to require governmental neutrality on the very existence of God.[1] This established an agnostic secularism as the implicitly official religion of the nation. In public schools, for example, moral questions have to be treated without affirmation of the law of God or of objective morality. "By 1961, our public philosophy had become thoroughly positivistic, but a lingering deference to God held matters in check. However, when the state declared its official indifference to God, the dam was breached. Thereafter, the Court would treat such issues as abortion only in secular and wholly amoral terms. Under those rules, the unborn child never had a chance."[2]

The second change in the 1960s came with the marketing of the Pill. Contraception prevents life while abortion kills life. Both, however, involve the deliberate separation of the unitive and procreative aspects of sex. A contraceptive society needs abortion as a failsafe remedy. When, through contraception, man (of both sexes) makes himself the arbiter of when and whether life begins, it is no surprise when, through abortion and euthanasia, he makes himself the arbiter of when it shall end. The issues converge also through the definition of early abortifacients as contraceptives.

Legal Realism: Might makes Right

The legalization of abortion was in accord with the trend of American jurisprudence over the preceding decades. In his classic 1942 article, Francis E. Lucey, S.J., accurately described the legal realism of Oliver Wendell Holmes, which decisively influenced American legal education and jurisprudence: "For [Holmes] the binding force in law is physical force. Might makes right. . . . Holmes saw clearly that the binding force in law had to be either a moral ought or physical force. He would have nothing to do with the moral ought. That meant a God, and all that was against his taste. Man for Holmes was merely a passing ganglion. People put too much importance on human life. . . . This ganglion was something to be used by society, the state, or to be more precise, the dominant group in the state."[3] For Holmes, truth is "the majority vote of the nation that could lick all others."[4]

For decades prior to *Roe*, American legal education had been dominated by a pragmatic positivism. "Only in the past two generations, in my lifetime," wrote Harold Berman, "has the public philosophy of America shifted radically from a religious to a secular theory of law, from a moral to a political or instrumental theory, and from a historical to a pragmatic theory. . . . Rarely does one hear it said that law is a reflection of an objective justice. . . . Usually it is thought to reflect . . . the community sense of what is expedient; and more commonly . . . the more or less arbitrary will of the lawmaker. . . . The triumph of the positivist theory of law – that law is the will of the lawmaker – and the decline of rival theories . . . have contributed to the bewilderment of legal education. Skepticism and relativism are widespread."[5]

A relativist epistemology will generate a jurisprudence of legal positivism, of which the clearest exposition is the "pure theory of law" of Hans Kelsen. He rejected "philosophical absolutism," the view "that there is an absolute reality . . . that exists independently of human knowledge."[6] He espoused "philosophical relativism" which he thought would lead to democracy and tolerance of differing views. "Only if it is not possible," he said, "to decide in an absolute way what is right and what is wrong is it advisable . . . to submit to a compromise."[7] Law, for Kelsen, is a system of coercive "legal norms." A law is valid and binding if it is enacted according to the prescribed procedures. "Any content whatsoever can be legal; there is no human behavior which could not function as the content of a legal norm."[8] "Justice," he said, "is an irrational ideal."[9] Therefore, no law can rationally be criticized as unjust.

Kelsen had the honesty to acknowledge later that under positivist theory "the law under the Nazi government" was valid law.[10] "The legal order of totalitarian states authorizes their government to confine in concentration camps persons whose opinions, religion, or race they do not like; to force them to perform any kind of labor; even to kill them. Such measures may morally be violently condemned; but they cannot be considered as taking place outside the legal order of these states."[11]

Human Beings as Persons or Grapefruits?

How are legal positivism and Kelsen relevant to *Roe v. Wade*? In its 1972 decision upholding New York's permissive abortion law, the highest court of that state found as a fact that the unborn child is a human being "upon conception." But then it cited Kelsen and others for the conclusion that "What is a legal person is for the law . . . to say . . . [U]pon according legal personality to a thing the law affords it the rights and privileges of a legal person (e.g., Kelsen General Theory of Law and State, pp. 93–109. . . .). . . . [I]t is a policy determination whether legal personality should attach and not a question of biological or 'natural' correspondence."[12] The Supreme Court followed this approach in *Roe v. Wade*[13] and *Doe v. Bolton*,[14] which cases did not involve, as did *Byrn*, a lower-court finding of fact that the unborn child is a human being. In *Roe*, the Court declined to decide whether the unborn child is a human being. Instead, it ruled that, whether or not he is a living human being, the unborn child is a nonperson within the meaning of the Fourteenth Amendment. He therefore has no more constitutional rights than a mosquito or a grapefruit.

In a legal system where personhood is the condition for possessing rights, natural justice requires that every human being be regarded as a person. In *Roe*, the Supreme Court said that if the unborn child is a "person," the pro-abortion case "collapses for the fetus' right to life is then guaranteed by the [Fourteenth] Amendment."[15] The Court indicated that if the child were a person, abortion would not be permitted even to save the life of the mother.[16] The principle underlying legalized abortion is the principle that underlay the Nazi extermination of the Jews and other classes, that an innocent human being can be declared to be a nonperson, deprived of his rights and subjected to death at the discretion of others. Thus the Nuremberg Laws of 1935 effectively deprived Jews of personhood by depriving them of citizenship and political rights.[17] The response of the German legal profession to those laws and to each further step that led the nonpersons to the gas chambers was submissive. Even under the earlier Weimar Republic (1919–33), "the greatest obstacle to the recognition of natural law was the doctrine of positivism which assigned to the legislator full discretion as to the . . . content . . . of the law."[18] During the Hitler years, positivism "made German jurists and lawyers defenseless against laws of arbitrary or criminal content."[19]

Lawyers and the Compromising Pro-Life Movement

In Germany, "[t]he newly-united National Socialist regime confronted a weak and vulnerable private bar which capitulated in the face of the Nazi assault."[20] The response of the American legal profession to the legalized execution of the innocent decreed by *Roe* was better, but it was mixed. Pro-abortion elements welcomed *Roe*, and ideological positivists submissively accepted it as the law. Pro-life lawyers opposed *Roe* but quickly divided on strategy. Some initially insisted on a reversal of *Roe* on its essential holding that the unborn child is a nonperson. Others responded with a variant of "Let's Cut a Deal." They advocated compromises to forbid abortion with exceptions for the life or health of the mother, rape, or incest. Or they promoted the states' rights solution, under which each state could decide whether to forbid, permit, or merely restrict abortion. All such compromise solutions, however, affirm the basic nonpersonhood holding of *Roe v. Wade.* If your life is subject to extinction at the discretion of a legislative body or of somebody else, you are a nonperson. If, under the states'-rights approach, each state may decide whether to permit your execution, you have no supervening right to life under the United States Constitution. Even the Justices of the Supreme Court who today are "pro-life" can bring themselves to advocate nothing more than the states'-rights approach.[21] The Court today is 9-0 in support of the basic holding of *Roe* that the unborn child is a nonperson.[22] When compromising pro-life entities talk about the "overruling" of *Roe,* they usually mean the adoption of that nonpersonhood, states'-rights approach. By urging that approach, or seeking incremental restrictions on abortion, they contribute to a perception of the pro-life movement as a political operation that regards the right to life of the unborn as no less negotiable then a highway appropriation.[23]

The strategy of the compromising pro-life movement is primarily a lawyers' work product. It has generated a Gresham's law of politics. Politicians quickly learn that all it takes to get the endorsement of politicized "pro-life" groups is to be marginally better than one's totally pro-abortion opponent. This is seen in the tendency to make a legislator's position on partial-birth abortion the test of "pro-life" certification.

The campaign to prohibit partial-birth abortion (PBA) (a particular method of abortion which kills the child during delivery) raised consciousness as to abortion. But it also certified the moribund state of the compromising pro-life movement. In any civilized, free society, the relevant question is *whether* innocent human beings may be legally executed. The lawyers in the compromising movement have for decades framed the issue, by their advocacy of exceptions, incremental restrictions, and the states'-rights approach, not in terms of *whether* but in terms of *which* innocents may be legally executed. They have led the movement from one fall-back position – one defeat – to another. Because they sold the pass, by themselves adopting the nonpersonhood holding of *Roe,* the political pro-life movement is dead. Now, in their focus on PBA, those leaders have defined the issue not in terms of *whether*, and not even in terms of *which*, innocents may be legal executed, but in terms of *how* the killing is to be done.

The compromising lawyers and Beltway publicists are not exclusively to blame for leading the political pro-life movement into the pits. Space limits preclude discussion here of the Catholic lawyers in Congress who have effectively apostatized through their support of legalized abortion and, in the case of PBA, even infanticide. They ought to be excommunicated, or at least explicitly denounced, by the bishops. But that is not likely to happen, given the current state of the United States hierarchy. The American Catholic Church has been paralyzed by the liberalism of its leaders and their unfounded fear of losing their tax exemption. It is always safe for a timid lawyer to advise a timid bishop *not* to take a stand.

The Judges

What about the response of pro-life judges to *Roe*? No federal judge ever refused to enforce the pre-Civil War fugitive slave laws. The record on abortion over the past three decades in the United States is no better. Gustav Radbruch, the German legal philosopher who renounced positivism during the Hitler regime said that "law is the quest for justice . . . if certain laws deliberately deny this quest for justice (for example, by arbitrarily granting or denying men their human rights) they are null and void; the people are not to obey them, and jurists must find the courage to brand them unlawful."[24] After World War II, courts of the German Federal Republic followed Radbruch's advice and held void various laws of the Nazi regime. As one West German court said, "the positive legislative act . . . loses all obligatory power if it violates the generally recognized principles of international law or the natural law . . . or if the contradiction between positive law and justice reaches such an intolerable degree that the law . . . must give way to justice."[25] In the face of an unjust law, such as a law authorizing the execution of the innocent by abortion, it is not a sound response for a judge merely to recuse himself from the case or resign his position. The problem is not with the judge but with the law. As the German courts said after World War II, when the conflict between an enacted law and justice is "intolerable" or "unendurable," the proper response of a judge is to declare that unjust law void and refuse to enforce it.[26] With very few isolated exceptions, no American judges have taken this sort of stand on *Roe v. Wade.*[27]

Law and Culture

If the past three decades prove anything, it is that the solution to the culture of death symbolized by *Roe* will not be found in law and politics. Unlike the experience in Nazi Germany, voices in all segments of the American bar, including judges and legislators as well as practitioners and academics, have been raised in defense of life. But those defenders of the right to life, regrettably, are a small minority in the profession. Nor is it likely that such will change. Support for legalized murder of the unborn is a canon of the political correctness that dominates the mainstream law schools and the courts. "There seems to be no immediate prospect," Judge Robert Bork accurately predicted in 1990, "that the steady politicization of the law and its institutions will slow, much less be reversed."[28] The legal profession reflects, as well as influences, the prevailing culture.

We can be hopeful, nevertheless, about the future. Because of technology, the law is losing its ability to deal with abortion and euthanasia as practiced. Early abortifacients are making abortion a private matter between the woman and her physician, beyond the effective control of licensing and other legal restrictions. In such cases, how can you prove that an abortion actually occurred? With respect to euthanasia, the Supreme Court, in *Vacco v. Quill,*[29] upheld New York's prohibition of assisted suicide. The Court, however, gave the green light to sedation and other palliative care which can cause death: "Just as a State may prohibit assisting suicide while permitting patients to refuse unwanted lifesaving treatment, it may permit palliative care related to that refusal, which may have the foreseen but unintended 'double effect' of hastening the patient's death."[30] The law is a blunt instrument which will be unable to distinguish, apart from exceptionally clear facts, cases of legitimate sedation or removal of treatment from cases where the physician acted with homicidal intent.

Both abortion and euthanasia, therefore, are moving beyond the reach of the law. This is good because the battle is moving onto our turf – education and conversion – where the pro-life cause is strongest. For the foreseeable future, we will not be able to amend the Constitution or enact effective laws to restore the right to life. But we should maintain the effort to enact such measures, without compromise, as an educational device. Numerous laws can be proposed at the federal and state levels, without compromise of principle, to impede the abortion industry and save lives.[31] And we should refuse to vote for any political candidate for any office who himself favors the legalization of any abortion in any case. The objective is the reconversion of the American people, one by one and family by family, to the conviction that the right of the innocent to live is absolute because it is a gift of God. And it is increasingly evident that the answer to the culture of death will be found in the timeless moral and social teachings of the Catholic Church.

Four decades of law teaching have impressed this writer with the intensity and quality of the students, including Evangelicals, Catholics, and others, who have come to law schools recently to prepare themselves to fight for the Culture of Life. They are a small minority. Except in some schools where they are welcomed and can find intellectual and moral support.[32] Despite the collapse of the political pro-life movement, a bright, aggressive new generation of pro-life lawyers is waging legal guerrilla warfare, in the courts, against every aspect of the culture of death. They save lives of unborn children, among other ways, by protecting against repression of the rights of students and others to voice the true pro-life message in schools, outside abortuaries, and elsewhere. The Thomas More Law Center in Ann Arbor,[33] the International Center for Law & Justice,[34] and the American Center for Law and Justice[35] are examples. The Blackstone Fellowship,[36] a project of the Alliance Defense Fund, intensively trains every summer more than sixty carefully selected law students to prepare them to join this authentic grass-roots legal movement. The National Lawyers

Association[37] is a full-service bar association which offers an alternative to the pro-legalized abortion American Bar Association.

The pro-life movement, with the help of principled lawyers, can use the law to educate the public and to gain breathing space for persons and families to build the culture of life from the ground up. This is a great time for pro-life lawyers to be here. The culture of death is itself dying. It has nothing to offer.

"God is preparing," wrote John Paul II, "a great springtime for Christianity, and we can already see its first signs."[38] "Now is the time," he said on the twenty-fifth anniversary of *Roe v. Wade*, "for recommitment to the building of a culture of absolute respect for life from conception to natural death."[39] We have reason for hope and confidence that members of the legal profession will play an important role in the building of that "culture of absolute respect for life."

Charles Rice is Professor Emeritus at Notre Dame Law School and Visiting Professor at Ave Maria School of Law.

Endnotes

1   See *Torcaso v. Watkins*, 367 U.S. 488 (1961); *Engel v. Vitale*, 370 U.S. 421 (1962); *Abington School District v. Schempp*, 374 U.S. 203 (1963).

2   Charles E. Rice, *Beyond Abortion: The Theory and Practice of the Secular State* (1979), 59–60.

3   Francis E. Lucey, s.j., "Natural Law and American Legal Realism: Their Respective Contributions to a Theory of Law in a Democratic Society," 30 Georgetown L. J. (1942), 493, 497–99.

4   Oliver Wendell Holmes, *The Natural Law: Collected Legal Papers* (1920), 310.

5   Harold Berman, "The Crisis of Legal Education in America," 16 *Boston Coll. L. Rev.* 347, 348 (1985); see also, Roger C. Cramton, "The Ordinary Religion of the Law School Classroom," 28 J. Legal Ed. 247, 262–63 (1978).

6   Hans Kelsen, "Absolutism and Relativism in Philosophy and Politics," 42 Am. Pol. Sci. Rev. 906, 906, (1948).

7   *Ibid.*, 913.

8   Hans Kelsen, "The Pure Theory of Law, Part II," 51 Law Quart. Rev. 517, 517–18 (1935).

9   Hans Kelsen, "The Pure Theory of Law, Part I," 50 Law Quart. Rev. 474, 482 (1934).

10   Hans Kelsen, *Das Naturrecht in der politischen Theorie* (F. M. Schmoelz, ed., 1963), 148, quoted in translation in F. A. Hayek, *Law, Legislation and Liberty* (1976), vol. 2, 56.

11   Hans Kelsen, *Pure Theory of Law* (1967), 40.

12   *Byrn v. New York City Health and Hospitals Corp.*, 31 N.Y.2d 194, 199, 201 (1972), appeal dismissed, 410 U.S. 949 (1973).

13   410 U.S. 113 (1973).

14   410 U.S. 179 (1973).

15   410 U.S. at 156–57.

16   410 U.S. at 157, n. 54.

17   See Hannah Arendt, *Eichmann in Jerusalem* (1964), 39.

18   Ernst von Hippel, "The Role of Natural Law in the Legal Decisions of the German Federal Republic," 4 Natural Law Forum 106, 109 (1959).

19   Heinrich Rommen, "Natural Law in Decisions of the Federal Supreme Court and of the Constitutional Courts in Germany," 4 Nat. L. Forum 1, 1 (1959).

20   Matthew Lippman, "Law, Lawyers, and Legality in the Third Reich: The Perversion of Principle and Professionalism," 11 *Temple Int'l & Comp. L.J.* 199, 211, 225 (1997).

21   See *Planned Parenthood v. Casey*, 505 U.S. 833, 944, 979 (1992) (Opinions of Chief Justice Rehnquist and Justice Scalia, in both of which Justices White and Thomas joined.).

22   *Ibid.*

23   See, for example, *Sojourner T. v. Edwards*, 974 F.2d 27 (5th Cir., 1992), holding unconstitutional the Louisiana law proposed by the Louisiana Catholic bishops and endorsed by the National Right to Life Committee, which prohibited abortion except in cases of life of the mother, rape, and incest. The bishops and NRLC refused to support a true "no exception" bill introduced by Rep. Woody Jenkins. See The Wanderer, June 27, 1991, p. l; N.Y. Times, June 21, 1991, p. A7.

24   Quoted in Ernst von Hippel, "The Role of Natural Law in the Legal Decisions of the German Federal Republic," 4 Natural Law Forum 106, 110 (1959).

25   Heinrich Rommen, "Natural Law in Decisions of the Federal Supreme Court and of the Constitutional Courts in Germany," 4 Natural Forum 1, 11 (1959).

26 See discussion in Charles E. Rice, *50 Questions on the Natural Law* (2d ed. 1999), 115–21; Charles E. Rice, *The Winning Side: Questions on Living the Culture of Life* (2d ed., 2000), 100–104.

27 See Randall J. Hekman, "Judging: By What Standard?" 4 Christian Legal Society Quarterly 19 (1983).

28 Robert Bork, *The Tempting of America* (1990), 349.

29 521 U.S. 793 (1997).

30 521 U.S. at 807–8, n. 11.

31 See Charles E. Rice, The Winning Side, *supra*, at 243–55.

32 Ave Maria School of Law, which opened in Ann Arbor in 2000–2001 and which has gained provisional accreditation, has raised Catholic legal education to a new level of competency and commitment. Ave Maria is unique in its combination of a sound technical formation with a systematic study, in each year, of the social and moral teachings of the Catholic Church as those teachings apply to the law.

33 3475 Plymouth Road, Ann Arbor, MI 48105 (734-827-8040).

34 New Hope, KY 40052 (502-549-5454).

35 1000 Regent University Drive, Virginia Beach, VA 23464.

36 15333 N. Pima Road, Suite 165, Scottsdale, AZ 85260.

37 P.O. Box 26005, Kansas City, MO 64196 (816-471-2994).

38 *Redemptoris Missio* (1990), no. 2.

39 Message of Dec. 29, 1997; 43 *The Pope Speaks* 167 (1998).

Only Liars Need Apply
Terence P. Jeffrey

On the thirtieth anniversary of *Roe v. Wade*, Americans may discover that the U.S. Senate will no longer confirm an honest person to the U.S. Supreme Court. Powerful pro-death forces seek to impose one non-negotiable condition on all nominees (call it "the mendacity test"): If you are not willing to lie about the meaning of the Constitution, you are not qualified to be a Justice. In short, only liars need apply.

If successful, the liars-only condition will mean the rule of law has joined 42 million dead babies among the victims of *Roe*.

How did we arrive at this threshold?

The Moral, Intellectual, and Legal High Ground

Since *Roe*, the abortion lobby has persistently escalated demands made not only of court nominees but also of the Senators who confirm them. They have required unwavering fidelity to their cause from their allies in political office. Pro-lifers, by contrast, are less demanding, and frequently forgive their faithless political partners. They have practiced patience and forbearance as self-described pro-life office-holders backpedaled from one retreat into another. The result? The judicial mandate for abortion on demand is more firmly entrenched than ever.

In 1973, *Roe* was decided by a 7-2 majority of U.S. Supreme Court Justices. Only one member of that Court, dissenter William Rehnquist, remains on the Court today. He was elevated to Chief

Justice by President Reagan in 1986. The other dissenter, Byron White, retired in 1993, and was replaced by President Clinton with pro-*Roe* Justice Ruth Bader Ginsburg.

All seven *Roe* signatories have retired, and Republican Presidents have nominated replacements for six of these seven. Four of these six (John Paul Stevens, Sandra Day O'Connor, Anthony Kennedy, and David Souter) later voted to uphold *Roe*. Republican pro-life Presidents Ronald Reagan and George Bush nominated three of these four pro-*Roe* Justices (O'Connor, Kennedy and Souter). Two of these three (O'Connor and Souter) were predictably pro-*Roe* at the time of their nominations. The third (Kennedy) had raised suspicions among careful pro-life observers (notably, Senator Jesse Helms).

And, although Robert Bork came close to doing so, no Republican nominee has ever unambiguously challenged the validity of *Roe* during a confirmation hearing.

If pro-life Republican presidents had enforced an anti-*Roe* litmus test as consistently as the abortion lobby has enforced its pro-*Roe* litmus test, the decision might have been overturned by now. That test, by the way, could simply say: If you believe that *Roe* was correctly decided, you are a judicial activist – that is, a judge who reads his own policy preferences into the Constitution and thereby imposes them on everyone – and you are therefore unqualified to serve on the Court.

Considering the strong moral, intellectual, and legal ground occupied by the pro-life view, its current weak political position was neither predictable nor preordained. Indeed, it was the other side that was plagued by uncertainty at the beginning. In *Roe*, for example, the Court's majority struck an almost apologetic tone. It conceded, for starters, that the "Constitution does not explicitly mention any right to privacy." It wasn't quite sure, therefore, where it should "find" such a right. (It also explicitly affirmed society's valid interest in protecting the child subject to abortion – "prenatal life" – calling that interest "compelling" at some point during pregnancy.)

Finally, it declared feebly that "the Fourteenth Amendment's conception of liberty" included an unstated "right to privacy broad enough to encompass a woman's decision whether or not to terminate her pregnancy." Then-Associate Justice William Rehnquist destroyed this argument with a single retort. "By the time of the adoption of the Fourteenth Amendment in 1868," he wrote,

> [T]here were at least 36 laws enacted by state or territorial legislatures limiting abortion. . . . Twenty-one [21] of the laws on the books in 1868 remain in effect today. . . . The only conclusion possible from this history is that the drafters did not intend to have the Fourteenth Amendment withdraw from the states the power to legislate in respect to this matter.[1]

Rehnquist's point was irrefutable. This was the "only conclusion possible." The seven justices in the *Roe* majority simply lied about the meaning of the Constitution, and their successors continue this lie to this day.

Since 1973, Supreme Court nominees could adopt three basic positions on *Roe*: (1) they could side with the *Roe* majority, arguing that the Fourteenth Amendment included a right to abortion; (2) they could side with Rehnquist, arguing that the Fourteenth Amendment could not include a right to abortion, since so many anti-abortion laws were in force both before and after the Amendment was ratified; or (3) they could argue that the unborn child was a person and that the Fourteenth Amendment therefore required all states to *ban* abortion, a position actually pondered by Justice Harry Blackmun in his majority opinion.

But, as we shall see, nominees have steered clear of stating positions (2) and (3) in the confirmation process even though it turned out later that some nominees clearly believed in position (2). While the Senate did elevate – grudgingly – Rehnquist to chief justice, knowing his dissent in *Roe*, in all other circumstances nominees have either refused to spell out their position on *Roe* during confirmation hearings, or have expressly adopted the majority opinion that the Fourteenth Amendment includes a "right" to abortion. Tellingly, the two nominees who stated their support for *Roe* (Ruth Bader Ginsburg and Stephen Breyer) were confirmed by overwhelming majorities. But the two nominees who did not directly state their views on *Roe* in committee (Robert Bork and Clarence Thomas) became the objects of character assassination by the abortion lobby. Only one of these two (Thomas) managed to win confirmation to the Court.

This is doubly ironic because nominees who endorse *Roe* deceive the public about the Constitution and therefore assassinate their own characters.

Post-*Roe* Nominations and the "Litmus Tests"

A brief review of the post-*Roe* nominations demonstrates how the political allies of the pro-life cause have retreated, while the pro-death lobby and its allies have advanced.

John Paul Stevens (President Ford): pro-*Roe* but opposed by the abortion lobby

In 1975, Justice William Douglas, an appointee of President Franklin Roosevelt, became the first *Roe* signatory to resign. Pro-abortion Republican President Gerald Ford nominated John Paul Stevens to replace Douglas. *Roe* was only two years old at the time and its 7-2 majority was not threatened by a one-vote change. Stevens, in any event, did not appear to threaten that change. He was cast in the same establishment Republican mold as several justices who had signed *Roe* (including Chief Justice Burger and Associate Justices Harry Blackmun, William Brennan, Potter Stewart, and Lewis Powell). The National Organization for Women (NOW) opposed Stevens anyway, citing what it called his "record of antagonism to women's rights."[2] It did not have much impact. A Democratically controlled Senate quickly confirmed Stevens 98-0.

Sandra Day O'Connor (President Reagan): "the high water mark"

In 1980, the Republican Party adopted a national platform that said: "We support the appointment of judges to all levels of the judiciary who respect traditional family values and the sanctity of innocent human life."[3] Ronald Reagan was elected president in a landslide. Perhaps more importantly, the Republicans won a major-

ity in the Senate and pro-life Republican Strom Thurmond of South
Carolina took over the chairmanship of the Senate Judiciary
Committee from pro-death Democrat Ted Kennedy of
Massachusetts. While running on the plank calling for pro-life
judges, President Reagan also promised to nominate the first
woman to the Supreme Court. These, of course, need not have been
contradictory positions.

In June 1981, Justice Potter Stewart, an Eisenhower appointee,
became the second *Roe* signatory to retire. The White House
instantly announced there would be no "litmus test" for his
replacement.[4] There wasn't. On July 7, Reagan nominated Sandra
Day O'Connor, a judge who had been appointed to the Arizona
Court of Appeals by Democratic Governor Bruce Babbitt.
O'Connor had a long pro-abortion record as a politician. As a state
senator, she had voted for a bill to legalize abortion, and she had
voted against an amendment to prohibit abortion at the University
of Arizona hospital. She had also voted against a resolution asking
Congress to pass a Human Life Amendment.

At the press conference announcing O'Connor's nomination,
Reagan was asked about her record on abortion. "Mr. President,
yours is a pro [-life] position on that; can you give us your feelings
about that pro [-life position]," a reporter asked. "I am completely
satisfied," Reagan said. "On her right-to-life position?" a reporter
asked. "Yes," said Reagan. "And did you interview her first personally?" a reporter asked. "Yes," said Reagan. At the same press
conference, when O'Connor was asked about her stand on abortion, she said: "I'm sorry, I can't address myself to substantive
questions pending the confirmation hearing."[5]

The Washington Post the next day quoted White House
Spokesman Larry Speakes as saying that O'Connor had told
Reagan "she is personally opposed to abortion." Speakes added,
"She also feels the subject of the regulation of abortion is a legiti-
mate subject for the legislative area."[6] Given her record, pro-life
groups opposed O'Connor and pro-death forces supported her.
NOW President Eleanor Smeal called her nomination "a major vic-
tory for women's rights."[7] Visiting with senators prior to her con-

firmation hearing, O'Connor declined to answer questions about *Roe*. In testimony, she stressed her personal "abhorrence of abortion." "It is a practice in which I would not have engaged," she said.[8]

National Right to Life Committee President John C. Willke boldly told the Judiciary Committee that the Senate should impose a pro-life litmus test on justices and reject O'Connor. "Those who do not recognize this fundamental right should be considered disqualified for the federal bench," he said. "This is a once-in-a-century issue, such an abominable evil that, while being a single issue, it should be a disqualifying issue."[9]

Republican Senate leaders, defying the platform that had won them a majority, scoffed at the notion. Republican Senator Robert Dole of Kansas said in the same hearing where Willke testified that he did not believe "we can subscribe to the position that she must repudiate" *Roe* to be confirmed. "I was hoping that you would have found it possible to have a change of heart," Dole told a pro-life witness who opposed O'Connor.[10] Elsewhere, Republican Senator Orrin Hatch of Utah said, "I also have real questions whether any single issue should be able" to stop the confirmation of a Justice.[11]

The Republican-controlled Senate voted 99-0 to confirm O'Connor. Democratic Sen. Max Baucus of Montana missed the vote but indicated he would have voted for confirmation. O'Connor went on not only to be a pro-*Roe* Justice, but also to provide the crucial swing vote in *Stenberg v. Carhart*, the 5-4 decision in June of 2000 which extended constitutional protection to partial-birth abortion, a procedure which kills the baby during delivery.[12]

Yet, in some ways O'Connor's confirmation process set the high-water mark for pro-life forces: President Reagan frankly admitted discussing abortion with her before nominating her. Despite evidence to the contrary, he believed she was pro-life. Furthermore, a prominent pro-life leader, Dr. Willke, publicly insisted the Senate should apply a pro-life litmus test for judges. In the elections of 1982 and 1984, the Republicans maintained their majority in the Senate and President Reagan was reelected. But, as it turned out, Reagan and the Republican Senate would not get another unambiguous opportunity – as they had with the retirement of Potter Stewart – to make a net pro-life gain on the Court.

Justice Scalia (President Reagan): Not "proper" to answer

In 1986, it appeared that the existing Court might be changing its mind on *Roe*. In *Thornburgh v. American College of Obstetricians and Gynecologists*, it split 5 to 4 in invalidating a Pennsylvania law that required abortion providers to give women detailed information about the physical and psychological risks of abortion. (This early opinion targeted abortion regulation, not *Roe* itself, and O'Connor joined the dissenters.) The near loss shocked pro-death forces. But so, too, did the apparent conversion of Chief Justice Warren Burger, who declared in a dissent that *Roe* should be reconsidered. The *New York Times* put it this way:

> [T]he narrowing margin of support for *Roe*, the unusually harsh dissenting opinions and, in particular, a shift in Chief Justice Warren Burger's position, suggested that the Court might consider reversing itself and restricting or even abandoning constitutional abortion rights if any member of the majority were replaced by a new Justice who shared the dissenters' views.[13]

Almost immediately, Burger resigned. Reagan named Rehnquist to replace him as Chief Justice, and Antonin Scalia, a judge on the U.S. Circuit Court of Appeals for the District of Columbia, to replace Rehnquist as Associate Justice. Rehnquist was well known for his dissent in *Roe*. Scalia, a Catholic with nine children, was also suspected of being anti-*Roe*. In a speech transmitted by satellite from the Oval Office to the Annual Convention of the Knights of Columbus, Reagan made sure to point out that Scalia was "the first Italian-American to be nominated to the Supreme Court in history."[14]

Neither Rehnquist's nor Scalia's confirmation would tip the Court's perceived 5-4 pro-*Roe* balance. And a still-Republican Senate was not going to do anything to hinder the confirmation of Reagan's nominees. Nonetheless, Rehnquist's ascent to Chief Justice was confirmed by a vote of 65-33 – the most votes in opposition that any justice confirmed to the Court had received up to that time.

Scalia had it easier. Ted Kennedy asked him in committee if he planned to overrule *Roe*. Scalia followed O'Connor's strategy of refusing to comment on the case. "I don't think it would be proper for me to answer that question," he said.[15] He was confirmed 98-0. He became an outspoken opponent of *Roe* both in and outside the Court.

Robert Bork (President Reagan): Adopt *Roe* or We Destroy You (Round I)

But then in November 1986, electoral disaster befell the Republican Party and the pro-life cause. The Democrats won a 55-45 majority in the Senate. Joseph Biden, a pro-death Catholic who harbored presidential ambitions, became chairman of the Judiciary Committee. In June 1987, Lewis Powell, another *Roe* signatory, resigned. Given the Court's perceived 5-4 pro-*Roe* majority, it was conceivable that the person Reagan nominated to replace Powell would cast the deciding vote to reverse *Roe*.

Reagan nominated Robert Bork, another judge from the U.S. Court of Appeals for the District of Columbia. Bork was a man of profound integrity. "I am convinced, as I think most legal scholars are," he had told a Senate subcommittee in 1981, "that *Roe v. Wade* is, itself, an unconstitutional decision, a serious and wholly unjustifiable judicial usurpation of state legislative authority."[16]

Pro-death forces went on a wilding spree. Democratic Sen. Ted Kennedy of Massachusetts threw the first punch. "Robert Bork's America," Kennedy told reporters, "is a land in which women would be forced into back alley abortions, blacks would sit at segregated lunch counters, rogue police could break down citizens' doors in midnight raids, schoolchildren could not be taught about evolution, writers and artists could be censored at the whim of government, and the doors of the federal courts would be shut on the fingers of millions of citizens."[17]

In the Judiciary Committee, Bork came closer than any Republican nominee – before or since – to challenging the validity of *Roe*. "*Roe v. Wade* contains almost no legal reasoning," he said in an exchange with Republican Sen. Orrin Hatch of Utah.[18] But he also said in testimony that as a general principle "[o]verruling should be done sparingly and cautiously," and, while describing how a Justice could challenge *Roe* and build a case for overturning it, he stopped short of saying it should be overturned.[19]

But Bork also refused to lie and give pro-death forces what they wanted: Explicit recognition of a Fourteenth Amendment right to abortion. Pro-death Republican Senators joined the lynch mob. Arlen Specter of Pennsylvania became Bork's chief inquisitor on the committee. Bob Packwood of Oregon threatened to filibuster the nomination on the Senate floor. John Warner of Virginia, who had married and divorced, in sequence, heiress Catherine Mellon and actress Elizabeth Taylor, said on the Senate floor that the "record is incomplete . . . as to the character of this man."[20]

Rather than withdraw his nomination, Bork forced the Senate to vote. It voted 58 to 42 against confirmation.

Pro-death forces had laid down their marker for future nominees: Adopt the lie of *Roe*, or we will destroy you.

Kennedy (President Reagan): "searching" (judicial activism by another name)

After the Bork defeat, Reagan nominated Douglas Ginsburg, who withdrew his name when it was discovered that he used marijuana in the 1970s.

Reagan then made a third try at replacing Powell by nominating Anthony Kennedy, a judge on the U.S. Circuit Court of Appeals in San Francisco. Kennedy told the Judiciary Committee that the Reagan Administration had never queried him on any issue that might come before the Court, and when pressed on *Roe* in particular, he stated that he did not have a "fixed" view.[21] But Kennedy openly rejected the theory of original intent, distinguishing himself sharply from Scalia and Bork: "Any theory which is predicated on the intent of the framers having reference to what they actually thought about is just not helpful," he said at one point in his testimony.[22] "I do not have an overarching theory, a unitary theory of interpretation," he testified later. "I am searching, as I think many judges are, for the correct balance in constitutional interpretation."[23]

Thus, pro-death forces had not just trashed Bork; they also managed to trash the serious and lawful doctrine of original intent *with a Reagan nominee*. The "searching" doctrine was just another name for judicial activism – judges making, rather than interpreting, the law.

The Senate confirmed Kennedy 97-0. On the Court, he would vote to uphold *Roe* in the 1992 decision, *Planned Parenthood of Southeastern Pennsylvania v. Casey*.[24]

David Souter (President Bush): pro-abortion record, opposed by abortion lobby

In 1990, Justice William Brennan resigned. This gave President George H.W. Bush his first chance to replace a *Roe* signatory. He nominated David Souter, a judge on the U.S. Circuit Court of Appeals in Boston, who had formerly served as a justice on the New Hampshire Supreme Court. He came recommended by Republican Senator Warren Rudman of New Hampshire, one of the most strident pro-abortion Republicans in Congress. In committee, Biden asked Souter if he believed in the "right of privacy" as established in *Griswold v. Connecticut* (the case that set the stage for *Roe*). Said Souter:

> I believe that the Due Process Clause of the Fourteenth Amendment does recognize and does protect an unenumerated right of privacy.[25]

While Souter refused to comment directly on *Roe v. Wade*, for those who had studied his record, his stand was no mystery. Conservative Caucus Chairman Howard Phillips testified in the Judiciary Committee that Souter, as a trustee of Concord Hospital in New Hampshire, had voted in 1973 to allow abortions there.[26]

Still, the pro-death lobby played hard to get. "Just as we stopped Robert Bork, we must stop any nominee who is not pro-choice," National Abortion Rights Action League Director Kate Michelman said in a letter to NARAL's membership when Souter was nominated.[27] A few days later Michelman said, "I don't think the public will accept, nor should the Senate confirm, a nominee who does not openly recognize that the Constitution protects an individual's right to privacy and right to choose."[28] NARAL opposed Souter all the way to the Senate floor.

The confirmation vote was 90-9. All dissenters were Democrats. On the Court, Souter has voted consistently to uphold *Roe*, and, like O'Connor, expanded the abortion "right" to include partial-birth abortion in *Stenberg*.

Clarence Thomas (President George H.W. Bush): "We're Going to Bork Him"

In 1991, Justice Thurgood Marshall resigned. The first African-American ever to serve on the Court and a legitimate hero of the civil-rights movement, Marshall also was a *Roe* signatory. President Bush nominated another African-American, Judge Clarence Thomas, to replace him.

Thomas, who personified the American Dream, appeared to be an untouchable nominee. Abandoned by his father as a boy, he was raised by his mother and grandparents, first in tiny Pinpoint, Georgia, then in segregated Savannah. He attended parochial school, studied briefly for the priesthood, graduated from Holy Cross College, and earned his law degree from Yale.

Before being appointed to the U.S. Circuit Court of Appeals for the District of Columbia, he had worked as Assistant Attorney General for Missouri, headed the civil-rights division of the U.S. Department of Education, and served eight years as Chairman of the Equal Employment Opportunities Commission.

Pro-death forces strongly suspected Thomas was anti-*Roe* and they wanted a declaration to the contrary. "I'm through reading tea leaves and voting in the dark," said Democratic Senator Howard Metzenbaum of Ohio, a Judiciary Committee member. "I will not support yet another Reagan-Bush Supreme Court nominee who remains silent on a woman's right to choose and then ascends to the Court to weaken that right."[29] NARAL's Kate Michelman said, "The 'Souter model' of silence and evasion that we saw last year is absolutely unacceptable."[30]

At the twenty-fifth anniversary celebration of the National Organization for Women, feminist Flo Kennedy told the Associated Press: "We're going to Bork him. We need to kill him politically."[31]

The Administration responded with what has been called the "don't ask, don't tell" policy. "Judge Thomas has not stated a public position on abortion," the White House said. "There will be efforts to assign him a position such as this attempt, but we will not comment on these kinds of speculation."[32]

Before the Committee, Thomas refused to comment directly on *Roe*, but did seem to follow Souter by accepting the idea of a Fourteenth Amendment "right to privacy," while refusing to say what that might mean for *Roe*: "My view is that there is a right to privacy in the Fourteenth Amendment," he said.

Pushing the question, Biden asked: "Well, Judge, does that right to privacy in the Liberty Clause of the Fourteenth Amendment protect the right of a woman to decide for herself in certain instances whether or not to terminate a pregnancy?" Thomas replied,

> Senator, I think that the Supreme Court has made clear that the issue of marital privacy is protected, that the State cannot infringe on that without a compelling interest, and the Supreme Court, of course, in the case of *Roe v. Wade* has found an interest in the woman's right to – as a fundamental interest – a woman's right to terminate a pregnancy. I do not think that at this time that I could maintain my impartiality as a member of the judiciary and comment on that specific case.[33]

Despite the resemblance between Thomas's and Souter's testimony, Democratic Senator Patrick Leahy of Vermont – who had voted for Souter – rejected Thomas, a clear example of how the abortion lobby was increasing the demands it made of its friends (while pro-life groups were doing just the opposite). Leahy explained:

> So let me make this very clear, Judge Thomas. In recent years, we've danced around the question of where nominees stand on a woman's fundamental right to abortion. Now, this is one of the burning social issues of our time. It

is the single issue about which this Committee and the
American people most urgently wish to know the nominee's views. And yet the Senate and the nation have been
frustrated by polite, albeit respectful stonewalling.[34]

Yet, at this point, the opposition of hardcore pro-death forces was
not enough to defeat Thomas. Before the Judiciary Committee
could vote, Democratic Senator Bennett Johnson of Louisiana
announced that he supported Thomas. So, too, did Senator Arlen
Specter, a pro-abortion Republican committee member. Democratic
Senator Dennis DeConcini of Arizona, another committee member,
soon followed.

The Circus: Adopt *Roe* or We Destroy You (Round II)

On September 27, the committee split 7-7 on whether to recommend Thomas for confirmation, and voted 13-1 to send his nomination to the full Senate. Thomas's victory seemed assured.

Then, someone leaked an unsubstantiated affidavit given to the
committee by University of Oklahoma Law Professor Anita Hill.
She had accused Thomas of sexually harassing her when she
worked as his assistant at the Department of Education and at the
EEOC in the early 1980s. Under oath, Thomas adamantly denied
the charges, and ferociously turned the tables on committee
Democrats. "This is a circus," he said in a nationally televised hearing. "It's a national disgrace. And from my standpoint as a black
American, as far as I'm concerned, it is a high-tech lynching for
uppity blacks who in any way deign to think for themselves, to do
for themselves, to have different ideas, and it is a message that
unless you kowtow to an old order, this is what will happen to you.
You will be lynched, destroyed, caricatured by a Committee of the
U.S. Senate rather than hung from a tree."

"The Supreme Court is not worth it," said Thomas. "No job is
worth it."[35]

The Senate voted 52-48 to confirm him. Thomas thus bested
Rehnquist's record for most negative votes received by a confirmed
justice. Vindicating his enemies and supporters alike, Thomas
became one of the finest Justices ever to serve on the Court, joining

Rehnquist and Scalia as one of the Court's three great anti-*Roe* constitutionalists.

Ruth Bader Ginsburg (President Bill Clinton): "clearly pro-choice" and well beyond *Roe*

President Clinton did not adopt a "don't ask, don't tell" policy for Supreme Court nominees. He openly applied the pro-death litmus test. In 1993, Justice Byron White resigned. White had been the only Justice to join Rehnquist in dissenting from *Roe*. Replacing him with a pro-*Roe* Justice would move the balance of the Court decisively back in the pro-*Roe* direction.

Clinton picked Ruth Bader Ginsburg, another judge on the U.S. Circuit Court of Appeals for the District of Columbia (to which she had been appointed by President Carter). In the 1960s and '70s, she had been director of the Women's Rights Project of the American Civil Liberties Union.

At the press conference announcing the nomination, Clinton said Ginsburg was "clearly pro-choice," to reassure certain death advocates who did not like a pro-abortion lecture she had given earlier that year at New York University.[36] In that lecture, Ginsburg argued that Justice Blackmun's opinion in *Roe* had been politically inept. A right to abortion, she argued, could have been more firmly established if it had been based on the Equal Protection Clause of the Fourteenth Amendment rather than on the right to privacy. Furthermore, she argued, by legalizing abortion in one fell swoop, *Roe* had moved too far too fast, inciting "a well-organized and vocal right-to-life movement" that "succeeded, for a considerable time, in turning the legislative tide in the opposite direction."

The Court should write its own laws to effect "social change," she believed, but should do so incrementally so as not to alarm voters, who then might demand that Congress or state legislatures overturn laws written by the Justices. "I do not suggest," she lectured, "that the Court should never step ahead of the political branches in pursuit of a constitutional precept. . . . But without taking giant strides and thereby risking a backlash too forceful to contain, the Court, through constitutional adjudication, can reinforce or signal a green light for social change."[37]

When asked before the Judiciary Committee whether there was a constitutional right to abortion, Ginsburg said, "This is something central to a woman's life, to her dignity. It's a decision that she must make for herself. And when government controls that decision for her, she's being treated as less than a fully adult human responsible for her own choices."[38]

This argument went well beyond *Roe*, which held that the state had an interest in protecting the life of the unborn child, particularly after viability. In Ginsburg's "equal protection" argument, the unborn child had no protection at all. It was as if the child did not exist.

Ginsburg and Republicans: "fawning and obsequious"

How did Republican Senators, still in the minority, react to Ginsburg's radical viewpoint? They fawned over her. Orrin Hatch accepted Clinton's pro-death test as a *fait accompli*. "Oh well," said Hatch on CNN's Inside Politics, "I don't know anybody that is going to agree with any particular member of the Judiciary Committee on everything, but it's – there's no question, I'm pro-life, she is pro-choice, just to give you one illustration; but, you know, the President said that he's going to have a litmus test, so that's a given as far as I'm concerned."[39]

But that was not all Hatch said. "Conservatives out there ought to be pleased," he told NBC.[40] "She's going to make an excellent Justice," *Bloomberg News* quoted him as saying.[41] When Ginsburg visited the Senate, Hatch told her he would like her autographed picture.[42]

Senate Republican Leader Bob Dole was equally obsequious. "I expect her nomination will be well-received," he told CNN. "She is also a neighbor in the same building we live in and it's a good non-partisan, bi-partisan building and we're happy to have her on board."[43]

"President Clinton made a good choice," Dole said in a release. "Ginsburg undoubtedly has the experience and the intellect to hit the ground running."[44]

She would run all the way, as it turned out, to joining Republican-nominated Justices O'Connor, Souter, and Stevens in the *Stenberg* decision, which declared near-infanticide (partial-birth abortion) a constitutional right. The Senate confirmed her 96-3, with only Republican Senators Jesse Helms of North Carolina, Don Nickles of Oklahoma, and Bob Smith of New Hampshire in opposition.

Stephen Breyer (President Clinton): The Pro-*Roe* Litmus Test and Beyond

It took twenty years, but pro-death forces had finally succeeded. They had imposed an explicit pro-*Roe* litmus test on a Supreme Court nominee, a Democratic president had used it, and Republican senators had acquiesced to it. The abortion lobby now only had to hold its ground.

But it would stay on the offensive, pushing the pro-death cause beyond *Roe* and beyond the Supreme Court.

When Blackmun announced his retirement in the spring of 1994, President Clinton nominated Stephen G. Breyer to replace him. Breyer was a judge on the U.S. Circuit Court of Appeals in Boston. A long-time Harvard Law professor, he had also worked as an aide to Senate Judiciary Committee Democrats. In 1979–80, he served as the committee's chief counsel when Ted Kennedy served as chairman. He was Teddy's guy – and Teddy was, and remains, a Senator most intent upon imposing a pro-death litmus test.

Touted as a "moderate" because he had worked on deregulation of the airline industry and appeared to be modestly pro-business for a Kennedy Democrat, Breyer's view on abortion was truly radical.[45] And it was in plain view for anyone who wanted to look at it. In the 1990 appellate court case of *Massachusetts v. Secretary of Health and Human Services*, he joined an opinion (later overturned by the Supreme Court in *Rust v. Sullivan*) stating that the First Amendment's free speech clause required U.S. taxpayers to subsidize Planned Parenthood and other organizations that promoted abortion as a method of birth control and who referred pregnant women to abortionists. In other words, Breyer believes the First Amendment requires taxpayers to pay people ("counselors") who steer women to abortion.[46]

This did not dampen the enthusiasm of Bob Dole and Orrin Hatch for Clinton's second nominee. "He's a fine man," Hatch said the day Clinton announced the choice. "He's very honest. He's compassionate. He's got a big heart. And frankly, an excellent legal scholar and I think he'll make a wonderful addition to the Supreme Court."[47] In a press release that day, Dole said Breyer was "a top-notch intellect and a person of integrity."[48] He predicted Clinton's second explicitly pro-abortion nominee would have no trouble winning confirmation.

In committee, Strom Thurmond asked Breyer what he thought of Blackmun's opinion in *Roe*. While declining to talk about secondary questions relating to abortion regulation, Breyer unhesitatingly took and passed the pro-death test. "The case of *Roe v. Wade* has been the law for 21 years, or more, and it was recently affirmed by the Supreme Court of the United States, in the case of *Casey*," he said. "That is the law."[49] To Democratic Senator Carol Moseley Braun, he gave a more involved answer, but it concluded succinctly enough. "The source [of the abortion right]," he stated, "is the Fourteenth Amendment and that word liberty," he said.[50]

This, in a word, is the pro-death lie that now pervades our judiciary and our politics: Abortion is liberty.

The Senate confirmed Breyer 87-9. All nine opponents were Republicans. On the Senate floor, Hatch defended Breyer against his detractors. "This is an honest man," said Hatch. "He's a man of immense qualifications. He's a man of immense integrity. He is a person who has a tremendous judicial and legal mind. He is a person who is fair and open. He is a person who I think will have an appropriate temperament for the Court."[51] Breyer would go on to actually write the Court's 5-4 decision in *Stenberg*, making partial-birth abortion a constitutional right.

In 1994, the Republicans won back control of the Senate. But Bill Clinton never appointed another Supreme Court Justice, so a Republican majority was never faced with the question of whether to accept or reject a death-tested nominee.

Upping the Ante to Appellate Courts

In 2001, pro-death Republican Senator James Jeffords of Vermont switched parties, returning control of the Senate to the Democrats. Another Vermonter, pro-death Democrat Patrick Leahy became chairman of the Judiciary Committee. As a preemptive strike against any Supreme Court nominees that might be made by President George W. Bush, Leahy has started to apply the pro-death test at the appellate level.

Many of President Bush's nominees to appellate courts have languished in Leahy's committee. Miguel Estrada, nominated for the U.S. Circuit Court of Appeals in the District of Columbia, was given a hearing, but no committee vote. His nomination expired with the end of the 107th Congress. Pro-life federal judge Charles Pickering, nominated to the U.S. Circuit Court of Appeals in New Orleans, suffered a baseless Bork-style character assassination, and was then rejected on a party-line vote. Texas Supreme Court Justice Priscilla Owen, who wrote a brilliant dissent from the Texas Court's decision that watered down the state's parental notification law, was also nominated to the U.S. Circuit Court of Appeals in New Orleans. She told Leahy's committee that *Roe* was the "law of the land" and that she would apply it, as modified by *Casey*, as an appellate court judge.[52] But she, too, lost a party-line committee vote and never made it to the Senate floor.

Conclusion

The strategy of appeasement has failed. Every step backward by "friends" of the pro-life movement has meant a step forward by pro-death forces. While intimidating Republicans with accusations of "litmus tests," the abortion lobby has succeeded in imposing its own. Having conquered the Supreme Court, they have now moved to the appellate courts. The endgame is a thoroughly corrupted judiciary that works to annihilate law itself: If U.S. judges will not defend the right to life of innocents against unjust aggressors, how can we expect them to defend property or liberty?

St. Paul told the Christians of Rome that God wrote the natural law on the hearts of all – believers and nonbelievers alike. In the

1960s, the Rev. Martin Luther King used this truth to win equal rights for African-Americans. Birmingham was desegregated. In the 1980s, Pope John Paul II and Ronald Reagan used this truth to defeat the evil empire of Soviet Communism. Without any violence, Mikhail Gorbachev *did* tear down that wall.

President Bush, and all future presidents who call themselves pro-life, should tear down the wall that blocks honest men and women from sitting on our highest courts. They should apply an unapologetic test to all nominees – that embodies the pro-life principles incorporated into every Republican platform since 1980: All must admit the truth, knowable in every heart, that abortion is wrong. All must be ready to attest, under oath before the Judiciary Committee, as Chief Justice Rehnquist argued so potently thirty years ago, that *Roe* was wrongly decided.

Pro-life presidents should follow a strategy first advocated by Pat Buchanan in his 1992 campaign for the Republican presidential nomination: Send men and women who will bear witness to these truths to the Senate for confirmation, and keep sending them.[53] Soon, the liars will lie low. Hearts will open. Votes will change. Truth shall triumph. And the forces of death at last will be overcome.

Terence P. Jeffrey is a nationally syndicated columnist and Editor of Human Events – The National Conservative Weekly. *He was formerly an editorial writer for the* Washington Times, *and served as National Campaign Manager for Patrick J. Buchanan's 1996 presidential campaign.*

Endnotes

1   Dissent of Justice William Rehnquist in Roe v. Wade 410 U.S. 113 (1973).

2   "Stevens Confirmation Hearings," *Facts on File World News Digest* (December 13, 1975), p. 929, F2.

3   As cited in Bill Peterson, "Reagan Choice for Court Decried by Conservatives But Acclaimed by Liberals," *The Washington Post* 8 July 1981: A7.

4   Michael Putzel, "Reagan: 'Always' Looking for Woman for High Court," *The Associated Press*, June 18, 1981.

5   "Transcript of Remarks by Reagan and Nominee to High Court,"
     New York Times 8 July 1981: A12.
6   Lou Cannon, "Reagan Names Woman to Supreme Court," *The
     Washington Post* 8 July 1981: A1.
7   Bill Peterson, *supra* note 2.
8   Elizabeth Olson, *United Press International*, September 9, 1981.
9   Fred Barbash, "O'Connor Rejected by Abortion Foes, Defended by
     Wide Range of Senators," *The Washington Post* 12 September 12, 1981:
     A2.
10   *Id.*
11   Fred Barbash, "Conservatives Feud in Wake of O'Connor Choice,"
     The Washington Post 9 July 1981: A1.
12   See opinion of the court, delivered by Justice Breyer in *Stenberg v.
     Carhart*, 530 U.S. 914 (2000). In describing partial-birth abortion,
     Breyer cites Nebraska's law banning partial birth abortion, which
     was challenged in the case. Writes Breyer: "The statute defines 'par-
     tial birth abortion' as: 'an abortion procedure in which the person
     performing the abortion partially delivers vaginally a living unborn
     child before killing the unborn child and completing the delivery.' . . .
     It further defines 'partially delivers vaginally a living unborn child
     before killing the child' to mean 'deliberately and intentionally
     delivering into the vagina a living unborn child, or a substantial por-
     tion thereof, for the purpose of performing a procedure that the per-
     son performing such procedure knows will kill the unborn child and
     does kill the unborn child.'"
13   Stuart Taylor Jr., "Justices Uphold Abortion Rights by Narrow Vote,"
     New York Times 12 June 1986: A1.
14   "Knights of Columbus, Remarks at the Annual Convention in
     Chicago, Il.," *Public Papers of the Presidents* (August 5, 1986), 22
     Weekly Comp. Pres. Doc. 1047.
15   "Won't Bring Conservative Agenda to Court – Scalia; Refuses to
     Give Stand on Abortion," *The Los Angeles Times* 5 August 1986: 1.
16   "A Bork Primer and Guide," *The National Law Journal*, 21 September
     1987: 32.
17   Lou Cannon, Edward Walsh, "Reagan Nominates Appeals Judge
     Bork to Supreme Court; Fierce Confirmation Battle Over
     Conservative Expected," *The Washington Post* 2 July 1987: A1.
18   "Bork Criticizes Supreme Court Ruling on Abortion," *United Press
     International*, September 15, 1987.
19   Glen Elsasser and Janet Cawley, "Bork Walks the Middle
     Line/Hearings Testimony Plays to Critics," *The Chicago Tribune* 16
     September 1987: 1.

20 R.H. Melton, "Warner's Vote on Bork Kindle's Va. GOP Leaders' Outrage," *The Washington Post* (October 24, 1987), p. A18.

21 Al Kamen, "Kennedy: No Fixed View on Abortion," *The Washington Post*, 15 December 1987: A1.

22 "Kennedy Passes the Confirmation Test," *Facts on File World News Digest*, 18 December 1987: 936 (D1).

23 *Id.*

24 Plurality opinion of Justices O'Connor, Kennedy and Souter in *Planned Parenthood of Southeastern Pa. V. Casey*, 505 U.S. 833 (1992).

25 "Hearing of the Senate Judiciary Committee; Subject: Confirmation of Judge David Souter to the Supreme Court," *Federal News Service*, September 13, 1990.

26 "Hearing of the Senate Judiciary Committee; Subject: Souter Nomination," *Federal News Service*, September 19, 1990, Witnesses: Howard Phillips, Chairman Conservative Caucus.

27 "Brennan, Key Liberal, Resigns Supreme Court Seat; Bush Nominates Souter, New Hampshire Judge, as Successor; President Avoids Abortion Issue," *Facts on File World News Digest*, 27 July 1990: 551 A1.

28 *Id.*

29 John E. Yang and Sharon LaFraniere, "Bush Picks Thomas for Supreme Court; Appeals Court Judge Served as EEOC Chairman in Reagan Administration," *The Washington Post*, 2 July 1991: A1.

30 Linda Greenhouse, "The Supreme Court: Bush Picks a Wild Card," *New York Times*, 2 July 1991: A1.

31 Beth J. Harpaz, "Feminists Say Clarence Thomas Must Be Rejected," *The Associated Press*, July 5, 1991.

32 Neil A. Lewis, "Court Nominee is Linked to Anti-Abortion Stand," *New York Times*, 3 July 1991: A1.

33 Reuters, "The Thomas Hearings: Excerpts From Senate Session on the Thomas Nomination," *New York Times*, 11 September 1991: A22.

34 "Hearing of the Senate Judiciary Committee; Morning Session; Subject: The Nomination of Clarence Thomas to the Supreme Court," *Federal News Service*, September 10, 1991, Witnesses: Clarence Thomas.

35 "Hearing of the Senate Judiciary Committee; Subject: Thomas Supreme Court Nomination," *Federal News Service*, October 11, 1991, Witnesses: Judge Clarence Thomas.

36 Steven Komarow, "Clinton says Ginsburg 'clearly pro-choice,'" *The Associated Press*, June 15, 1993.

37   Ruth Bader Ginsburg, "A Look at . . . *Roe v. Wade* v. Ginsburg: The Case Against the Case; Ruth Bader Ginsburg's Concerns About the Abortion Ruling," *The Washington Post,* 20 June 1993: C3.

38   Joan Biskupic, "Ginsburg Endorses Right to Choose Abortion, ERA," *The Washington Post,* 22 July 21993: A1.

39   Catherine Crier and Bernard Shaw, "Politicos Expect Ginsburg to Ace Confirmation Hearings," *CNN's Inside Politics,* June 14, 1993.

40   "Reaction From Key Senators and Others," *The Hotline,* June 15, 1993.

41   "Clinton Nominates Ruth Bader Ginsburg to Supreme Court," *Bloomberg News,* June 14, 1993.

42   Steven Komarow, "Ginsburg Visits Senate Leaders," *The Associated Press,* June 15, 1993.

43   Catherine Crier and Bernard Shaw, "President Clinton Makes Nomination Announcement," *CNN's Inside Politics,* June 14, 1993.

44   "Reaction From Key Senators and Others," *The Hotline,* June 15, 1993.

45   For examples of how Breyer was touted as a moderate, *see* Joan Biskupic, "A Moderate Pragamatist; Nominee Widely Admired in Legal Circles," *The Washington Post* 14 May 1994: A1; David Savage, "Nominee Unlikely to Take Predecessor's Liberal Path; Law: Breyer is Known for an Interest in Economics. His Opinions Tend to be Narrow and Technical," *The Los Angeles Times,* 14 May 1994: A1.

46   *Commonwealth of Massachusetts, et al. v. Secretary of Health and Human Services,* No. 88-1279, The United States Court of Appeals for the First Circuit; 899 F2d 53; 1990 U.S. App. LEXIS 4236 (March 19, 1990). As explained in the "Case Summary:" "The state and associations filed an action, in which the low income woman intervened, seeking declaratory and injunctive relief from the Secretary's regulations, which prohibited recipients of Title X funds from engaging in abortion counseling or referral. . . . The Court stated that the effect of the regulations was to infringe upon women's freedom of reproductive choice by denying them access to important information and by interfering with the physician-patient relationship. The Court further found that the regulations imposed a speech restriction that was both viewpoint and content-based, in violation of the First Amendment, because they prohibited advocacy related to abortion."

47   "Senators Hatch and Metzenbaum Offer Opinions on Breyer," *CNN,* May 13, 1994.

48   Bob Dole, Senate Minority Leader Senate Republicans, "Breyer Nomination," *Federal Document Clearing House, Inc. Congressional Press Releases,* May 13, 1994.

49   "Hearing of the Senate Judiciary Committee; Subject: Supreme
      Court Confirmation Hearing for Judge Stephen G. Breyer," *Federal
      News Service*, July 12, 1994, Witnesses: Judge Stephen G. Breyer.
50   "Hearing of the Senate Judiciary Committee; Subject: Supreme
      Court Confirmation Hearing for Judge Stephen G. Breyer, Afternoon
      Session," Federal News Service, July 13, 1994, Witnesses: Judge
      Stephen G. Breyer.
51   Carolyn Skorneck, "Breyer Wins Overwhelming Senate Approval
      for Supreme Court," *The Associated Press*, July 29, 1994.
52   "Afternoon Session of Panel II of a Senate Judiciary Committee
      Hearing; Chaired By: Senator Dianne Feinstein (D.-CA.); Subject:
      Nomination of Priscilla Owen to be a Circuit Court Judge for the
      Fifth Circuit," *Federal News Service*, July 23, 2002.
53   The author first heard this idea expressed by Republican presiden-
      tial candidate Patrick J. Buchanan in 1992, when the author was
      working as Buchanan's Issues Director. At the 1992 Conservative
      Political Action Conference, for example, Buchanan said: "I will tell
      you what I will do. I don't think we ought to be afraid of Kennedy
      and Biden and Metzenbaum and all the rest. I don't think we ought
      to be afraid of their questioning our nominees of where they stand.
      I will find in this country the most qualified, able, experienced fed-
      eral judges who are constitutionalists and conservatives who have
      taken a stand and stood on each of these issues and I will send them
      up to the Senate Judiciary Committee and tell them to state their
      beliefs and not back down, even if they are defeated. We will send
      one after another up until we break that monopoly in the Senate
      Judiciary." *See* "Remarks by Pat Buchanan, Republican Presidential
      Candidate, to the Conservative Political Action Conference, Omni
      Shoreham Hotel, Washington, D.C.," *Federal News Service*, February
      20, 1992.

Let the People Decide
Clarke D. Forsythe

"[B]y foreclosing all democratic outlet for the deep passions this issue [abortion] arouses, by banishing the issue from the political forum that gives all participants, even the losers, the satisfaction of a fair hearing and an honest fight, by continuing the imposition of a rigid national rule instead of allowing for regional differences, the Court merely prolongs and intensifies the anguish."
– Supreme Court Justice Antonin Scalia, dissenting, in *Planned Parenthood v. Casey* (1992)

"In this and like communities, public sentiment is everything.
"With public sentiment, nothing can fail; without it, nothing can succeed.
"Consequently, he who molds public sentiment, goes deeper than he who enacts statutes or pronounces decisions. He makes statutes and decisions possible or impossible to be executed."
– Abraham Lincoln, Ottawa, IL (1858 Lincoln-Douglas Debates)

Thirty years after the Supreme Court overturned the abortion laws of all fifty states and legalized abortion-on-demand nationwide, many believe that the issue is irresolvable. The passage of time, however, may bring American society closer to progress. It takes time to document the experience of a social revolution and catalogue its negative effects. And it takes time to answer the arguments that prompted the revolution in the first place. This was true in the fight against the slave trade in England in the 1780s and in the fight against slavery in the United States in the 1850s. The solutions to the tragedy of abortion may be more feasible in 2003 – when legal abortion has aggravated the very problems it promised to solve – than they were in 1973 – when many still believed that abortion would help women.[1]

Nevertheless, thirty years has changed the nature of our challenge. Abortion is now not just a legal issue, but a broadly based cultural problem, requiring a broadly based cultural strategy, with social, political, and educational elements. While changes in law must be part of any effective, long-term solution, the law alone cannot solve the problem.

The Supreme Court's 1973 decision in *Roe v. Wade* made abortion a *constitutional* issue, taking the question from the people and investing the federal courts with the power to invalidate state and federal laws.[2] The Court's most recent abortion decision, *Stenberg v. Carhart*[3] in 2000 – striking down Nebraska's ban on partial-birth abortion (and thereby invalidating similar laws in twenty-nine other states) highlights the problem. Public opposition to this method of abortion – which destroys the child during delivery – was profound and widespread, with thirty states acting to prohibit it. But the federal courts stepped in to block all those laws. Unelected federal judges simply wiped out public sentiment. Clearly, one of the biggest obstacles to a culture of life in America is the interference of the federal courts in obstructing the people's will.

Because of *Roe*'s revolutionary impact, efforts were made to overturn *Roe* through a constitutional amendment (from 1973 to 1983) and then through test-case litigation (1983–1992). For cultural, political, and institutional reasons, which I will outline, those efforts did not prevail and were necessarily put on hold during the Clinton Presidency. But, with the end of the Clinton Presidency and the Supreme Court as pro-abortion as ever, what now?

Two essential problems – one structural, one democratic – must be solved to change our law and culture: the federal courts must be removed as an obstacle, and public opinion must be roused to change the national rule of abortion-on-demand. In order to do that, the myth of abortion as a "necessary evil" must be dispelled. This can be done by raising public consciousness of the negative impact of abortion on women. Also, a "federalism" constitutional amendment must be pursued to return the abortion issue to popular control at the state level. In pursuing these objectives, Middle America (the 60 percent in the middle) must become the primary audience.[4]

How Abortion Became a Constitutional Problem

A little history of abortion law is in order. Professor John Noonan summarized the evolution of abortion over two decades from a problem of local law enforcement into a constitutional issue: "In America . . . moral issues become legal issues, and legal issues become constitutional issues."[5]

Prior to 1958, abortion was prohibited in virtually all states. These laws were actively and effectively enforced against abortion doctors and no influential social institutions called for abortion's legalization.[6] John Harlan Amen's work in New York in the 1940s is the best-documented example of vigorous and effective prosecutorial efforts to inhibit illegal abortion. As an Assistant Attorney General in New York State during the 1930s and 1940s, Amen encouraged use of these laws in prosecutions and effectively curbed illegal abortion. Abortion was not a constitutional issue; it was a social and local law-enforcement matter.

Four myths about the pre-*Roe* era have distorted thirty years of public debate. First, it is widely believed that 1 to 2 million illegal abortions occurred annually before 1973, and that thousands of women died annually. Second, many think that abortion law targeted women rather than abortionists. Third, most believe that abortion laws did not reduce abortion. And finally, people think legalized abortion has been good for women.

Mary Calderone, the Medical Director for Planned Parenthood, pointed out that "[I]n 1957, there were only 260 deaths in the whole country attributed to abortions of any kind. . . ."[7] In fact, statistics from the Centers for Disease Control (CDC) for 1972 show that thirty-nine women died from *illegal* abortion and twenty-seven died from *legal* abortion.[8] No evidence supports a figure of millions of illegal abortions or thousands of deaths.[9] The nearly uniform state policy for a century before 1973 was to treat the woman as the second victim: laws were enforced against abortionists, not mothers.[10] Finally, legalized abortion – directly and indirectly – has been devastating for women's health: from its physical and psychological toll, to the epidemic of sexually transmitted diseases; from the general coarsening of male-female relationships, to the three-fold increase in repeat-abortions; from the increase in hospitalizations for ectopic pregnancies, to the decline in future fertility and the increased risk of breast cancer.[11]

In 1958, the American Law Institute (ALI) became the first elite organization to support the loosening of abortion laws by creating broad exceptions to general prohibitions. "Exceptions" were the focus during the 1960s, with legalization efforts to follow. Colorado and California legalized abortion under certain conditions in 1967, for example, and approximately fifteen states liberalized their laws prior to 1970. Other states, however, rejected legalization as late as November of 1972. Between the fall elections of November 1970 and the *Roe* decision in January 1973, only one state – Florida – loosened its abortion law – and that was due to a state-court decision, not popular demand.[12] The momentum of the abortion-reform movement may have been spent by November, 1970.

We will never know, of course, because the U.S. Supreme Court decisions in January of 1973, *Roe v. Wade*[13] and *Doe v. Bolton*,[14] legalized abortion-on-demand nationwide, eliminating both the traditional laws that prohibited abortion (except to save the life of the mother) and the newer laws that allowed abortion for broad exceptions. The Supreme Court made abortion a *constitutional* issue by creating a constitutional right to abortion that supersedes state and federal laws and by empowering federal courts to enforce that right. If the Court had treated abortion in 1973 the way it treated assisted suicide in 1997 (rejecting a constitutional "right" to assisted suicide and allowing states to handle the issue), abortion would have remained a political, educational, legislative problem for the people in their states.[15] But *Roe* read abortion into the Constitution and dismantled democracy on the question. The public will cannot be expressed on abortion, as it is on most other controversies in a democratic society. As long as *Roe* exists, abortion will be a *constitutional* issue.

Roe sparked a ten-year effort, between 1973 and 1983, to pass a constitutional amendment on abortion in Congress. These efforts were suspended (in fact if not by design) between 1976 and 1980, but then revived with the election of Ronald Reagan in 1981. Hearings were held on constitutional amendments until June 28, 1983, when a vote on the Hatch-Eagleton Amendment failed in the Senate, 49-50.[16] That amendment stated simply: "A right to abortion is not secured by this Constitution." By overturning the national right to abortion, it would have effectively returned the issue to the states, which is the essence of a "federalism" amendment on abortion.

In June 1983, barely two weeks before that vote, the Supreme Court decided *City of Akron v. Akron Center for Reproductive Health,*[17] from which Justice Sandra Day O'Connor (appointed by President Reagan) dissented with two other justices. Based on Justice O'Connor's dissent and the anticipation of additional changes in the Supreme Court through President Reagan's nominations, a concerted effort – "a course of responsible and effective litigation" – was made to overturn *Roe* through the courts between 1983 and 1992.[18] This effort was suspended with the Court's reaffirmation of *Roe* by a 6-3 vote in *Planned Parenthood v. Casey* in June, 1992.[19]

The Campaign to Overturn Roe in the Courts

There are only two ways to overturn a Supreme Court decision interpreting the Constitution: through a constitutional amendment or by the Supreme Court reversing itself. When the amendment vote failed in June of 1983, a court-reversal strategy was emphasized.

The decade-long effort to overturn *Roe* through the courts was consciously predicated upon specific conditions. These included: 1) the reduction in the pro-*Roe* majority on the Supreme Court from 7-2 in 1973, to 6-3 in 1983, to 5-4 in 1989; 2) the refutation of historic and constitutional justifications for *Roe*; 3) the obsolescence of the Court's trimester framework as medicine and technology advanced and conclusively demonstrated the humanity of the unborn child;[20] and 4) the Court's willingness to return the issue to the states. (The campaign understood and expected that reversing *Roe* would simply return the issue of abortion to the people.)[21]

Evidence for these predicates grew with a series of decisions from *Akron* in 1983 to *Webster v. Reproductive Health Services* in 1989.[22] During this time, many believed the effort to overturn *Roe* through the courts was going to be successful, including activists on both sides of the issue and members of the media. For example, Notre Dame Law Professor Charles Rice wrote as early as 1988 of the "coming retreat from *Roe v. Wade*."[23] Commentators of all political stripes predicted *Roe*'s demise again in the spring of 1992, at the time of the Supreme Court arguments in *Planned Parenthood v. Casey*.

However, the Court eliminated the predicates in its 1992 decision in *Planned Parenthood v. Casey*, which reaffirmed *Roe*. In *Casey*, the Court created a completely *new* rationale for a national abortion right. It made the sociological and political determination that American women need abortion-on-demand for equal opportunity in American society. In their dramatic joint opinion, three Justices – O'Connor, Kennedy, and Souter (three Reagan-Bush Justices) – "call[ed on] the contending sides of a national controversy to end their national division by accepting a common mandate rooted in the Constitution" while *simultaneously* admitting that they could *not* demonstrate that any such mandate was rooted in the Constitution.[24]

Thus, the justification for *Roe* shifted from law to sociology. The decision emphasized "reliance interests" in abortion:

> [F]or two decades of economic and social developments, people have organized intimate relationships and made choices that define their views of themselves and their places in society, *in reliance on the availability of abortion in the event that contraception should fail*. The ability of women to participate equally in the economic and social life of the Nation has been facilitated by their ability to control their reproductive lives.[25]

Cultural and political factors simply overwhelmed legitimate legal and constitutional considerations.[26]

The impact of abortion on women was the defining theme of the joint opinion in *Casey*.[27] If the Court had had a strong sense of abortion's harm to women, these three Justices might have joined with Chief Justice Rehnquist, Justice Scalia, and Justice Thomas to create a 6-3 majority to overturn *Roe* and return the issue to the states. But the plurality assumed that legal abortion was not only good for women but *necessary for their equal participation in American society*. This belief apparently persuaded Justices O'Connor, Souter, and Kennedy to stand by *Roe*.

Shortly thereafter, President Clinton successfully nominated two pro-abortion justices to the Supreme Court (Justice Ginsburg in 1993 and Justice Breyer in 1994), creating the current Court's 5-4 pro-abortion majority. The change in rationale, the changed positions of O'Connor, Souter, and Kennedy, and the confirmations of Justices Ginsburg and Breyer, mean that the conditions to reverse *Roe* through the courts do not exist at this time.

Some of the conditions for overturning *Roe* were realized, however. In 1973, the Court held that *Roe* was justified because a "right" to abortion existed in Anglo-American history. With *Webster* in 1989, a majority of the Court dropped that rationale, implicitly acknowledging that it was false. No majority of Justices since *Webster* has suggested a constitutional foundation for the original decision, referring to *stare decisis* alone as a reason *not* to *overturn Roe*.[28] In addition, a series of decisions by the Court indicated that *Roe* and its progeny were based – in Justice O'Connor's words – on a series of "inconsistent" and "unworkable" policy judgments about abortion practice.[29]

What Happened?

Why did *Casey* come out the way it did? There may be dozens of reasons – political, legal, cultural, personal. But four stand out.

First, as a result of the November, 1986, U.S. Senate elections, pro-abortion Senators took over the chairmanship of the Senate Judiciary Committee, which reviews and approves Supreme Court nominees. The summer before saw the confirmations of Chief

Justice Rehnquist and Justice Scalia; the following summer saw the Bork debacle, and the nomination process has never been the same.[30]

Second, the litigation strategy, devised a decade after *Roe*, focused on intricate legal aspects of constitutional litigation – and not the cultural considerations that formed the "reliance interests" concern of the Supreme Court.[31] Indeed, the litigation strategy barely addressed the presumption that abortion was good for women.[32] The litigation campaign knocked out the legal pillars to *Roe*, as evidenced by the reasoning in *Webster* and *Casey*, only to see them replaced with sociological/political ones.

Third, abortion proponents countered with a strategy focused on "an audience of one" – Justice Sandra Day O'Connor, the first woman justice on the Supreme Court.[33] Justice O'Connor proved to be highly influenced by the "reliance interests" arguments, and she, in turn, obviously influenced the votes of Kennedy and Souter. Her approach grew even more extreme in her *Carhart* concurring opinion in 2000. Whereas she had once written in her *Akron* dissent in 1983 that the opinions of national medical organizations should *not* determine the outcome of abortion cases, she agreed with the Court's position in *Carhart* that the views of a vague "significant body of medical opinion" could determine the Court's view of the "safety" of partial-birth abortion and the constitutionality of laws prohibiting it.[34]

Fourth, the cause for life adopted an "inside" strategy – focused on persuading the Court, litigating cases correctly, and observing legal precedents and nuances. When the "inside" strategy seemed to be gathering steam (as evidenced, for example, by Supreme Court decisions between 1983–1992 and by media predictions of *Roe*'s demise), abortion proponents adopted an "outside" strategy of political and personal lobbying and media pressure. In a sense, the "inside" strategy of reason and logic and legal analysis was overwhelmed by the "outside" strategy of political maneuvering and rhetoric and marketing. The outside strategy obviously won. In light of this experience, the cause for life should be wary of adopting an exclusively "inside" strategy again, thinking that "only a Justice or two will do it." Such thinking overlooks the difficulty of the confirmation process and the importance of public and professional opinion and their impact on individual Justices.

Democratic Obstacles to Constitutional Change: The Myths

The key challenge for the cause for life in the coming decade is mobilizing public opinion to bring about constitutional change. At the outset, that will require understanding what public opinion is and why, and shifting the focus of public education to "Middle America."[35] The central problem is public "ambivalence" over legalized abortion.[36] That ambivalence is grounded in the myths that abortion is a "necessary evil" and good for women. We must dispel those myths.

The Myth that Public Opinion is "Polarized"

One view – an erroneous one – is the notion that public opinion is "polarized" over abortion. This metaphor is often used by the media and is shared by the majority of the Supreme Court. Justice Breyer's opinion in *Carhart* suggests that the Court employs Solomon-like wisdom in deciding contentious issues like abortion that cannot be left to the people to decide – the Court as national psychologist:

> We understand the controversial nature of the problem. Millions of Americans believe that life begins at conception and consequently that an abortion is akin to causing the death of an innocent child. . . . Other millions fear that a law that forbids abortion would condemn many American women to lives that lack dignity, depriving them of equal liberty and leading those with least resources to undergo illegal abortions with the attendant risks of death and suffering. Taking account of these virtually irreconcilable points of view, aware that constitutional law must govern a society whose different members sincerely hold directly opposing views . . . this Court . . . has determined . . . that the Constitution offers basic protection to the woman's right to choose.[37]

This turns the Constitution on its head. Whereas the Founders believed that all but a few issues are left for the people to decide through the democratic process, the Supreme Court believes it is free to remove certain controversies from the democratic process.[38] This is a dangerously anti-democratic notion. And it is particularly dangerous because at its most arrogant, the Court is most ignorant. The Court's perception of public opinion on abortion is fundamentally wrong.

The majority in *Carhart* assumes that Americans are evenly divided between those who see abortion as a fundamental right and those who see the life of the unborn child as inviolable – an "all or nothing" divide. With public opinion so divided and so irreconcilable, the Court has to intervene, mediate, and decide the issue. The Court's view may reflect the interest groups that come before it, but it does not accurately represent the view of most Americans.[39]

This is clearly demonstrated by the most in-depth and thorough survey of American attitudes toward abortion ever undertaken, the 1991 Gallup Poll on "Abortion and Moral Beliefs." University of Virginia sociologist James Davison Hunter designed the survey instrument, and Hunter and sociologist Carl Bowman analyzed the results in their path-breaking 1994 book, *Before the Shooting Begins: Searching for Democracy in America's Culture Wars*. As Hunter concluded, "[t]he majority of Americans morally disapprove of the majority of abortions currently performed."[40]

Forty-nine percent of respondents considered abortion "murder," while an additional 28 percent considered abortion to be "the taking of human life." Other polls confirm these findings.[41] And yet, while many Americans see legalized abortion as an evil, they see it as "necessary." The *Chicago Tribune* aptly summarized the situation in a September, 1996, editorial: "Most Americans are uncomfortable with all-or-nothing policies on abortion. They generally shy away from proposals to ban it in virtually all circumstances, but neither are they inclined to make it available on demand no matter what the circumstances. They regard it, at best, as a necessary evil."

The Myth of Abortion as a "Necessary Evil"

If Middle America sees abortion as an evil, why is it thought to be "necessary"? Although the 1991 Gallup Poll did not probe this question directly,[42] the data made clear that Americans don't view abortion as necessary to secure equal opportunity for women. For example, less than 30 percent believe abortion is acceptable in the first three months of pregnancy if the pregnancy would require a teenager to drop out of school (and the number drops below 20 percent if the abortion is beyond three months). Likewise, less than 20 percent support abortion in the first three months of pregnancy if the pregnancy would interrupt a woman's career (and that support drops to 10 percent if the abortion is after the third month).

Although the Gallup Poll does not provide specific answers, many Americans may see legalized abortion as "necessary" to avert "the back alley." This view follows directly from the myths outlined earlier: that one to two million illegal abortions occurred annually before legalization, that thousands of women died as a result, that pre-*Roe* abortion laws targeted *women* rather than abortionists, and – more recently – that legalized abortion has been good for women. A generation of Americans educated by these myths sees criminalization as counter-productive and sees no alternative to legalization. Prohibitions on abortion would mean no fewer abortions and would only push thousands of women into "the back alley" where many would be killed or injured. *That* would be worse than the status quo.

Middle America's sense that abortion is a "necessary evil" explains a lot, and may get us beyond our current stalemate. First, it explains the seemingly contradictory polls that half of all Americans believe abortion is *murder* but should be *legal*. (This must be distinguished from the notion that abortion is *murder* and *moral*, which the public does *not* adhere to.) The most committed pro-life Americans see legality and morality to be inextricably intertwined and therefore view the polling data as contradictory. But Middle America understands "legal" versus "illegal" not in moral terms but in practical terms. Based on the historical myths,

Middle America believes that criminalizing abortion would only aggravate a bad situation.

Second, it explains the power of the "choice" rhetoric. For the most committed abortion proponents, "choice" means moral autonomy. But there are less ideological meanings. According to the choice rhetoric, Americans can persuade women to make another choice, but they can't make abortion illegal, because that would mean no fewer abortions and would simply push women into the back alley. Thus, Middle America supports virtually any regulation – short of criminalization – that will encourage alternatives and reduce abortions.

The coat hanger is an especially powerful symbol for the "necessary evil" mindset. For example, when Congress first began to consider bills prohibiting partial-birth abortion, abortion advocates bought a full-page advertisement in the *New York Times* showing a large coat hanger and the caption, "Will this be the only approved method of abortion?" The coat hanger recalls desperate women and the back alley, and reinforces the notion that there are two and only two alternatives: legal abortion or the back alley.

Finally, the myth of abortion as a "necessary evil" also explains why 50 percent of Americans may believe that abortion is "murder" without translating this into fervent social or political mobilization. Middle Americans view abortion as *intractable*. Accordingly, they view fervent campaigns to prohibit it as unrealistic if not counterproductive, while they are drawn to realistic alternatives and regulations. Abortion is not a galvanizing *electoral* issue for Middle America because Middle America does not see that much can be done about it legally or politically.

What to do?

The myth of abortion as a "necessary evil" has profound implications for future public education.

First, it means that abortion opponents have *won* the essential debate that the unborn child is a human being and not mere tissue. In fact, the whole thrust of the "choice" argument admits this and seeks to sideline Americans' moral qualms by telling Americans that, *even if* it is a human life, the most that can be done is to persuade women not to have abortions. Second, it means that the ideological arguments of both sides ("choice" v. "child") often miss the much more practical concerns of many Americans. Third, it indicates that Americans balance the fate of the woman and the fate of the child. Although they understand the fate of the child to be fatal, they want to avoid the same result for women and believe that legalized abortion has been better, on balance, for women. This means that emphasizing the fatal impact of abortion through, for example, graphic pictures of aborted babies, is not a "silver bullet" that will transform public opinion. Indeed, emphasizing the negative impact on the baby alone may only heighten public anxiety over abortion and make it seem more intractable, which reinforces "pro-choice" rhetoric: Since abortion is intractable, many think, it must be left to women in their individual circumstances.

The most direct and effective response to the myth of abortion as a "necessary evil" is to raise public consciousness of the negative impact of abortion on women. If it can be shown that abortion harms women as well as the unborn, it will not be seen as "necessary." This is a very clear-cut objective and can be effectively tracked through public opinion polls.

The Abortion Experiment: The Disasters Behind the Façade

The past three decades of abortion-on-demand have been an unprecedented experiment on women (and on society). Cataloguing all its effects is beyond this chapter's scope,[43] but any list would include:

DIRECT HARM
Physical injury and death
Psychological trauma
Increased risk of breast cancer

INDIRECT HARM
Sexual promiscuity and the increased incidence of STDs
(including increased incidence of cervical cancer)
Coarsened relationships between men and women

Domestic abuse

Child abuse

Increase in the repeat abortion rate

These disasters lie behind the façade of women's "freedom" of abortion. Abortion has actually aggravated the very problems – illegitimacy, child abuse, and domestic abuse – that it promised to solve. It has isolated women in their pregnancies and made them more vulnerable to violent abuse from uncommitted men. This is the real, enduring legacy of *Roe v. Wade*.

We need to learn from history. The "necessary evil" myth is not unique to abortion. The fight against slavery, both here and abroad, also encountered the "necessary evil" myth. Many in England and the United States believed that slavery was necessary to the economy. Abolitionists simply had to dispel that myth.[44] The cause for life in America must do the same.

Incremental Measures: Strategically Necessary and Morally Appropriate

Since *Roe*, democratically elected representatives have made efforts to limit abortion's impact as much as possible through many types of important legislation (parental involvement laws, informed consent provisions, regulations on abortion clinics, and partial-birth abortion prohibitions). These measures *seek to limit abortion when it is not possible – socially, legally, politically, or physically – to prohibit it*. Legislation of this type is sometimes called "incremental" legislation or "incrementalism." Given the constitutional and political obstacles imposed by *Roe*, this legislation is both morally appropriate and strategically necessary.

Roe effectively stripped the states of the *power* to prohibit abortions. Lawmakers responded with legislation that would at least limit it. To have any real impact, these laws must incorporate boundaries imposed by the Supreme Court. Otherwise, federal courts will strike them down, and attorneys' fees will go to abortion clinics and their attorneys – a senseless and humiliating end for pro-life legislators. The cause for life has only two options: It can stay out of the legislative process and do nothing, or work within the legal and political constraints imposed by the Supreme Court. This has been true since 1973.

The intent of such "incremental" legislation is clearly not to endorse abortion or *Roe*, but to limit its effect. These state regulations recognize the *power* of *Roe*, not its authority. By "limiting the harm done" or "lessening the negative consequences," we do not support the rest of the evil that we do not have the power (legal, political, or social) to limit now. This moral reasoning is aptly summarized by Pope John Paul II in his encyclical, *Evangelium Vitae*:

[W]hen it is not possible to overturn or completely abrogate a pro-abortion law, an elected official whose absolute personal opposition to procured abortion was well known, could licitly support proposals aimed at *limiting the harm* done by such a law and at lessening its negative consequences at the level of general opinion and public morality. This does not in fact represent an illicit cooperation with an unjust law, but rather a legitimate and proper attempt to limit its evil aspects.[45]

Incremental legislation follows this formula completely.

An "all or nothing" approach, by comparison, is not morally required and is almost always futile, for three major reasons. First, in a democratic society, a wide spectrum of views exists. Legislative outcomes lean toward the middle, and voices at either end of the spectrum (on *any* public issue) usually do not command majority support.

Second, most people oppose dramatic change and are usually open, if at all, to change a little at a time. In a democratic society – where political power is so diffused, freedom of speech is almost unlimited, and public opinion plays such a dominant role – advocating a policy change dramatically at odds with the status quo (abortion-on-demand in every state) creates a stark contrast of absolutes – with a Grand Canyon in between – and no means of bridging that gap in public discourse.

As a practical matter, an "all or nothing" approach means abandoning the legislative arena. Incremental legislation, in contrast, raises pointed issues in the state legislatures and requires legislators to debate real issues and stand up on real votes. And this is all done with the recognition that incremental legislation seeks to limit the abortion license to the greatest extent possible. Incremental legislation is an "all or *something*" approach.

We must pursue a vision of complete justice, of complete legal protection for human life. But, in the democratic process, we must always pursue the ideal in such a way that progress is made with the willingness to accept "something" when "all" is not achievable due to social, legal, or political obstacles beyond our control.

A Federalism Amendment for Constitutional Change

The *Carhart* decision vividly demonstrates that no progress can be made as long as the federal courts can thwart the public will expressed through legislation. But the Court's current composition, the pro-abortion majority in the U.S. Senate, and the changed (and charged) nature of the Supreme Court nomination process make overturning *Roe v. Wade* through the courts highly unlikely in the next decade.

Rather than focusing exclusively on judicial selection, the cause for life should focus on a *long-term* plan to achieve a "federalism" amendment on abortion. [46] A federalism amendment would overturn the primary holding in the *Roe/Doe* decisions – i.e., that a right to abortion is protected by the federal constitution – thereby returning the abortion issue to the states where it resided before 1973.

The traditional goal of the cause for life, a Human Life Amendment (amending the Constitution to explicitly provide protection to human life from conception to natural death) is simply not possible without first opening up the state political and legislative process. A federalism amendment would do this, allowing democratic forces to build consensus, state by state, to protect the unborn. A federalism amendment should be seen, therefore, as a prerequisite to any Human Life Amendment, rather than a substitute.

A national strategy to ratify a federalism amendment to the Constitution would complement a Court reversal strategy by mobilizing the public nation-wide and by putting pressure on the Court to correct its own mistake. But the prospects for the latter are still low: President Bush may well have the opportunity to appoint 4-5 new justices by 2008, if elected to a second term. But his chances to actually confirm 4-5 new, strong justices (like those who have repeatedly and forthrightly argued for the overturning of *Roe*) are slim. Senator Jeffords's decision to become Independent in the spring of 2001 put Senate committees into pro-abortion hands. And the Senate confirmation process has changed significantly since Justice O'Connor was nominated in 1983. As former U.S. Senator and federal judge James Buckley recently wrote:

> Thirty years ago, when I was privileged to serve in the Senate, nominees of [the caliber of John Roberts and Miguel Estrada] would have been confirmed within weeks after their names had been submitted, regardless of party affiliation. In those days, a candidate's personal opinions were deemed irrelevant as long as he was qualified by training, experience and tem perament to interpret and apply the law dispassionately. The confirmation process has changed dramatically for the worse since then.[47]

Even with such successful nominations, the Court would only reverse *Roe's* finding that the Constitution contains a right to abortion. It would *not* declare the unborn child a "person," and therefore protected by the Constitution (under the Fourteenth Amendment, for example). Even Justices Scalia and Thomas – the two most pro-life Justices on the Court – have rejected that argument. They believe that the Constitution is silent on abortion, and that the issue is therefore for the people, not the Court, to decide. If returning the issue to the states is the most the Court would do anyway, why not work toward that goal directly?

A federalism amendment would require an enormous effort and a creative educational strategy. But it could galvanize Americans by: 1) recognizing and seizing upon public ambivalence; and 2) showing that abortion has not benefited women and is therefore not a "necessary" evil. A federalism amendment would say, in effect: The national rule of abortion-on-demand has not worked; let the states try alternative policies. And it would do this without establishing, in words or principle, that anything less than a life-protective policy is encouraged in the Constitution itself.

Conclusion

Political and legal changes in American society since 1983 demonstrate that a litigation campaign to overturn *Roe* through the courts will be futile for the foreseeable future. These include: the *Casey* and *Carhart* decisions, which confirm the pro-abortion direction of the Supreme Court; the growth of pro-abortion sentiment in the U.S. Senate, the corresponding political obstacles to successfully change the Court by nomination; and the myth of abortion as a "necessary evil" – believed by the Court as well as many Americans. A coherent and sustained strategy to secure a federalism amendment, along with a creative public education campaign to raise public awareness of the negative impact of abortion on women, is necessary to open up the political and democratic processes at the state and federal level to create a culture of life in America.

Clarke D. Forsythe earned his B.A. at Allegheny College, 1980, and J.D. at Valparaiso University, 1983; he is President, Americans United for Life (AUL), a national public policy and educational organization.

Endnotes

1   See generally, Paige C. Cunningham & Clarke D. Forsythe, "Is Abortion the First Right for Women?" in J. Douglas Butler and David F. Walbert, eds., *Abortion, Medicine and the Law* (4th ed. 1992); Elizabeth Ring-Cassidy & Ian Gentles, *Women's Health after Abortion: The Medical and Psychological Evidence* (The deVeber Institute for Bioethics and Social Research 2002); Theresa Burke, *Forbidden Grief: The Unspoken Pain of Abortion* (2002); Thomas W. Strahan, ed., *Detrimental Effects of Abortion: An Annotated Bibliography with Commentary* (3d ed. 2001); Thorp, Hartmann & Shadigian, *The Long-Term Health Consequences of Abortion*, Ob. Gyn Survey (January 2003).

2   410 U.S. 113 (1973). The Court may not have specifically held that abortion was itself a "right" in *Roe*, and the Court's decision in *Harris v. McRae*, 448 U.S. 297 (1980) (upholding restrictions on federal fund-

ing of abortion) may not have been possible if abortion was denominated a fundamental right. It now seems, however, that a majority of the Court has come to regard abortion itself as a constitutional right. See e.g., *Stenberg v. Carhart*, 530 U.S. 914, 920 (2000) (referring to "the right to an abortion").

3   530 U.S. 914 (2000).

4   James Davison Hunter, *Before the Shooting Begins: Searching for Democracy in America's Culture Wars* (1994). "Middle America" is the 60 percent of the American public which is neither consistently pro-life and consistently pro-abortion. See supra text at pp. 6–8 and accompanying notes.

5   John T. Noonan, Jr., ed., *The Morality of Abortion* ix (1970).

6   Clarke D. Forsythe, "The Effective Enforcement of Abortion Law Before *Roe v. Wade*," in Brad Stetson, ed., *The Silent Subject: Reflections on the Unborn in American Culture* (1996).

7   Mary Calderone, "Illegal Abortion as a Public Health Problem," 50 Am. J. Pub. Health 948, 949 (1960). See U.S. Dept. of Health, Education and Welfare, Public Health Service, Vital Statistics of the United States, 1957 cxxxix (1959) (Table CZ) (citing 260 deaths attributed to abortions of all kinds out of total of 1,746 maternal deaths from all causes).

8   U.S. Public Health Service, Centers for Disease Control, Abortion Surveillance 61 (Nov. 1980).

9   Clarke D. Forsythe, "The Effective Enforcement of Abortion Law before *Roe v. Wade*," in Brad Stetson, ed., *The Silent Subject: Reflections on the Unborn in American Culture* (1996); Germain Grisez, *Abortion: The Myths, the Realities, and the Arguments* (1970).

10   Clarke D. Forsythe, "The Effective Enforcement of Abortion Law before *Roe v. Wade*," in Brad Stetson, ed., *The Silent Subject: Reflections on the Unborn in American Culture* (1996).

11   See generally, Paige C. Cunningham & Clarke D. Forsythe, "Is Abortion the First Right for Women?" in J. Douglas Butler & David F. Walbert, eds., *Abortion, Medicine and the Law* (4th ed. 1992); Elizabeth Ring-Cassidy & Ian Gentles, *Women's Health after Abortion: The Medical and Psychological Evidence* (The deVeber Institute for Bioethics and Social Research 2002); Thomas W. Strahan, ed., *Detrimental Effects of Abortion: An Annotated Bibliography with Commentary* (3d ed. 2001); Joel Brind et al., "Induced Abortion as an Independent Risk Factor for Breast Cancer: A Comprehensive Review and Meta-Analysis," 50 J. Epidemiology & Community Health 481 (1996); Janet R. Daling et al., "Risk of Breast Cancer Risk

Among Young Women: Relationship to Induced Abortion," 86 J. Nat'l Cancer Inst. 1584 (1994); John Kindley, "The Fit between the Elements for an Informed Consent Cause of Action and the Scientific Evidence Linking Induced Abortion with Increased Breast Cancer Risk," 1998 Wis. L. Rev. 1595.

12   Paul Benjamin Linton, "Enforcement of State Abortion Statutes after *Roe*: A State-by-State Analysis," 67 U. Det. L. Rev. 157 (1990).

13   410 U.S. 113 (1973).

14   410 U.S. 179 (1973).

15   *Vacco v. Quill*, 521 U.S. 793 (1997); *Washington v. Glucksburg*, 521 U.S. 702 (1997).

16   See Lynn Wardle, "Judicial Appointments to the Lower Federal Courts: The Ultimate Arbiters of the Abortion Doctrine," in Dennis J. Horan, Edward R. Grant & Paige C. Cunningham, *Abortion and the Constitution: Reversing Roe v. Wade Through the Courts*, 216–17 (1987).

17   462 U.S. 416 (1983) (striking down the following requirements: that all first trimester abortions be performed in a hospital; that parental consent be obtained for abortions on minors under the age of fifteen; that detailed informed consent be obtained; that a twenty-four-hour waiting period be observed; and that disposal of remains be "humane").

18   See generally, Dennis J. Horan, Edward R. Grant & Paige C. Cunningham, eds., *Abortion and the Constitution: Reversing Roe v. Wade Through the Courts* (1987); Rex Lee, Foreword, p. xv, in Horan, Grant & Cunningham.

19   505 U.S. 833 (1992).

20   For example, extensive scientific and medical data on the humanity of the unborn child have been submitted to the Supreme Court through numerous briefs from *Roe* through *Carhart*. Clearly, the current justices know the facts about fetal development but do not care.

21   See e.g., Rex Lee, Foreword, Horan, Grant & Cunningham, *Abortion and the Constitution*, at xiv.

22   492 U.S. 490 (1989).

23   Charles E. Rice, Implications of the Coming Retreat from *Roe v. Wade*, 4 J. Contemp. Health L. & Pol. 1 (1988).

24   *Casey*, 505 U.S. at 833, 867. Cf. 505 U.S. at 853 ("the reservations any of us may have in reaffirming the central holding of *Roe* are outweighed by the explication of individual liberty we have given combined with the force of *stare decisis*.").

25   505 U.S. at 856 (emphasis added).

26 The notion of "reliance interests" was not entirely unforeseen. Dean Robert Bennett of Northwestern Law School, who unsuccessfully argued against the constitutionality of the Hyde Amendment in 1980, voiced a similar formulation in 1986: "*Roe* has aroused expectations and induced patterns of behavior, so that, quite apart from one's views of the merits of the abortion controversy, any move to overrule brings social costs that must be taken into account." Bennett, "Judicial Activism and the Concept of Original Intent," 69 Judicature 219, 223 (1986), quoted in Richard S. Myers, "Prolife Litigation and Civil Liberties," in Horan, Grant & Cunningham, pp. 53–54 n.90.

27 Paul Benjamin Linton, "*Planned Parenthood v. Casey*: The Flight from Reason in the Supreme Court," 13 St. Louis U. Public Law Rev. 15, 43 (1993) ("This . . . is the heart of the Joint Opinion and the real reason the Court did not overrule *Roe v. Wade* in *Casey*," citing 112 S.Ct at 2809). This notion was also referred to in the first paragraph of the Court's opinion in *Carhart*: "Other millions fear that a law that forbids abortion would condemn many American women to lives that lack dignity, depriving them of equal liberty and leading those with least resources to undergo illegal abortions with the attendant risks of death and suffering." 530 U.S. at 920.

28 *Casey*, 505 U.S. at 854–69 (joint opinion of Justices O'Connor, Kennedy and Souter).

29 *Akron*, 462 U.S. at 452, 454 (O'Connor, J., dissenting). See also *Thornburgh v. American College of Obstetricians and Gynecologists*, 476 U.S. 747, 814 (O'Connor, J., dissenting) ("unworkable scheme"). See also, Clarke D. Forsythe, "A Legal Strategy to *Overturn Roe v. Wade* After *Webster*: Some Lessons from Lincoln," 1991 B.Y.U. L. Rev. 519.

30 See text and accompanying note, citing James L. Buckley, "Obstruction of Justice," *Wall Street Journal*, June 13, 2002, at A16.

31 There was some recognition that this was needed but it was not developed into a full-scale public education effort. See e.g., Rosenblum & Marzen, "Strategies for Reversing *Roe v. Wade*," in Horan, Grant & Cunningham, *Abortion and the Constitution: Reversing Roe v. Wade through the Courts*, at 206: "Secondary tasks, the development of statistical data demonstrating the social and medical harm caused by abortion, have barely begun, and the creation of social, economic, and legal policies assisting the pregnant woman to carry her child to term and thereafter are even further behind." *Id*. at 205 ("[T]he Court's predominant concern was the social, psychological,

and economic 'detriments' and 'stigmas' attached to pregnancy. From this perspective, a fully convincing case for abolition of the *Roe* doctrine can be made only in the context of a social and legal milieu in which these stigmas and detriments are alleviated or erased.")

32   *Abortion and the Constitution*, p. 36.

33   See e.g., Susan Estrich, "Abortion Politics: Writing for an Audience of One," 138 U. Pa. L. Rev. 119, 122–23 (1989). ("[T]he real audience is one woman. Sandra Day O'Connor, the only woman in American history to sit on the United States Supreme Court, is in the position single-handedly to decide the future of abortion rights.").

34   Cf. *Akron*, 462 U.S. at 456 (O'Connor, J., dissenting) (dismissing ACOG Standards) with *Carhart*, 530 U.S. at 948 (O'Connor, J., concurring).

35   See *infra* note 4.

36   James Davison Hunter, *Before the Shooting Begins: Searching for Democracy in America's Culture War* (1994), Chapter 4 ("The Anatomy of Ambivalence"), Chapter 5 ("The Culture of Ambivalence").

37   530 U.S. at 920–21. Justice O'Connor seems to be of the same mindset. See also Justice O'Connor's concurring opinion, 530 U.S. at 947 ("difficult questions that, as the Court recognizes, involve 'virtually irreconcilable points of view.'. . .").

38   The most recent example of six justices doing this is the Supreme Court's June 20, 2002, decision in *Atkins v. Virginia*, holding that the execution of the mentally retarded is unconstitutional under the Eighth Amendment based on public opinion polls. 122 S.Ct. 2242 (2002).

39   In fact, the abortion policy imposed by the Supreme Court (abortion-on-demand throughout pregnancy) reflects the views of only the 15–20 percent who are committed to abortion-on-demand. See Hunter, supra note 36; Lynn D. Wardle, "The Quandary of Pro-life Free Speech: A Lesson from the Abolitionists," 62 Albany L. Rev. 853, 963 (Appendix 4), 964 (Appendix 5), 966 (Appendix 6) (1999).

40   Hunter (& Bowman) at 98.

41   Raymond J. Adamek, *30-plus Years of Abortion Polls: What Have We Learned* (Ad Hoc Committee in Defense of Life 2002).

42   See Hunter, *supra* note 4, at 122 ("But where does the ambivalence come from? Here the survey findings provide us with little insight.")

43   See generally, Paige C. Cunningham & Clarke D. Forsythe, Is Abortion the First Right for Women? in J. Douglas Butler & David F. Walbert, eds., *Abortion, Medicine and the Law* (4th ed. 1992); Elizabeth Ring-Cassidy and Ian Gentles, *Women's Health after Abortion: The*

Medical and Psychological Evidence (The deVeber Institute for Bioethics and Social Research 2002); Thomas W. Strahan, ed., *Detrimental Effects of Abortion: An Annotated Bibliography with Commentary* (3d ed. 2001); Jonathan Klick & Thomas Stratmann, "The Effect of Abortion Legalization on Sexual Behavior: Evidence from Sexually Transmitted Diseases" (George Mason University School of Law Working Paper 02-11 2002).

44 See e.g., Thomas Clarkson, *An Essay on the Impolicy of the African Slave Trade* (1788) (Books for Libraries Press Reprint 1971).

45 Pope John Paul II, *The Gospel of Life* (Evangelium Vitae) 135 (Times Books/Random House 1995) (emphasis in original).

46 For a fuller explanation of the reasons for a "federalism" amendment on abortion, see Clarke D. Forsythe, "A New Strategy," *Human Life Review* (Fall 1999); Clarke D. Forsythe, "First Steps," *National Review* (Dec. 20, 1999).

47 James L. Buckley, "Obstruction of Justice," *Wall Street Journal*, June 13, 2002, at A16.

Seeing the Dragon Cloud

John Manning Regan, Sr.

Byron R. White, United States Supreme Court Justice from 1962 to 1993, died in Denver, Colorado, at age 84 in the spring of 2002.

Justice White did not share, nor did he support in his decisions, the politically correct ideologies of the legal and cultural elite, most particularly, their contentions that the Constitution protects a pregnant women's choice to have an abortion. For this repudiation of their dearest philosophy, his reward is current obscurity in the archives of American jurisprudence. For these reasons alone, the pro-life organizations and their members should demonstrate their appreciation for his important contributions to the pro-life cause, rendered on the field of battle where they count the most – the Federal Judiciary.

In 1963–64, I was a graduate student at Yale Law School. White had received his LL.B. from Yale in 1946. President Kennedy had appointed him to the Court in 1962, and his judicial performance – even then – was causing a mild stir among the faculty. I took a seminar, *Supreme Court Today*, under Professor Fred Rodell, and wrote a term paper on the newly appointed Justice.[1] As many know, Byron R. White was an all-American running back for the University of Colorado football team. On the gridiron, his teammates called him "Whizzer." He also played running back for the NFL's Pittsburgh Steelers and the Detroit Lions. In 1954, at age 37, he was inducted into the National Football League Hall of Fame (the only Supreme Court Justice so honored). He was also a Rhodes scholar, and a Navy pilot in World War II. Accordingly, I entitled my paper "Goal to Go," capitalizing on a familiar football analogy; but the title also reflected the growing anxieties about White's judicial views, which did not conform to the paradigms of the Yale Law School faculty.

The purpose of this article is to examine White's judicial opinions on the constitutional right to abortion – specifically, his dissenting opinions in *Roe v. Wade* and *Thornburgh v. American College of Obstetricians*.[2] This article could be titled "Touchdown," because White achieved his goal not only of becoming an outstanding football player, but also of becoming an outstanding Supreme Court Justice. White never succumbed to the deconstruction of our Constitution. Instead, he remained steadfast in observing sound principles of constitutional judicial review whereby the language of the document and the original intent of its authors (and of those who voted its approval), supersede the personal policy preferences of judges.

The Dragon Cloud

*Sometimes we see a cloud that's dragonish;
A vapour sometimes like a bear or lion:
A tower'd citadel, a pendent rock,
a forked mountain, or blue promontory,
with trees upon't, that nod unto the world,
and mock our eyes with air:
Thou hast seen these signs:
They are black vesper's pageants.

from *Antony and Cleopatra*; by Wm. Shakespeare
Act IV, Sc. XIV: Antony to Eros

Justice White's Dissenting Opinion in Roe v. Wade

If ever there was an example of a Judge seeing the dragon cloud of judicial despotism, it was Justice White's dissent in *Roe*:

The Court simply fashions and announces a new constitutional right for pregnant mothers, and, with scarcely any reason or

authority for its action, invests that right with sufficient sub-
stance to override most existing state abortion statutes ... [it is]
an exercise of raw judicial power. . . .[3]

Three external and objective forces transcend and constrain the
subjective personal preferences of federal judges while they perform the process of judicial review. The first, and most important,
is their oath of office to support the Constitution, which Article VI
imposes on all judicial officers of the United States (and, upon
every state judge also). The second is the doctrine of *stare decisis*,
which compels a judge to decide issues before him in the same
manner as prior courts have decided them so long as the precedent
remains tenable. Third, are the principles of constitutional and
statutory interpretation, which become obligatory whenever ambi-
guities arise in the intentions of the lawmakers, and/or in the language of statutes or constitutional provisions (a duty exists, for
example, to interpret laws in such a way as to avoid constitutional
conflict, if possible). What is not permitted, nor authorized in any
manner, is the supplanting of the lawmakers' intentions with the
personal predilections of the judge. Because, as is obvious in the
latter case, the judge would then usurp the law-making function,
and arrogate to himself, the legislative power which Article I, sec.
1, of the Constitution vests in the Congress, or the amending
power, which Article V vests in the Congress and the states.

White's dissent proclaims that the majority in *Roe* is guilty of
usurping both the legislative and amending functions when it
announces "a new Constitutional right" to abortion. He sees the
announcement as bereft of both reason and authority, and an overt
exercise of raw judicial power. This decision lets loose the dragon
of judicial irresponsibility – tantamount to tyranny – which
"mock(s) our eyes with air" and transforms the Judiciary, under the
pretext of Constitutional interpretation, into Supreme autocrats
answerable to no one.

That dissent is a serious indictment of his colleagues' personal
integrity. White, in effect, has charged them with violating their
oaths of office, and with inserting into the Constitution a right to
abortion which nowhere exists in the language of that document.

He sees in this act of malfeasance a deliberate displacement of the judgment of State Legislatures, democratically chosen in political processes calculated to ascertain the "consent of the governed," and a substituting for that legislative judgment a contrived constitutional barrier and an order of priorities, only the judges themselves prefer.

White's further comments on the morality of abortion – *per se* – are equivocal. His circumlocutions allow the inference that he may approve of therapeutic abortions, though no firm conclusion is possible from what he has written.[4] Unequivocal is his conclusion that the Court has embarked upon a perilous journey; that it has left its proper moorings of oath-bound fidelity to the language of the Constitution, and to the intentions of its framers; and that it has begun to drift into the open sea of ideology and politics, thus putting at risk the rule of law, the judicial process, the integrity of judges, and the legitimacy of the Court itself – truly a dragon cloud to dread.

Justice White's Dissenting Opinion in Thornburgh

Thirteen years after *Roe*, in 1986, White calls, in another dissent (thirty pages long), upon the Court to repudiate *Roe* on the ground that its premises are still "fundamentally misguided."

> I was in dissent in *Roe v. Wade*, and I am in dissent today.

> Fundamental liberties and interests are most clearly present when the Constitution provides specific textual recognition of their existence and importance.

> As for the notion that choice in the matter of abortion is implicit in the concept of ordered liberty...the values animating the Constitution do not compel recognition of the abortion liberty as fundamental. In so denominating that liberty, the Court engages, not in Constitutional interpretation, but in the unrestrained imposition of its own extra constitutional value preferences.[5]

White's dissent in *Thornburgh* is much more detailed and elaborate than in *Roe*, though his ultimate opinion remains the same.

What has changed is White's moral conscience. In *Roe*, he only superficially observes that the Court chooses maternal interests ("convenience") over developing fetal life. In *Thornburgh*, however, White classifies the abortion decision as *sui generis* because it "involves the destruction of the fetus" and therefore it is "different in kind from the decision not to conceive."

The White-Stevens Exchange

Justice White's charges in *Thornburgh*, that the Court had betrayed its oath of office, its responsibilities to precedents, and its duty to interpret state laws in a manner to avoid, if possible, a constitutional confrontation, so riled his colleague, Justice John Paul Stevens, that Stevens wrote a separate concurring opinion mildly rebuking White for both inconsistency and incoherence.[6]

Stevens's first salvo is that White concurred with the Court's decisions in *Griswold v. Connecticut* (striking down Connecticut's ban on contraceptives as applied to married persons),[7] which spawned both *Eisenstadt v. Baird* (extending right to contraception to unmarried persons)[8] and *Roe*, and which, for Justice Stevens, is also the binding precedent that should invoke White's concurrence, not his dissent, in those subsequent cases. Thus, Stevens alleges that White is being inconsistent in his *Roe* and *Thornburgh* dissents:

> (Justice White) has not disavowed the Court's prior approach
> to the interpretation of the word "liberty" or, more narrowly,
> the line of cases that culminated in the unequivocal holding ...
> that the Constitution protects individual decisions in matters
> of child bearing from unjustified intrusion by the State.[9]

Stevens' next thrust is to White's logic. He declares that White agreed in both *Griswold* and in *Thornburgh* that a woman's ability to choose whether to conceive a child is a "species of liberty" which the Fourteenth Amendment protects, but that White now holds her Fourteenth Amendment "liberty" interest is not *fundamental after* she has conceived a child. Stevens argues:

> [I]f one decision is more *fundamental* to the individual freedom
> than the other, surely it is the post-conception decision that is

the more serious. Thus, it is difficult for me to understand how Justice White reaches [his] conclusion.[10]

Finally, Stevens assails Justice White's characterization that the life of the developing fetus makes the decision to abort "different in kind from the decision not to conceive," and that the state's interest in fetal life trumps the mother's liberty to abort:

> Justice White is surely wrong in . . . protecting fetal life…during the entire period from the moment of conception until the moment of birth. Again, I recognize that a powerful theological argument can be made for that position, but I believe our jurisdiction is limited to the evaluation of secular state interests.[11]

To which criticisms, White makes the following replies:

> The Court's opinion in *Roe* itself convincingly refutes the notion that the abortion liberty is deeply rooted in the history or tradition of our people, as does the continuing and deep division of the people themselves over the question of abortion.
>
> The State's interest is in the fetus as an entity in itself, and the character of this entity does not change at the point of viability . . .
>
> [T]his is no more a "theological" position than is the Court's own judgment that viability is the point at which the State's interest becomes compelling.[12]

White's *Thornburgh* dissent presses upon the Court the legal issue of whether the fetus is a "person" under the Fourteenth Amendment, *and* the moral issue of the Court's preferring the "convenience" of the woman over the life of the fetus. For White, the presence of a separate and distinct living human being makes the abortion decision "different in kind from the others (privacy rulings) that the Court has protected under the rubric of personal . . . autonomy." White summarizes as follows:

> [O]ne must at least recognize, first, that the fetus is an entity

that bears in its cells all the genetic information that character-
izes a member of the species *homo sapiens* and distinguishes an
individual member of that species from all others[13] [including,
of course, the mother].

White thus insists that the Court deal with the pro-life positions
that abortion is the equivalent of murder, that the fetus is a separate, distinct human being apart from the mother, and is – or ought
to be – recognized as a "person" under the Fourteenth Amendment
to the Constitution; and that the classification of the right to abortion as a protected "liberty," under the Constitution is both a
flawed and illegitimate act of judicial despotism because the
Justices are merely substituting their value preferences, under the
pretense of Constitutional interpretation, for those that state legislatures have made on the question of abortion regulation.

While Justice White was not the sole dissenter in either *Roe* or
Thornburgh,[14] he is the only Justice who forthrightly challenged the
Court on the moral quality of its judgment by asserting the indisputable fact that abortion takes a human life and that to allow that
homicide under the rubric of Constitutional liberty is to create a
dragon cloud of doubt, suspicion, and illegality over the workings
of the Court itself.

The Jurisprudential Struggle of Natural Law versus Legal Realism

To understand *Roe* and *Thornburgh*, and the White-Stevens
exchange described above, it is necessary to understand the
jurisprudential struggle within the judicial system which preceded
it. This struggle began before the Civil War and culminated in the
post-World War II era. It involved the earlier dominance of
jurisprudential theories of Natural Law, and of the judicial process
as a search for truth, with the later emergence of the doctrine of
Legal Realism as the superior claimant to the attention and dedication of both legislators and judges. Natural Law jurisprudence
relied upon the proposition that truth is both reasonably ascertain-
able and a precondition to justice. Legal Realism, however,
advanced the proposition that lawmakers (legislators and judges),

who imposed rules on society from positions of institutional authority, and who made legal decisions – whatever they were, were themselves, together with their pronouncements, the ultimate "LAW." The medieval maxim – *"lex injusta non est lex"* (an unjust law is not a law) had no place in the minds of these Legal Realists, because they rejected the truth/justice correlation that Natural Law had taught.[15]

In England, these theories of realism originated with John Austin in the 1840s and were expanded by Austin's disciple, H.L.A. Hart. These theorists described their realist philosophies as Logical Positivism. In America, Roscoe Pound, dean of the Harvard Law School, and Supreme Court Justice Oliver Wendell Holmes promoted the adoption of comparable jurisprudential thought throughout the legal community.[16]

Logical Positivism and Legal Realism share the notion that the lawmakers are identical with law itself. There is no transcendent authority such as truth, or Natural Law, or moral obligation, to channel the boundaries of legislation or to limit the scope of judicial decisions. The reality is the process, and the process is the substantive thing itself. This is the principle of self-authentication or self-validation, where laws are deemed legitimate and moral by reference only to the institutions that make them.

Some variations on these themes have developed over the years. Holmes's famous assertion that the life of the law is not logic, but experience, introduced both history and pragmatism as influential factors in the formation of laws and judicial decisions. And Pound advocated a test of social acceptance as a validating mechanism for enactment of laws.[17] But the core philosophy of all of them is that law does not exist apart from the processors who promulgate it.

The idea, expressed in our Declaration of Independence, of the self-evident truth that man's inalienable rights derive from a Creator, was thus abandoned as a tenet of modern legal theory, and was replaced with a theory that legal rights derived solely from the dictates of the legal institutions themselves. Obviously, this is a form of totalitarianism.

Positivism and the Individual

Now, if the principle of self-authentication is good enough to justify what our legal institutions do, why is it not also applicable to justify the behavior of individuals? To ask this question is to posit the answer because the response is not a mighty leap, but a simple step.

For these reasons, individuals within the legal elite sought the same right to determine what they should do in their lives, by a process of their own will rather than by any adherence to rules of moral behavior established by a transcendent authority which the political and legal institutions no longer recognized as in existence.[18] And, as the grip of Legal Realism tightened around the soul of American Jurisprudence, this legal elite – which saw the potential for totalitarianism – reacted by seeking refuge in the "liberty" language of the Constitution's Fourteenth Amendment. There they carved out an area of life into which the law could not trespass – the island of privacy (now known as "personal autonomy"), with all its penumbras, wherein they, like the institutions they feared, could commit acts whose legitimacy and morality only they would decide. [19] The relevant question was no longer "Is it moral?" but "Did I choose?"

Authentic Human Freedom

It was into this maelstrom of clashing jurisprudential theories that President Kennedy plunged Byron R. White in 1962. Since legal scholars measure changes in jurisprudence by centuries, and not by generations, no one knows whether White was aware of this process of jurisprudential transformation. We can and do know, from his work on the Court, that he did *NOT* manifest any agreement with the principles of Legal Realism – especially the principle of self-authentication.

In the White-Stevens exchange, White says that "liberty" requires the recognition that the decision "not to conceive" is vastly different from the decision "to abort" because, in the latter case, the abortion decision deprives another human being of his life and liberty. The "liberty" of the mother, correctly understood, becomes a responsibility to safeguard the life and "liberty" of the fetus. Stevens, contrariwise, argues that the post-conception decision is more *fundamental*, more *serious*, and that therefore it implicates individual freedom to a greater degree, wherefore he concludes, in such circumstances, it is *more* important to confirm the independence and privacy of the will of the mother to abort.

Such disparities merely exemplify the failure of these Justices to know, in any philosophical sense, what human freedom actually means. White assents to the component of responsibility in human freedom; Stevens declares the indomitability of the human will.

These are ancient and competing definitions of the concept of human freedom. For Thomas Aquinas, freedom was a means to achieve, by an exercise of reason and will, an experience of truth and goodness; but for William of Ockham, freedom was simply the exercise of unfettered willfulness, a matter of asserting the power of personal choice.[20] Aquinas wrote in the thirteenth century, Ockham in the fourteenth.

Clearly, at present, the Court has assumed the power to govern on social issues through the vehicle of constitutional Judicial Review as comprehended in the jurisprudence of Legal Realism.[21] On this battleground, Justice White both began and ended his judicial career in the minority.[22] This cannot be classified as a failure. For he saw the dragon cloud of an imperialist judiciary, an oligarchy governing by fiat rather than by reference to the text of the higher authority of the written Constitution, the moral law and the search for justice through deference to the truth. And his foresight has proved to be accurate. Legal Realism has corrupted the judicial process to the extent that the Courts now threaten our freedoms rather than safeguard them.[23]

Realism has brought irresponsibility, and irresponsibility has fetched oligarchy from democracy. The judicial system has removed all transcendent authority. It is not simply that God is dead – that is an anachronistic idea from the 1960s. What is asserted today is that man is god.[24]

Several generations of law students have already become accustomed to the precepts of Legal Realism, and its doctrine of judicial supremacy. What's more, these doctrines have permeated the popular culture, and ordinary people can no longer distinguish between what is legal and what is moral. And the law, like the bad seed, has become not only a force for evil, but a black vesper's pageant.

John Manning Regan is an attorney and retired trial court judge, having served a ten-year term. He continues his practice of law of over forty years on an "of counsel" basis at Regan & Regan, P.C., in Rochester, New York.

Endnotes

1   Rodell's most famous work, *Nine Men*, advanced the theory that Supreme Court Justices' rulings were the product of their environment and experience, and not independently creative thoughts. Rodell died in 1980.

2   *Roe v. Wade*, 410 U.S. 113 (1973) and *Thornburgh v. American College of Obstetricians*, 476 U.S. 747 (1986).

3   *Roe*, 410 U.S. 113, at 221–222.

4   *Id.* ("[W]hether I agree with that marshalling of values, I can in no event join the Court's judgment . . .").

5   *Thornburgh*, 476 U.S. 747, at 786, at 790 and at 793–94.

6   More than you ever wanted to know about the White-Stevens Exchange in *Thornburgh* can be found in "Two ships passing in the Night," *St. Louis Univ. Public Law Review* (Vol.6), at pp. 229–311 (1987).

7   381 U.S. 479 (1965).

8   405 U.S. 438 (1972).

9   *Thornburgh*, 476 US at 779–80.

10 *Id.*, at 776.

11 *Id.*, at 778.

12 *Id.*, at 793, 795.

13 *Id.*, at 792.

14 Justice Rehnquist authored the one other dissenting opinion in *Roe*. In *Thornburgh*, Chief Justice Burger, Justices Rehnquist, White, and O'Connor all dissented.

15 The Latin phrase is translated: "An unjust law is not a law." Cf. Suarez, Francisco (1548–1617), Professor of Philosophy / Theology

at the University of Coimbra (Spain), in *De Legibus Ac Deo Legislatore* (Concerning Laws and God as Legislator), wherein he defends regicide as an acceptable means to dethrone an unjust sovereign, observing that unjust decrees do not bind the subjects. To Suarez, there was no "Divine Right of Kings."

16   For a more trenchant discussion of this history, see Rev. Edward J. Richard, "Law And Morality," in *National Lawyers Association Review* (Winter 1999).

17   In fairness to Pound, I should observe that he parted company with the most radical of the Legal Realists. He used social science as an ameliorating check on judicial activism. And, consequently, over the years, Pound's theories developed into a sociological jurisprudence which kept intact the idea that the law is somehow related to social justice as its end. See Roscoe Pound, *The Ideal Element in Law* (Calcutta, India: University of Calcutta Press, 1958; reprinted Indianapolis: Liberty Fund, 2002).

18   Despite our claims to democracy, this conflict involved *only* the elites, the *cognoscenti*, who were aware of the threat Legal Realism posed to their freedoms. The rise of *privacy* as a legal right was part of their answer. See Christopher Lasch, *Revolt of the Elites* (New York: W.W. Norton Co., 1995), pp. 232–33 (1995). Moreover, these individuals who brought *Griswold*, *Eisenstadt*, and *Roe* before the Supreme Court knew enough about the state of the judicial system at the time to believe that the Court would accept their challenges and decide them despite the reality that, in all three cases, the facts were both contrived and essentially false, and the controversy a despicable sham. They were right!

19   "The right to privacy" originated in 1890. See Warren and Brande, *The Right to Privacy*, 4 Harvard L. Rev. 193 (1890). Its adoption as a constitutional legal doctrine was first on the agenda of the legal elites.

20   Consult the excellent article in *First Things* magazine, by George Weigel, "A better concept of Freedom" (March, 2002) wherein he discusses at length how two medieval writers, Aquinas and Ockham, diverge along these same lines of philosophical analyses of the nature of human freedom.

21   A much-expanded presentation of this thesis can be found in Raoul Berger, *Government by Judiciary*, 2nd Edition (Indianapolis: Liberty Fund, 1997).

22   The abortion cases, the parochial school cases, and affirmative action issues all found White in dissent.

23   A conclusion Judge Robert H. Bork reached in his book *Slouching Towards Gomorrah* (New York: HarperCollins, 1996),Chapter 6 at 117.

24   And that assertion may cause the courts themselves to die. How many anti-majoritarian rulings will it take to produce the counter-reaction of constitutional reform to harness the powers of a runaway Supreme Court?

Part II
Medicine and Science

Reflections of the Abortion King

Dr. Bernard Nathanson

The Abortion King!

That, among other less-felicitous designations, was my unoffi-cial title in the obstetrical-gynecological community in the United States in the late 1960s (others ranged from Baby-killer to Dr. Hit Man). I was then one of the co-founders of the National Association for the Repeal of Abortion Laws (NARAL), later metamorphosing into the National Abortion and Reproductive Rights Action League. I was, as co-founder, a member of the Executive Committee and Chairman of the Medical Committee, actively tes-tifying at hearings on abortion law, inspecting abortion clinics (after the restrictive law in New York State had fallen in 1970), organizing NARAL action groups in other states across the country, and twice annually retreating with Lawrence Lader, the Executive Committee Chairman and mastermind of NARAL, to an island in the Caribbean to plan the national pro-abortion strategy for the next six months. In short, on the political front, I was as busy as the proverbial one-armed paper-hanger.

Transport yourself, if you will, back to the roiling maelstrom of the hirsute sixties. Something momentous had transpired across the nation (change, *blowin' in the wind*) with the shattering confla-tion of the assassinations of John F. Kennedy, Robert Kennedy, and Martin Luther King, Jr.; the slow murderous descent into the Vietnam quagmire; the emergence of the baby-boomer countercul-ture; the visceral dislike and distrust of the nation's leader, Lyndon Johnson. The time was ripe for a frontal challenge to complacent institutions, to old-line established authority. The pillars of certainty were cracking and crumbling, and into the void rushed the tie-dyed, shaggy, half-stoned counterculture and its malformed handmaiden, the sexual revolution.

It is impossible to date precisely the event in question. Suffice it to say that the introduction of the oral contraceptive in 1960 (after a seven-year "field trial" of the drug on women in Puerto Rico, one of the most shameful, uncontrolled, irresponsible experiments in the annals of medical history) is a reasonable entry point. Admittedly, some would date the revolution from 1965, concurrent with the U.S. Supreme Court decision in *Griswold v. Connecticut*, which struck down laws prohibiting contraception, but it is my conceit that that decision probably flowed from the gathering momentum of the anti-authoritarian tsunami and was thus a spawn of the sexual and social revolution convulsing the nation.

American Medicine and the Hippocratic Oath

The medical establishment in the U.S. had historically condemned induced abortion. James Mohr, a preeminent historian of abortion in America, holds that nineteenth-century organized medicine advocated extremely tight limits on abortion to spare pregnant women the dangerous ministrations of unqualified midwives, unskilled rogue nurses, and a host of non-medical personnel posing as medical professionals dispensing noxious concoctions and lethal surgical interventions. This is undoubtedly true in part, although there is reliable evidence that as far back as 1847 the American Medical Association took due notice of the ethical and moral aspects of abortion. Even as late as 1970 (after restrictive abortion laws had been struck down in thirteen states), the AMA still waffled on the abortion issue, although in that same year an editorial in an obscure California state medical journal called for a new ethic in medicine, proposing that the old ethic (largely derived from the Hippocratic Oath) was outmoded, outdated, and antiquarian. The editorial was widely cited, not only in medical but in lay circles as well, in support of loosening the legal reins on abortion.

And what of that monumental document authored by a Pythagorean physician on the island of Cos some twenty-five hundred years ago? The original Oath includes the following:

> I will give no deadly medicine to anyone if asked, nor suggest any such counsel; and in like manner I will not give a woman a pessary [a device inserted into the vagina then thought, erroneously, to induce abortion] to produce an abortion . . .

A forthright, take-no-prisoners deontology.

The remarkably long life of this Oath is probably attributable to its compatibility with orthodox Christian doctrine; indeed, there is said to be a strictly Christian version of the Oath, written in the tenth or eleventh century by person or persons unknown which is entitled *From the Oath according to Hippocrates Insofar as a Christian May Swear It.* However, in 1964 (the turbulent sixties, again), Dr. Louis Lasagna, professor of Medicine, Pharmacology and Experimental Therapeutics at Johns Hopkins Medical School, took it upon himself to revise and update the Oath. In his version he eliminated the strictures against abortion, euthanasia, sexual relations with patients, specific obligations to those who had taught him his art, and the unambiguous sense of obligation to do good and avoid harming those in his charge. His version of the Oath reads as follows:

> Most especially must I tread with care in matters of life and death. If it is given to me to save a life, all thanks. But it may also be within my power to take a life; this awesome responsibility must be faced with great humbleness and awareness of my own frailty. Above all, I must not play God.

This Uriah Heepish Lasagna revision has gained wide circulation in American education, most especially in those courses, seminars, and instructions concerning medical ethics. It is still recited at graduation ceremonies even today despite its clumsy and inelegant phrasing and its tentative moral "suggestions."

Whether the Lasagna revision prophesied or reflected the utilitarian zeitgeist gathering hurricane force in the mid-sixties is impossible to say, even at this remove. Surely there is a moral insouciance at work in this document regardless of the artless disclaimer at the end: When we speak of taking life, even the tiny innocent life of the nascent child within the womb, we *are* "playing God." To terminate human life at any stage in its natural trajectory from nascence to senescence is to foray precariously into Orwell country.

Empty Shibboleths and the Perversion of Autonomy

When I was high in the inner councils of NARAL, one of my unofficial duties was to coin attractive, catchy slogans tailored for the sound-bite-sized argument. Among my many seductive inventions were: "a woman's right to control her own body" and "freedom of choice." I smile indulgently now when I hear such empty shibboleths flung at *me* – their designer – in the course of the interminable abortion debate. Why do I discount them as duplicitous nonsense, heuristic claptrap? Because morally – and even legally – we do not have absolute, unlimited sovereignty over our own bodies: we cannot sell them; we must not inject controlled substances into them; we are barred from killing them. We cannot voluntarily place our bodies into servitude (slavery) – consult the Thirteenth Amendment to the U.S. Constitution.

With respect to freedom of choice, the ethical argument runs something like this: A morally legitimate choice involves the selection of one or more alternatives provided the alternative(s) are morally and ethically unexceptionable. In short, selection of an alternative tainted with gratuitous violence, and egregiously at odds with normative moral standards, is not an acceptable choice. Indeed, the structuring of a choice in which one alternative entails the deliberate destruction of human life is itself an immorality, an act of moral illegitimacy.

Autonomy – self-governance – is highly prized in our society. And it should be. But autonomy (read freedom of choice) is itself subject to rules and limits, e.g., the choices made by any individual within a society must be made with due regard to the moral boundaries, communal bonds, and ethical texture set by that society.

Violence – and abortion is an act of pure, unfettered violence – is and must remain outside those boundaries of acceptable choices. To permit an act of violence against another defenseless human being, to persevere in the pantheon of choices, is a perversion of autonomy – it is autonomy run wild, unbridled.

Remorseless Indifference: The Future of Medical Science?

It is a dismaying fact that after thirty years of *Roe v. Wade*, abortion has become institutionalized. Generations of medical students, physicians, nurses – even bioethicists – have aged to maturity with abortion an element of the background white noise of society: available on the cheap, vaguely discomforting. Its very omnipresence, its avowed indifference to nascent life, has contaminated the cultural currency of life, cheapened our pristine American-style panvitalism, and – most woefully – coarsened the ethical texture of our heretofore most respected profession: medicine. No longer dedicated to preserving and protecting all life, it has succumbed to the irresistible lure of the utilitarian siren song – no Ulysses contrast either!

With the coarsening of the fine and sensitive strands which compose the ethical and moral tapestry of our society, who can be surprised at other equally egregious offenses against the polity? I refer here to physician-assisted suicide (a particularly fulsome variation on Weimar-era *Rassenhygiene*) now flourishing in the state of Oregon and on the political agenda of a dozen or more of the sovereign states. Muscling onto the national stage is human stem-cell research that utilizes "spare" embryos created within *in-vitro* fertilization laboratories (are prisoners on death row slated to die by execution "spare" humans available for use in lethal experimentation?); the poisonous reach of the geneticists for germ-line engineering, forever altering the steady course of natural evolution to create their version of bigger, better, and a higher order of posthumans, waits patiently in the wings.

These are mass-scale programs, as ambitious and as deadly as any set forth in the Wannsee Conference of 1942. The ultra-structure of our professional kenosis is to be discerned in the daily reportage of the remorseless indifference and even collegial venality of that once revered sodality (physicians, now called "healthcare providers"). How else to account for the inaction of Dr. Josefino S. Santos of Chesapeake, Virginia, who passively watched as Velma Poynter died of large infected bedsores while under Santos's care at the Chesapeake HealthCare Center, where he was Medical Director? (It took six years before the Virginia Board of Medicine took serious notice of such feckless criminal neglect and brought disciplinary action against the doctor.) Note that Mount Sinai Hospital in New York City allowed Mike Hurewitz, a reporter for the *Albany Times Union* and a liver donor for his brother, Adam, to die asphyxiating on his own blood in the post-operative unit of the hospital three days following the procedure. How could the Florida Board of Medicine allow Dr. James Graves of Pensacola to continue to sell prescriptions of OxyContin, a powerful narcotic, to the extent that four "patients" died of overdose of the drug? (Ultimately Graves was apprehended, tried, and found guilty on four counts of manslaughter, one count of racketeering, and five counts of unlawful delivery of a controlled substance; he faces thirty years in prison.)

More? Efren Saldivar, a respiratory therapist at the Glendale Adventist Medical Center in California, confessed to killing more than forty elderly patients at that institution and admitted he had "contributed" to anywhere from one to two hundred other deaths there and at other hospitals in which he had worked. How could Harold Shipman, practicing in the British town of Hyde (Americans do not have a monopoly on slaughterous medical conduct), systematically put to death 215 patients (there were another 45 "suspicious" deaths) over 23 years before he was apprehended? He is said to have used a lethal injection of heroin strong enough to have killed 360 people as his weapon. In counterpoint, 200 to 300 physicians in this country account for 1.5 million deaths a year, plying their odious arts in the abortion clinics of the nation.

But why go on? I am working from an eight-inch thick file of police reports, newspaper clippings and Internet data labeled "Bad

Docs;" it contains medical malefactions that stagger the imagination, and I have barely skimmed the surface. This is evidence that demands a verdict: Rank indifference to the sanctity of life invites a brutish Zeitgeist as ferocious and as inhumane as any in the bestial, late twentieth century.

Dogged Perseverance and Prayer

Operation Rescue foundered in the courtrooms of this land; murdering abortion doctors is as vile an act as abortion itself. Reversing *Roe v. Wade* in the U.S. Supreme Court will only throw the conflict back into the individual state legislatures from when it arose; some states will opt to remain abortion sanctuaries, other abortion free. Sound familiar? It should: It was the political *mise-en-scene* in the late 1850s – slavery was the issue then. It was a proem to the bloodiest and most heart-breaking war in our history.

What is to be done? Dogged perseverance in the courts and on the political hustings; boundless faith in the righteousness of the cause; and prayer – continuous, fervent, rhapsodic. Powerful enough to topple the battlements of Jericho and then some. Until, like slavery, abortion is banished from the land, forever.

Bernard Nathanson is a doctor in obstetrics and gynecology and a bioethicist. A former abortionist who worked arduously to legalize and promote abortion in the 1960s, he became pro-life after working in the field of fetology, the study and science of the human unborn. He now writes and speaks on behalf of the pro-life cause.

Abortion Wounds
The Deeply Damaging Impact of Abortion on Women and the Family
Philip G. Ney, MD, FRCP(C), MA, FRANZCP, RPsych

Abortion is practiced as if it were medicine. However, physicians who perform abortion, as well as the medical licensing bodies, legislators and judges who should regulate it, do not treat it as such.

Four universally recognized tenets of medical care should apply to all medical branches. They are:

1   *Benefit.* Physicians must determine that any medical, surgical, or psychiatric procedure is (a) necessary, (b) efficacious, and (c) reasonably safe, before using it on a patient. They must carefully examine each patient before recommending treatment and demonstrate that the recommended procedure is either free from deleterious side effects, or that the benefits outweigh the hazards.

2   *Informed Consent.* Physicians must always obtain fully informed consent for a given procedure, ensuring that the patient knows the long- and short-term risks, as well as the alternative treatments.

3   *Exploitation.* Physicians must not exploit a patient's dependency, or use their authority or position to unduly influence patient decision-making.

4   *Do no harm.* Physicians must not harm their patients. *Primum non nocere.* If they cannot help or heal, they cannot intervene.

If the practice of abortion were governed by these tenets, abortion would be very rare indeed, for it is neither necessary, nor efficacious, nor safe. Abortion is most frequently performed without informed consent and often exploits a couple's fears at a time of acute crisis. Abortion harms women, men, and children (the surviving "wanted" children), as well as the medical professionals who do it.

Medically speaking, pregnancy is not a disease. Like sleep, it is a normal, self-limiting, bio-rhythm. It begins at conception, and progresses through various psychological and physiological changes (some dramatic), until the mother gives birth. This is the natural ending to a natural condition, just as waking up is the natural ending of sleep. By contrast, abortion is a brutal, sudden, artificial, and traumatic truncating of a bio-rhythm. It should be no surprise that it has so many untoward consequences.

No Benefit

Extensive research must precede the use of any new surgical procedure on humans. The effects of abortion on live pregnant laboratory animals should have been carefully analyzed before any abortion procedure was allowed on humans. Scientists would then monitor all procedures for short- and long-term consequences. After this, clinical follow-up, medical reviews, and government regulation would control the procedure's use.

The usual trials and standards were not applied to abortion before medical and legal bodies permitted it. No abortion studies were conducted on pregnant laboratory animals, even though such research would not have been complicated. The search terms "abortion" and "psychiatric benefit" produce no references in the National Library of Congress "Pub Med" files. Thus, according to the world's largest medical library, no study supports the claim that abortion has psychiatric benefits. Yet physicians continue to use psychiatric illness to justify abortion.

No psychiatric indications exist for abortion. Standard psychiatric textbooks make clear that abortion aggravates every psychiatric illness: The more psychiatrically ill a person, the worse is the abortion outcome. This is particularly true for suicide. Whereas being pregnant and having children are known to protect a woman against suicide, research shows that women who abort are 200 to 600 percent more likely to commit suicide.[1]

Professors of obstetrics and gynecology at all four medical schools in Ireland state that no medical condition requires abortion. Some argue abortion should be performed on compassionate grounds, especially in cases of rape or incest. But the criteria of science must apply to these cases too. No evidence supports the claim that abortion in cases of rape or incest benefits the woman. If it is not beneficial, it is not compassionate.

Similarly, there is no compassion in aborting babies who would be born "deformed" or "defective." The claim that abortion removes the anguish of raising a handicapped child, or spares the child discomfort, or a low quality of life, is unsupported. Suicide among handicapped children is relatively low, indicating that these persons do appreciate being alive. Raising a handicapped child matures parents and bestows more meaning on life, not less.

Babies with abnormalities incompatible with life should not be aborted. A few hours in the arms of loving parents is unquestionably good for child and parent. To be able to hold, accept, name, welcome, and bury the baby makes complete grieving possible. Killing the baby before birth, because s/he is more helpless, can cause biologically based guilt, which complicates mourning immeasurably. Such complications often result in pathological grief, which frequently leads to depression, which often interferes with the immune system. As a result, there may be more infections and cancer.[2]

Being too young for motherhood is not a medical indication for abortion. Data from our family-practice study show that teens have as high a rate of normal, full-term pregnancies as any age group.[3]

Cycles of Tragedy

Abortion is dangerous and dehumanizing. Cycles of human tragedy overlap, with abortion the dark apex. While conducting research on child abuse and abortion in the '70s, I discovered a reciprocal connection between the two. This discovery began with a clinical observation. A young mother told me that although she had a supportive husband, wonderful home, a good pregnancy and delivery that produced a beautiful baby, she couldn't touch the baby or breastfeed as she yearned to. I was puzzled until she told me she had aborted her previous child. With subsequent research, the reasons for this became much clearer: Women who abort are statistically more likely to abuse and neglect their children, while women who were neglected or abused as children are more likely to abort.[4]

Margaret Sanger, the birth-control advocate of the 1920s and founder of Planned Parenthood, first promoted the now widely accepted view that, "the first right of every child is to *be wanted*." Ms. Sanger argued that *wanted* children would not be abused or neglected, and that freely available abortion would therefore lessen the incidence of childhood maltreatment. We hardly hear this position anymore because the facts so clearly refute it. Yet this nice-sounding but pernicious philosophy has helped cause the death of countless lives, mostly of the pre-born, but also of the handicapped and the elderly. "Wantedness" now determines who lives and who

Table 1

ABORTION AND CHILD ABUSE

BRITISH COLUMBIA*				ONTARIO**	
Year	Abortions	Children admitted to care for physical abuse	Cases of probable abuse	Abortions	Cases of alleged physical ill treatment
1971	7,045	52		16,173	422
1972	8,179	75		20,272	491
1973	9,192	94		22,661	598
1974	10,024	81	145	24,795	562
1975	10,076	120	262	24,921	769
1976	10,704	124	417	26,768	746
1977	11,271		450	27,782	1,045
1978					1,762

Note: Abortion was legalized in Canada in 1969.

Sources: * Family and Children's Service, Ministry of Human Resources

** Child Welfare Branch, Ministry of Community and Social Services

dies, despite the fact that abortion not only has *not* prevented child abuse, but appears to contribute to it. Table 1 shows that child abuse and neglect cases increase parallel to escalating numbers of abortion.[5] *Wantedness* also correlates positively with various kinds of child mistreatment.

It may seem paradoxical that wanted children are more likely to be abused. But often too much is expected by the parents of a wanted child. The more wanted the child, the more likely the child will fall short of his parents' expectations and consequently disappoint, frustrate, and anger them.

If wanting a child is not right, then what? A *welcome* accepts persons where they are, as they are, whenever they are. Being "wanted" is contingent upon pleasing people, looking nice, work-

Table 2
TOP REASONS A WOMAN CHOOSES ABORTION

Model 7	t	Sig.
Constant	-1.592	0.112
Emotional neglect: Were you emotionally or intellectually neglected: 0-9	3.217	0.001
Mother's abortion: Total # of abortions in first pregnancy of mother 0 or 1	2.908	0.004
Grieve: Were you able to grieve your loss 0-9	2.858	0.005
Sexual abuse: Were you sexually mistreated 0-9	2.203	0.028
Chances: Statistically my chance of being aborted: 0-9	2.806	0.005
Kill: I have tried to kill myself: 0-9	2.188	0.029
Possible: I was possible pregnancy loss, yes – 1, maybe – 2, no – 3	1.993	0.047

Stepwise regression analysis

ing hard. Being "welcome" gives a person intrinsic value. The first right of every child is *to be* and *to be here* and *to become* all that the Creator intended.

Among the 240 factors considered in one analysis, we found the most closely correlated reason a woman chooses abortion is that *she* was neglected as a child.[6] (Table 2) Other significant reasons include: She has insufficient support from her partner; and she aborted her first pregnancy. Race, religion, socio-economic conditions, education, etc., which some think are important, were not statistically significant.

Also, when a woman becomes pregnant after having aborted a baby, she tends to be more anxious during her pregnancy,[7] and more depressed following the baby's birth.[8] Unresolved pregnancy losses interfere with parent-infant bonding.[9] Children who are less well bonded are more likely to be abused and neglected.

Women who have aborted are also sometimes revolted by contact with the flesh of a newborn baby. In their imaginations they have seen the flesh of their baby being torn apart in the abortion. Women who have aborted are often reluctant to hold a naked infant, and consequently are less likely to breastfeed. Breast milk is the only natural source of essential fatty acids that are necessary in brain development. Research indicates that children who are not breastfed are not as bright or as quick as they are designed to be.[10]

Men and women who have participated in abortion weaken their ability to restrain their own aggression. As parents, they fear their own anger, and can have difficulty being even-handed in the discipline of children. They either over- or under-react because they intuitively recognize their lack of restraint. These people are also likely to project their aggression into others. Women who abort tend to project their aggression into men. This may explain why many post-abortion women report being so frightened of men.[11]

In medicine it is vitally important to treat the underlying causes, not just the symptoms. I believe post-abortion counseling must address and resolve the following underlying conflicts: (1) many forms of guilt, including a biological guilt (that is, feeling guilty for doing something destructive to one's species); (2) the most complicated kind of grief; (3) rage at being misled and mistreated, including by the abortionist; (4) fear that instinctual restraint to aggression is weakened; (5) despair, or the knowledge that the innocent attitude toward life is lost; (6) distrust, born of the awareness that they have been abandoned by those they depended on in crisis, and the fact that they abandoned the baby who depended on them; (7) broken relationships; (8) difficulty bonding; and (9) vicarious pain.

Vicarious Pain Syndrome (VPS)

A patient told me of a persistent and tearing pain in her every muscle and joint. I realized that the onset of her pain coincided with her abortion. After investigation, I had to conclude that her pain, like the pain of some other women suffering with fibromyalgia, isn't her pain at all. It is the vicariously experienced pain of her child being torn apart within her. That pain was transmitted across the placental barrier by hormones generated from tearing flesh.[12] The pain now resides in her head and feels as if it comes from her body. Like other forms of severe trauma, the pain will probably stay there.[13] She cannot forget the child who was once within her, partly because of the child's pain, and partly because the child's DNA is indelibly inscribed in her mind.

Recent evidence demonstrates just how damaging abortion is to a woman.[14] In an analysis of government-collected data from a large sample, women who abort are more likely to die from suicides, homicides, accidents, heart attacks, strokes, and AIDS, when compared to those who deliver. (Table 3) The statistics and conclusions are valid. The reasons need further investigation, but possible reasons for the increased incidence of AIDS are: (a) to complete her pregnancy biorhythm, the aborted woman tries to become pregnant again. But because of her guilt, grief, and anger, she is reckless and promiscuous; (b) the residual post-abortion bleeding makes an ideal medium in which the HIV virus can grow.

Lack of Partner Support (LOPS)

It appears that when a woman is emotionally neglected – particu-

Table 3
ABORTION AND CAUSE OF DEATH
Number of deaths
Rate per 100,000

Cause of death	Delivery of first pregnancy and no abortions 195.4	Abortion of first pregnancy 807.0	Controlling for age & psychiatric history adjusted relative risk
Suicide	19.1	63.0	3.12*
Homicide	66.7	137.4	1.93*
AIDS	23.8	68.7	2.96*
Mental disease	14.3	45.8	3.21*
Circulatory disease	42.9	85.9	2.00*
Cerebrovascular disease	7.2	28.6	4.42*

p <.05

Risk of death by specific causes in eight subsequent years for women with only one known pregnancy, those with an abortion compared to those with a delivery.

larly by her father – she seeks to correct this by finding a mate who will "truly love her." Because people tend to re-enact unresolved conflicts, the woman finds and then coaches her partner into treating her as her father did.[15] When pregnant, she hopes her baby will be welcomed and she will be lovingly nurtured. Instead, her man rejects her and demands that she abort the baby. Threatened with abandonment, as she was when she was a child, she too readily capitulates. After the abortion, the man leaves anyway. Small wonder she becomes bitter and distrustful. Our study of women responding to a post-abortion women's help-line shows that 80 percent of relationships break up following an abortion.

Parents of a premature infant don't bond well with the baby because they anticipate he or she may die. Similarly, fathers of unborn children, who know that mothers can and may abort their children without their knowledge or consent, are reluctant to bond with their children before birth. When fathers are reluctant this way, they don't support the mother. Without the father's support, the mother is more likely to have an abortion. Because the mother is more likely to have an abortion, the father is less likely to be involved in the pregnancy. So goes another vicious cycle.

Men know they cannot legally restrain women from aborting their children. This undercuts their protective instincts. Now that men are unable to protect their unborn children, they are less protective of dependent or young life generally. Up against women's awesome power to decide who lives and who dies, men feel both impotent and angry. That sense of helplessness can result in sexual impotence. Sexual inadequacy coupled with rage can combine to cause rape.

Siblings as Survivors

Many years ago, a family physician referred a seven-year-old child to me for consultation. I saw the little girl with her mother, who told me that she, her only daughter, could not sleep because of a recurrent nightmare. The child was tired, irritable, and unable to eat, concentrate, or get along with others. The little girl told me she dreamed three siblings made a tunnel in a bank of sand, and they crawled inside. The tunnel collapsed, and the little girl's siblings were buried alive. I asked the mother to tell me about all her pregnancies. She revealed that she experienced three early miscarriages that her little girl "could not have known about." The nightmare clearly showed that the child did know, and that she was deeply disturbed that her three siblings had died.

Data confirm that children are painfully afflicted when their siblings die – especially when they die by abortion. I called this "Post Abortion Survivor Syndrome" (or PASS), which refers to the constellation of signs and symptoms that has existential guilt as its most prominent feature: "I feel I don't deserve to be alive."[16] Other closely correlated symptoms are: (1) a sense of impending doom (existential anxiety); (2) feelings that they have not used their lives well (ontological guilt); (3) a deep distrust of parents and parental figures; (4) pseudo-secrets that are most burdensome and intellectually interfering; (5) inexpressible rage toward all authority because nobody protected them when they were most vulnerable; (6) little desire to have children; (7) small concern for their aging parents; (8) risk-taking behavior with drugs, alcohol, cigarettes, sex, etc.; (9) trying to stay "wanted" and "wantable." (They know that they were chosen to live because they were "wanted." Now they feel they must continue to please others in order to stay alive); (10) the sense that life's value – their own lives and that of others – is relative.[17]

Health education initiatives aimed at reducing risk behaviors among PASS people often encourage rather than curb them, because abortion survivors are attracted to risk, not repelled by it. If up to 70 percent of North American women have had at least one abortion by age 45, then approximately 50 percent of the young people born in the USA since 1973 are abortion survivors.[18] If this is correct, it might explain why education programs directed at this age group about sex, cigarettes, drugs and safe driving, etc., are so ineffective. PASS might also help explain the interest in violence, terrorism, and disregard for authority among young people. After all, these were "wanted" children, who sense that the value of life is extrinsic and relative, and, because they feel guilty for being alive, it's "no big deal to get blown away."

Ex-Abortionists

There is a growing list of doctors, nurses, receptionists, technicians, and others who used to work as abortion providers but now cannot. I helped found a collegial organization for them called, "The Society of Centurions."[19] The Society recognizes the deep psychological and spiritual wounds left by the practice of abortion, and helps former abortion workers come to terms with their past. The name is derived from the Roman centurion who stood at the foot of Christ's cross and suddenly became aware of his role in that unjust crucifixion. As Christ died, this centurion dropped his sword and fell to his knees exclaiming, "Surely, this was an innocent man!"[20] Ex-abortionists feel that they are today's centurions. They have dropped their scalpels, and must now deal with the ramifications of their actions.

The Society works to help heal the ex-abortion providers' painful wounds. Reconciliation with all those injured is necessary. Some make contact with the women they aborted to apologize and to offer to pay for counseling. All are encouraged to deal with each abortion as a killing of an individual child of a specific sex, personality, and name. They know the healing process is slow, but necessary.

Hope Alive

The wounds in post-abortion women are also very deep and difficult to treat. Few medical professionals recognize or treat these wounds as they should. Many counselors try to cure women with methods that are neither honest nor scientific and often appear to be attempts at magic. Effective post-abortion healing must deal with the deep, underlying conflicts within women, about both abortion and antecedent childhood mistreatment.[21]

Because of this, I have developed a group-counseling program over the past thiry years called, "The Hope Alive" method for post-abortion women and men. It is now taught in over twenty countries, and is proving effective. From pre- and post-treatment data, we have found that some of the most significant improvements reported by women in the program are to depression and self-esteem.[22] Hope Alive emphasizes the necessity of reconciliation with all those who hurt them and all those they hurt, particularly surviving children.[23]

We are determined to be rigorously scientific, thoroughly professional, and unashamedly Christian with this method. Hope Alive welcomes everyone regardless of faith or orientation. While devoid of prayer, Bible reading, candles, ceremony, or song, those who are determined to know and grow come to know Christ spontaneously.

Still, Hope Alive is not perfect. We are constantly modifying the program. We are determined to provide experiential professional training. We carefully monitor cases and collect data on outcomes.

We keep confidential clinical records, and we constantly update our techniques. We give and accept supervision, criticism and scrutiny. Above all, we are determined to work as hard at prevention as treatment. I acknowledge the privilege of facilitating Christ's healing and wish to credit Him with any discovery and healing.

The Future

The following are basic but necessary recommendations for the future. We must:

1   Apply existing medical standards and legislation to abortion as we would to any other surgical or medical or psychiatric procedure;

2   Provide financial support to those able and interested in doing research on abortion's effects;

3   Insist that those who promote or provide abortion prove that it is necessary, beneficial, and safe (abortion proponents bear the burden of proof to show that abortion is good for women's health – and for men and children – they will not, because they cannot, but they must keep trying);

4   Insist that doctors tell their patients, "Until abortion is proven to be good treatment, I cannot recommend nor do this to you;"

5   Insist that medical licensing bodies prohibit abortion, and insist that governments stop funding it;

6   Welcome everyone, regardless of "wants;" welcome especially all newly conceived babies – don't "want" them but affirm their God-given right to be, to be here, and to become all God designed them to be.

Conclusion

After forty years as a consultant psychiatrist, clinical researcher, and university professor, I have no doubt that abortion is the most destructive and dehumanizing experience known to humanity. Unfortunately, it remains legal and commonplace, devastating the lives of children, mothers, fathers – of everyone.

But there is hope. First, the mounting scientific evidence of abortion's ill effects now make lawsuits against aborting physicians, hospitals, and nurses more possible. These suits are for damages, assault, lack of informed consent – among other negligent acts. Second, the testimony of those who performed abortion, or were harmed by it, will soon become well known.

And their anguish will be heard.

Philip Ney is a physician, child psychiatrist, and psychologist. He has taught at five universities in three countries. He has been academic and clinical chairman; full professor three times. Much of his research is in the area of child abuse and neglect. Since discovering the reciprocal connection between childhood mistreatment and abortion about thirty years ago, he has been concentrating his research on the damaging effects of abortion on the whole family. He and his wife, a pediatrician, also train counselors in the Hope Alive Group Counseling technique in many countries.

Endnotes

1   Gissler M., Hemminiki E., Lonnqvist J., "Suicides after Pregnancy in Finland: 1987–94" (register linkage study), *BMJ* 313: 1431–34, 1996; Reardon D. C., Ney P. G., Scheuren F. J., Cougle J. R., Coleman P. K., Strahan T., "Deaths Associated with Delivery and Abortion – A Record Linked Study," *South Med J* 95; 834–41, 2000.

2   Irwin, M., "Psycho Neuro Immunology of Depression: Clinical Implications," *Brain Behav. Immun.* 16:1–16, 2000; McGuire L., Kiecolt-Glaser J. K., Glaser, R., "Depressive Symptoms and Lymphocyte Proliferation in Older Adults," *J. Abnorm. Psychol.* 111:192–97, 2002; Siegel J. M. and Kuykendall D. H., "Loss, Widowhood and Psychological Distress Among the Elderly," *.J.Consult Clin. Psychol.* 8: 519–24, 1990.

3   Ney P. G., Fung T., Wickett A. R, et al, "The Effects of Pregnancy Loss on Women's Health," *Soc. Sci. Med.* Vol. 38: 1193–1200, 1994.

4   Ney P. G., Fung T., Wickett, A.R., "Relationship Between Induced Abortion and Child Abuse and Neglect: Four Studies," *Pre- and Perinatal Psychology Journal* 8: 43–63, 1993.

5   Ney P. G., "The Relationship Between Abortion and Child Abuse," *Can. J. Psychiatry* 24:610–20, 1979.

6   Ney P. G., Peeters-Ney M., Shiels C., "Psychological Factors that

Determine Pregnancy Outcome," presented at annual meeting Can. Academy of Child Psychiatry, Banff, AB, Nov. 2002.

7 Bradley C.F., "Abortion and Subsequent Pregnancy," *Canadian Journal of Psychiatry* 29: 494–98, 1984.

8 Kumar R. and Robson K., "Previous Induced Abortion and Ante-Natal Depression in Primiparae: A Preliminary Report of a Survey of Mental Health in Pregnancy," *Psychology Med.* 8: 711–15, 1978.

9 Lewis E., "Mourning by the Family after a Still Birth or Neonatal Death," *Arch. Dis. Child* 54:303–6, 1979; Klaus M. H., Kennell J. H.: *Maternal-Infant Bonding*, St. Louis: C. V. Mosby Co., 1976.

10 Mortensen E. L., Michaelsen K. F., Sanders S. A., et al, "The Association between Duration of Breastfeeding and Adult Intelligence," *JAMA* 287:2365–71, 2000; Quinn P. J., O'Callaghan M., Williams G. M., et al., *"The Effect of Breastfeeding on Child Development* at 5 years: a cohort study," *J. Paediatr. Child Health* 37: 465–59, 2001. If this is correct, wide-scale abortion may lower the average IQ of a nation.

11 Ney P. G., Deeply Damaged: An Explanation for the Profound Problems Arising From Infant Abortion and Child Abuse, Pioneer Publishing, Victoria BC, 1997.

12 Basbaum A. I., "Distinct Neuro Chemical Features of Acute and Persistent Pain," *Proc. Nat'l Acad. Sci. USA*, 96: 7739–43, 1999; Russell I. J., "Advances in Fibromyalgia: Possible Role for Central Neurochemicals," *Am. J. Med Sci* 315:377–84, 1998; McHugh J. M., McHugh W. B., "Pain: Neuroanatomy, Chemical Mediators, and Clinical Implications," *AACN Clin. Issues*, 11:168–78, 2000.

13 van der Kolk B. A. & van der Hart O., "The Intrusive Past: The Flexibility of Memory and the Engraving of Trauma," *American Imago*, 48:425–54, 1991.

14 Reardon D. C., Ney P. G., Scheuren F. J., Cougle J. R., Coleman P. K., Strahan T., "Deaths Associated with Delivery and Abortion – a Record Linked Study," *South. Med. J.* 95; 834–41, 2000.

15 Ney P. G., "Child Mistreatment: Possible Reasons for Its Transgenerational Transmission," *Can. J Psychiatry*: 34: 594–99, 1989.

16 Ney P. G., "A Consideration of Abortion Survivors," *J Child Psychiatry and Hum. Dev.* 13:3 168–79, 1983; Ney P. G., "Abortion and Family Psychology: A Study in Progress," *Canadian Journal of Diagnosis* 16:113–19, 1999; Ney P. G., Peeters-Ney M., *Abortion Survivors* (2nd Ed.) Pioneer Publishing, Victoria BC, 1996.

17 Ney, P. G., Shiels C., *Signs & Symptoms of Abortion Survivors*, present-

ed at annual meeting, Can. Academy of Child Psychiatry, Banff, AB, 1993.

18   Ney P. G., "Abortion and Family Psychology: A Study in Progress," *Canadian Journal of Diagnosis* 16:113–19, 1999.

19   Ney P. G., Peeters-Ney M., *The Centurion's Pathway – A Description of the Difficult Transition for Ex-Abortion Providers or Facilitators*, Pioneer Publishing, Victoria BC, 1997.

20   Luke 23:47 NIV.

21   Ney P. G., Peters A., *Ending the Cycle of Abuse – The Stories of Women Abused as Children and the Group Therapy Techniques that Helped Them Heal*, Francis Taylor Inc., New York NY, 1995.

22   Ney P. G., Shiels M., *Group Therapy for Those Damaged by Childhood Mistreatment and Pregnancy Loss,* Presented at the annual meeting of the American Group Psychotherapy Association, Los Angeles, 2000.

23   Ney P. G., *How to Talk with Your Children about Abortion*, Pioneer Publishing, Victoria BC, 1995.

Breaking the Silence
Elizabeth Shadigian, M.D.

Most of the medical literature since induced abortion was legalized has focused on short-term surgical complications, surgical technique improvement, and abortion-provider training. Long-term complications are not well studied due to politics – specifically, the belief that such studies would be used either to limit or expand access to abortion. The two commissioned studies that attempted to summarize the long-term consequences of induced abortion only concluded that future work should be undertaken to research long-term effects.[1]

The political agenda of every researcher studying induced abortion is questioned more than in any other field of medical research. Conclusions are feared to be easily influenced by the author's beliefs about women's reproductive autonomy and the moral status of the unborn.

Against this backdrop of politics is also a serious epidemiological concern: That researchers can only observe the effects of women's reproductive *choices*, since women are not exposed to induced abortion by chance. Because investigators are deprived of the powerful tool of randomization to minimize bias in their findings, research must depend on such well-done observational studies. These studies depend on information from many countries and include legally mandated registers, hospital administrative data, and clinic statistics, as well as voluntary reporting (or surveys) by abortion providers.[2]

Approximately 25 percent of all pregnancies (between 1.2 and 1.6 million per year) are terminated in the United States, so that if there is a small positive or negative effect of induced abortion on subsequent health, many women will be affected.[3]

A recent systematic review article, on which I am a co-author, critically assesses the epidemiological problems in studying the long-term consequences of abortion in more detail.4 It should be kept in mind that: (1) limitations exist with observational research; (2) potential bias in reporting by women with medical conditions has been raised and refuted; (3) an assumption has been made that abortion is a distinct biological event; (4) inconsistencies in choosing appropriate comparison groups exist; and (5) other possible confounding variables of studying abortion's effects over time also exist.

Nonetheless, given the above caveats, research suggests that a history of induced abortion is associated with an increased long-term risk of:

1. breast cancer
2. placenta previa
3. pre-term birth and
4. maternal suicide.

Current maternal mortality from induced abortion is also incompletely reported.

Outcomes Not Associated with Induced Abortion

Induced abortion has been studied in relation to subsequent spontaneous abortion (miscarriage), ectopic pregnancy, and infertility. No studies have shown an association between induced abortion and later spontaneous abortion. An increase in ectopic or tubal pregnancies was seen in only two out of nine international studies on the topic, while only two out of seven articles addressing possible subsequent infertility showed any increased risk with induced abortion.[5]

Outcomes Associated with Induced Abortion
1. Breast Cancer
Based upon my systematic review of the literature and my own

independent meta-analysis of spontaneous and induced abortion in pre- and post-menopausal women, induced abortion causes an increased risk of breast cancer in two different ways.[6] First, there is the loss of the protective effect of a first full-term pregnancy ("fftp"), due to the increased risk from delaying the fftp to a later time in a woman's life. Second, there is also an independent effect of increased breast cancer risk apart from the delay of fftp.

The medical literature since the 1970s has shown that a full-term delivery early in one's reproductive life reduces the chance of subsequent breast cancer development.[7] This is called "the protective effect of a first full-term pregnancy (fftp)." This is illustrated in Figure 1, which uses the "Gail Equation" to predict the risk of breast cancer for an eighteen-year-old within a five-year period and also within a lifetime. The Gail Equation is used to help women in decision-making regarding breast cancer prevention measures. In the first scenario, the eighteen-year-old decides to terminate the pregnancy and has her fftp at age thirty two, as compared to the

Figure 1
THE GAIL EQUATION
SCENARIO:
ALL FOUR WOMEN ARE PREGNANT AT AGE 18; #1 & #3 ABORT THEIR FIRST PREGNANCY AND DELIVER FULL-TERM IN THEIR NEXT PREGNANCY AT AGE 32.

Gail Variable	#1	#2	#3	#4
Race	Caucasian, Non-Black	Caucasian, Non-Black	Black	Black
Age	50	50	50	50
Menarche	12	12	12	12
Age 1st live birth	32	18	32	18
Number of first-degree relatives with breast cancer	0	0	0	0
number of previous breast biopsies	0	0	0	0
five-year breast cancer risk	1.3%	0.7%	0.8%	0.4%
Lifetime breast cancer risk	12.1%	6.5%	6.7%	3.6%

eighteen-year-old in the second example who delivers at term. The individual risk of these women is then assessed when the risk of breast cancer peaks. As Figure 1 shows, a woman's decision to have an abortion instead of a full-term pregnancy at age eighteen can almost double her five-year and lifetime risk of breast cancer at age fifty, regardless of race.

An independent effect of increased breast cancer risk apart from the delay of first full-term pregnancy has been controversial. Four published review articles have been written. Two of the reviews found no association between induced abortion and breast cancer,[8] while one paper found a "small to non-significant effect."[9] The sole published meta-analysis reported an odds-ratio (OR)[10] for breast cancer of 1.3 (95% CI=1.2, 1.4) in women with a previous induced abortion.[11] I have also performed an independent meta-analysis which found the OR=1.21 (95% CI=1.00, 1.45).[12] Brind et al. used older studies and translated non-English ones. He did not exclude any studies and used a different statistical approach. My study used exclusion criteria and only English language studies. Another finding was that breast cancer is increased if the abortion is performed before a first full-term pregnancy. Brind found an OR=1.4 (95% CI=1.2, 1.6), while our study showed OR=1.27 (95% CI=1.09-1.47). Although my study is not published yet (Brind's is), and although different methodologies were used, the results are nearly equivalent, are statistically significant, and do show that induced abortion is an independent risk factor for breast cancer.

In addition, the risk of breast cancer increases with induced abortion when (a) the induced abortion precedes a first full-term pregnancy;[13] (b) the woman is a teen;[14] (c) the woman is black;[15] (d) the woman is over the age of thirty;[16] (e) the pregnancy is terminated at more than twelve weeks gestation;[17] or (f) the woman has a family history of breast cancer.[18] One researcher (Daling) also reported that *all* pregnant teens with a family history of breast cancer who aborted their first pregnancy developed breast cancer.[19]

2. Placenta Previa

"Placenta previa" is a medical condition of pregnancy where the placenta covers the cervix, making a cesarean section medically necessary to deliver the child. In general, this condition puts women at higher risk, not just because surgery (the c-section) is necessary, but also because blood loss is higher, and blood transfusions may be necessary. There is also a higher risk of hysterectomy (the loss of the uterus), and therefore the need for more surgery.

Three studies with over 100 subjects each were found examining induced abortion and placenta previa, as well as one meta-analysis. The three studies found a positive association, as did the meta-analysis. Induced abortion increased the risk of placenta previa by approximately 50 percent.[20]

3. Pre-Term Birth (PTB)

Twenty-four studies explored associations between abortion and pre-term birth or low birth weight (a surrogate marker for pre-term birth). Twelve studies found an association which almost doubled the risk of pre-term birth.[21] Moreover, seven of the twelve identified a "dose response effect," which means a higher risk for women who've had more abortions.

Also notable is the increased risk of very early deliveries at twenty to thirty weeks (full-term is forty weeks) after induced abortion, first noted by Wright, Campbell, and Beazley in 1972. Seven subsequent papers displayed this phenomenon of mid-pregnancy PTB associated with induced abortion. This is especially relevant as these infants are at high risk of death shortly after birth (morbidity and mortality), and society expends many resources to care for them in the intensive care unit as well as for their long-term disabilities. Of particular note are the three large cohort studies done in the 1990s, twenty to thirty years after abortion's legalization. Each shows elevated risk and a dose response effect. Because these studies were done so long after legalization, one would assume that the stigma of abortion that might contribute to under-reporting would have waned.[22]

4. Suicide

Two studies have shown increased rates of suicide after induced abortion, one from Finland[23] and one from the United States.[24] The Finnish study (by Gissler et al.) reported an OR=3.1 (95%CI=1.6,6.0) when women choosing induced abortion were compared to women in the general population. The odds ratio increased to 6.0 when women choosing induced abortion were compared to women completing a pregnancy. The American study (by Reardon et al.) reported recently that suicide RR=2.5 (95%CI=1.1, 5.7) was more common after induced abortion and that deaths from all causes were also increased RR=1.6 (95%CI= 1.3, 7.0).

5. Maternal Mortality

Statements made regarding the physical safety of abortion are based upon incomplete and inaccurate data.

There is no mandatory reporting of abortion complications in the U.S., including maternal death. The Centers for Disease Control (CDC) began abortion surveillance in 1969. However, the time lag in CDC notification is greater than 12 months for half of all maternal deaths.[25]

Maternal deaths are grossly underreported, with nineteen previously unreported deaths associated with abortions having been identified from 1979–1986.[26] The CDC quotes approximately one maternal death for every 100,000 abortions officially.[27] Many women are at much higher risk of death immediately after an induced abortion: (a) black women and minorities have 2.5 times the chance of dying; (b) abortions performed at greater than sixteen weeks gestation have fifteen times the risk of maternal mortality as compared to abortions at less than twelve weeks; and (c) women over forty years old, as compared to teens, have three times the chance of dying.[28]

Conclusion

Induced abortion is associated with an increase in breast cancer, placenta previa, pre-term birth, and maternal suicide. Maternal deaths from induced abortion are underreported, do not include maternal suicide, and do not include deaths from all causes in the years immediately following abortion. These risks should appear on consent forms for induced abortion, but currently do not.

In its most recent Compendium of Selected Publications, the American College of Obstetricians and Gynecologists (ACOG) states:

> Long-term risks sometimes attributed to surgical abortion include potential effects on reproductive functions, cancer incidence, and psychological sequelae. *However, the medical literature, when carefully evaluated, clearly demonstrates no significant negative impact on any of these factors with surgical abortion*[29] (italics added for emphasis).

I am a member and fellow of ACOG and have demonstrated that a body of literature exists on the long-term effects of induced abortion. This literature should be acknowledged, analyzed, and explained to women. ACOG should be at the forefront of this scholarly undertaking.

The preceding quotation denies that this literature exists. I am deeply troubled that ACOG makes sweeping assurances to their membership and to women everywhere about the lack of long-term consequences of induced abortion. I challenge ACOG and all professional medical organizations to help women everywhere by bravely and objectively interpreting these studies. I challenge the United States government, and all governments, to fund studies that follow women throughout their lifetimes so that the long-term effects of induced abortion can be brought to light.

Elizabeth Shadigian, M.D., is a Clinical Associate Professor of Obstetrics and Gynecology at the University of Michigan in Ann Arbor. She is a Fellow at the American College of Obstetricians and Gynecologists (ACOG) and also now serves as the Secretary of the American Association of Pro-Life Obstetricians and Gynecologists (AAPLOG), a special interest group of ACOG.

Endnotes

1   Wynn, M., and Wynn, A., *Some Consequences of Induced Abortion to*

Children Born Subsequently, London Foundation for Education and Research in Childbearing, 27 Walpole Street, London (1972); "More on Koop's Study of Abortion," *Family Planning Perspectives* (1990), Vol. 22(1): 36–39.

2   Thorp, J. M., Hartmann, K. E, Shadigian, E. M., "Long-Term Physical and Psychological Health Consequences of Induced Abortion: A Review of the Evidence," *Obstet. Gynecol. Survey* (in press 2003).

3   *Supra* note 1.

4   Thorp, et. al., *supra* note 2.

5   *Id.*

6   *Id.*

7   McMahon, M., Cole, B., Lin T., et al. "Age at First Birth and Breast Cancer Risk," *Bull World Health Organ.* (1970); 43:209–21.

8   Wingo, P., Newsome, K., Marks, J., Calle, E., Parker, S., "The Risk of Breast Cancer Following Spontaneous or Induced Abortion," *Cancer Causes and Control* (1997) 8, at pp. 93–108; Bartholomew L., and Grimes D., "The Alleged Association between Induced Abortion and Risk of Breast Cancer: Biology or Bias?," *Obstet. Gynecol. Survey* 1998, Vol. 53(11) 708–14.

9   Michels K., Willett W., "Does Induced or Spontaneous Abortion Affect the Risk of Breast Cancer?" *Epidemiology* 1996, Vol. 7(5) 521–28.

10   The odds ratio of an event is the ratio of the probability of the event occurring, to the probability that the event does not occur. An "OR" equal to 1 (OR=1) indicates that there is no association with the disease. An OR which is greater than 1 indicates a positive association with the disease. An odds ratio of less than 1 indicates a negative association. Similarly, a relative risk (or "RR") of greater than 1 is said to be a risk factor between an exposure and the end event. "CI" refers to the "confidence interval." A confidence interval which is greater than 95 percent, where the numbers in question do not cross 1, is considered statistically significant and most likely not due to chance. *In this paper only statistically significant numbers are quoted.*

11   Brind J., Chinchilli V., Severs W., Summy-Long J., "Induced Abortion as an Independent Risk Factor for Breast Cancer: A Comprehensive Review and Meta-Analysis, *J Epidemiology Community Health* 1996; 50:481–96.

12   Shadigian, E.M. and Wolf, F.M., "Breast Cancer and Spontaneous and Induced Abortion: A Systematic Review and Meta-Analysis" (in review).

13   Brind, et al., *supra* note 10; and Shadigian & Wolf, *Id.*

14   Daling, J. R., Malone, K. E., Voigt, L. F., et al., "Risk of Breast Cancer Among Young Women: Relationship to Induced Abortion, *J Natl Cancer Inst.*, 1994; 86:1584–92.

15   Laing, A. E., Demenais, F. M., Williams, R. et al., "Breast Cancer Risk Factors in African-American Women: The Howard University Tumor Registry Experience," *J Natl Med Asso* 1993; 85: 931–99.

16   Daling, et al. (1994), *supra* note 13.

17   Melbye M., Wohlfahrt J., Olsen J.H. et. al., "Induced Abortion and the Risk of Breast Cancer," *N Engl J Med.* (1997); 336(2):81–85.

18   Daling, J. R, Brinton, L. A., Voigt, L. F., et al., "Risk of Breast Cancer Among White Women Following Induced Abortion," *Am J Epidemiol.* (1996); 144:373–80.

19   Daling, et al, (1994), *supra* note 13.

20   Thorp, et. al . (2002), *supra* note 2.

21   *Id.* (Risk ratio elevation of 1.3 to 2.0)

22   *Id.*

23   Gissler, M., Hemminki, E., Lonnqvist, J., "Suicides After Pregnancy in Finland," 1987–94: register linkage study, *BMJ* 1996; 313:1431–34. Reardon, D. C., Ney, P. G., Scheuren, F., Cougle, J., Coleman, P. K., and Strahan, T. W. "Deaths Associated with Pregnancy Outcome: A Linkage Based Study of Low Income Women," Southern Med. J. (2002), 95 (8): 834–41.

24   Reardon, D. C., Ney, P. G., Scheuren, F., Cougle, J., Coleman, P. K., and Strahan, T. W., "Deaths Associated with Pregnancy Outcome: A Linkage Based Study of Low Income Women," *Southern Med. J.* (2002), 95 (8): 834–41.

25   Lawson, H. W., Frye, A., Atrash, H. K., Smith, J. C., Shulman, H. B., Ramick, M., "Abortion Mortality, United States, 1972 through 1987," *Am J Obstet Gynecol* (171), 5, (1994).

26   Atrash, H., Strauss, L., Kendrick, J., Skjeldestad, F., and Ahn, Y., "The Relation between Induced Abortion and Ectopic Pregnancy, *Obstet. Gynecol.* 1997; 89:512–18.

27   Centers for Disease Control, MMWR (Morbidity and Mortality Weekly Report): Abortion Surveillance in the United States, 1989–present.

28   Lawson (1994), *supra* note 24.

29   Compendium of Selected Publications, the American College of Obstetricians and Gynecologists, 2002, Practice Bulletin #26, April 2001.

Putting It All Together

Margaret (Peggy) Hartshorn

The common names used for a pregnancy help center during the past thirty-plus years tell a lot about where we've been and where we are going. The earliest names were: Birthright and Emergency Pregnancy Services (EPS), then came Problem Pregnancy Centers (PPCs), then Crisis Pregnancy Centers (CPCs), and finally Pregnancy Resource Centers (PRCs). Now we also have "A Woman's Concern Health Centers" and "Life Choices Medical Clinics" among a host of other medical and professional-sounding names.

Our burgeoning numbers also tell much about our history. The first printed (i.e. mimeographed) directory of contact names and semi-organized centers in the United States contained about 75 entries; the latest Heartbeat International Directory contains about 3,400.[1] Approximately 2,300 of those are pregnancy centers (of which 350 have added medical services), and about 80 percent of those are members of one or more of nine affiliating organizations.[2] The rest are professional social service agencies, such as Catholic Charities (about 500), Christian maternity homes (about 350), non-profit, Christian adoption agencies (about 160), some hotlines (about 30), and some freestanding post-abortion programs (about 50).

The names, numbers, and variety of services reflect our response to the women, girls, and families who have been coming to us for help for over thirty years. These clients are, in a sense, "products" of a decaying culture, sometimes now called a Culture of Death. In the late '60s and '70s, we presumed that these women were in short-term crisis (hence "emergency"). Now we recognize them as the walking wounded who need much more than crisis intervention.[3] In the '70s, we thought our culture was in a short-term-memory lapse and would soon return to its Judeo-Christian values. Now we realize that we need to teach those values anew to a generation that has hardly heard of them – a generation with the scars to prove it.

The Original Vision: Mother-and-Baby-Centered Service

The birth of pregnancy centers in the U.S. was not a result of *Roe v. Wade* but of the earlier movement to liberalize abortion laws state by state. Concerned people realized that the carefully crafted message of abortion as a *reluctant, humane,* but sometimes *loving* choice, would influence some women to abort their babies unless they had help and support. (At that time, most pro-life people did not fully comprehend that the movement to change abortion laws was an integral part of a well-orchestrated strategy to break down traditional family and religious values and replace them with hedonistic and atheistic ones.)

Catholics, especially medical professionals and mothers, with their firm tradition of welcoming children and their consistent teaching on the sanctity of human life, were in the forefront of a movement to start alternatives to abortion, although they rarely saw this as a Catholic issue, or even a uniquely Christian mission. It was simply part of who they were. The work was primarily humanitarian: an outreach of one caring individual to another.

Birthright was the first formal organization to provide abortion alternatives. Founded in Canada in 1968, Birthright centers soon spread to the United States.[4] These centers follow a strict charter (1971). Birthright insists that you cannot save a baby without "saving" (or serving) a mother, and vice versa.

A similar woman-and-baby-centered vision was held by "Alternatives to Abortion," formed in 1971 (soon renamed

"Alternatives to Abortion International" and called AAI) in the United States.[5] The founders established a loose federation of independent organizations that could learn from each other, rather than a "franchise" model. This seemed right for the entrepreneurial United States, where a variety of small organizations had already sprung up, starting in the late '60s, from California to New York, some operating out of pro-life doctors' offices, some out of churches, and some even out of homes. (Interestingly, both the loose federation and the franchise model still exist among the nine pregnancy-center membership organizations thirty years later.)

While AAI often called itself the "service arm of the pro-life movement," they and Birthright considered themselves quite distinct from Right to Life, the lobbying and educational arm. The service organizations seemed cautious about losing their coveted 501(c)(3) status, so they shied away from any lobbying. Their role was primarily "crisis intervention," and then connecting women to friends and services in the community (medical care, housing, material aid, and social services). The presumption was that then their work had been a "success," the mother was safe, and therefore the baby would be safe.

A Civil Rights and Humanitarian Issue

Both Right to Life and the service organizations agreed on one thing: The pro-life issue was a civil-rights and humanitarian issue. The abortion movement, by contrast, tried to marginalize pro-life sentiment as something merely "Catholic." Indeed, an early tactic of the Religious Coalition for Abortion Rights (RCAR) was its attempt to have every major Protestant denomination sign statements depicting abortion as sometimes necessary and even the "Christian" response to a woman with a difficult pregnancy. They consistently tried to discredit any pro-life speaker with the question, "You're a Catholic, aren't you?" But the issue was never solely Catholic. Instead, the presumption was that our religious beliefs, and certainly the Judeo-Christian values shared by most of America, were a "given" and did not need to be explicitly stated.

As abortions continued and affected not only women but everyone connected with them, the culture became more accepting of "sex for recreation," sexually transmitted diseases surged, and AIDS emerged. Marriage also declined, causing the disintegration of the two-parent family. Our culture became more obviously hedonistic and amoral. The "disconnect" between our presumption of a Judeo-Christian ethic and reality was undeniable.[6] The pregnancy-center movement responded to this decay with new approaches.

The Baby-Centered Approach

First tried was the baby-centered approach. It brought centers, in the short-term, into disrepute, but, in the long-term, prompted an internal move toward real responsiveness, credibility, and promise.

In the late 1970s, perhaps due to frustration that the lobbying and educational branches had not passed a Human Life Amendment and that the numbers of abortions were skyrocketing, centers were urged to advertise alongside abortion clinics in the yellow pages (the phone book indexes referred readers to the same headings, such as *Clinics* and *Birth Control Information*, for both abortion and abortion alternatives),[7] to show slides of fetal development and aborted babies to clients, and, in general, to use every possible method to save the baby at risk for abortion.[8]

In 1987, Planned Parenthood, the world's biggest abortion promoter, became infuriated with this approach and orchestrated what can be called a smear campaign. Their undercover reporters, posing as clients, and using hidden cameras and tape recorders, entered centers to, ironically, collect "evidence" that the centers were being deceptive and misleading about their services. With the indispensable help of television shows and magazines, a controversy ensued. Congressional hearings were held, but pregnancy centers were forbidden from testifying in their own defense. Thus, in the public arena, pregnancy centers had a "black eye."[9]

The campaign's short-term effects were devastating. Many involved in centers felt embarrassment and shame, and centers began to be suspicious of each other. The boomerang effect even caused some to think they needed to "warn" potential clients, in ads and on the phone, of their pro-life values. Client numbers decreased in many areas.

Legal attacks followed. State attorneys general tried to dictate center advertising and phone scripts. Individuals filed suits against some centers. Court findings often went against these centers, and some were forced to pay damages and even close down.

But the long-term effects have been positive. To the dismay of our opponents, pregnancy help centers not only did not go away, but became stronger. In 1993, the National Institute of Family and Life Advocates (NIFLA) was founded specifically to provide legal education and training to help centers protect themselves from frivolous tort claims (such as assault and battery for touching a client without her permission), and NIFLA spearheaded the development of the first insurance program to protect centers from "counselor liability."[10]

The Medical Vision

Some centers in California had been accused of "practicing medicine without a license" for providing urine pregnancy tests, and the abortion lobby's wordsmiths began to label all centers "fake clinics." Meanwhile, in the medical field, ultrasound was emerging as a new diagnostic tool for pregnancy. NIFLA soon envisioned the centers as fully accredited medical clinics, not only doing pregnancy testing but also using ultrasound to medically confirm it. NIFLA pioneered a medical model for centers to become either licensed by the state, or to work under the license of a private physician. The potential of ultrasound to help abortion-vulnerable mothers bond with their babies was clear.

More and more centers today are adding ultrasound services for abortion-vulnerable clients. True to their entrepreneurial nature, centers are taking the original model even further, with some adding testing for sexually transmitted diseases (STDs), pap smears, natural family planning, prenatal care, birthing centers, and even well-baby care. Some are becoming "hub" medical clinics and encouraging other centers to refer clients to them for ultrasound and other medical services. As we partner with physicians and other medical personnel, we are beginning to see a small ripple effect in the medical community, to bring back a more pro-life and holistic approach to the care of women.

Predictably, our new strength invited a second attack, fourteen years after the first, led by NARAL. In 2000, NARAL published the *Choice Action Kit: A Step-by-Step Guide to Unmasking Fake Clinics*, a bald and brazen attempt to close down pregnancy centers offering true choice (just not abortion or birth control).[11] This time, the attack united pregnancy centers, and our national affiliating organizations quickly responded with our own guide, *Serving Clients with Care and Integrity*, which outlines our policies and procedures. The guide also contains *Our Commitment of Care*, which details ethical policies relating to advertising and client services, adopted officially by eight of the nine affiliating organizations.[12]

As a result of the new NARAL campaign, the New York attorney general began an investigation into advertising and medical practices of eight centers. But the centers responded with a united front, including both an effective legal defense and public relations strategy. In the end, a legal team, headed by the Christian Legal Society, was able to force withdrawal of all subpoenas.

While the ultimate outcome of this second attack is yet to be seen, no one can deny that our centers are now stronger and more united than ever. Ironically, the baby-centered approach, which provided ammunition to discredit us, eventually led to greater professionalism and efficacy. Also ironic was the result of our opponents' efforts, which sought desperately to eliminate baby pictures: Centers now provide one step better than still photographs – "live action" ultrasound with the help of licensed medical personnel. Women can see and bond with their babies at the earliest stages of pregnancy, helping them make more informed choices.

The Christian Vision

In the early 1980s, Evangelical Christians came into the pro-life service movement in large numbers, and they were a "breath of fresh air" to those who had been carrying the ball since the late '60s.

Christian Action Council (CAC) had been formed in 1975, primarily as a pro-life educational and lobbying organization.[13] But it soon saw the need for pregnancy centers and opened its first in 1980. This branch of CAC then took priority, and the organization was renamed "Care Net" in 1994, to emphasize its network of Crisis Pregnancy Centers (CPCs). Their vision is both woman-centered and baby-centered, but primarily Christ-centered, with the specific mission to evangelize.

For Evangelical Christians, abortion is more a religious issue than a civil-rights or humanitarian one. It is also a call to action for Christians. In 1984, CAC launched Sanctity of Human Life Sunday on the Sunday closest to January 22, in an effort to educate and motivate Evangelical churches nationwide. Dr. James Dobson's organization, Focus on the Family (FOF), has also been a great help to all centers, by developing an official program to support them with educational materials and a ministry office in the 1990s.

The mix of Catholics and Protestants of various denominations has strengthened centers nationally. Most now seem to consider their Christianity a part of their work in some way. This could be entirely through "service" (the root vision), sometimes called "being Christ" to a client, and/or through direct evangelization, "sharing Christ" with a client, or a combination of both. The former take their inspiration from the Biblical teaching, "Whatever you do for one of these the least of my brethren, you do it unto Me" (Matt. 25:40). The latter from the Great Commission, "Go, therefore, and make disciples of all nations" (Matt. 28:19). Heartbeat International, which as AAI called itself "non-denominational and non-sectarian," began calling itself Christian and interdenominational in 1993.

There is currently an effort to unite Christians within our movement, especially Catholics and Evangelicals, by developing materials, conferences, and other gatherings that focus on what we have in common, rather than on the theological differences that have divided Christians for centuries. Mutual respect is developing among very different organizations, evidenced at the national, state, and city levels.

The Healing Vision

In the early '70s, we began to see clients who had already had one or more abortion and were thinking of another, and we began to be approached by post-abortive women who wanted to help other women avoid the tragic mistake they had made. The term *post-abortion syndrome* had not yet even been coined. When we consulted professional counselors for help, they either denied that abortion had any ill effects or they cautioned us, as volunteers and nonprofessionals, not to get involved for fear that post-abortive women might become suicidal.

Early attempts were made in some AAI centers to create post-abortion programs that were nondenominational and nonsectarian. However, when centers were confronted with the need for post-abortion healing programs, many moved from the service model to a ministry model, realizing that they had to choose a basis for their "counseling" and the obvious choice was a Biblical one. Thus, centers were pioneers in developing post-abortion programs, and now many organizations have formed who have this as the sole mission.[14]

We have also come to realize that almost all clients have broken sexual integrity. They are wounded by casual sex and broken trust, sexual abuse, incest, date rape, and/or abortion. By the 1980s and certainly by the '90s, most of our clients had grown up in a post-Christian era (certainly, most were born after the "quaint" time when abortion was illegal and marriage was the default option if there was a crisis pregnancy).

Crisis intervention alone is sometimes effective in keeping such clients from jumping off a cliff (i.e., not choosing an abortion), but they are still left with broken limbs and severely damaged internal organs, like broken hearts and souls. Life change and healing are necessary. Our centers have sometimes become "revolving doors," where clients come back time and again for pregnancy tests. Providing healing, ongoing support, and education is becoming a priority in our movement, and new programs are being introduced in an effort to provide healing and restoration so clients can actually regain their sexual integrity.

The Prevention Vision

Abstinence education, like post-abortion healing, also had its beginnings in pregnancy centers, since we had to develop a counseling approach when the client had a negative test, a more common result than the positive test.[15] In the 1980s, as we witnessed more and more clients with multiple sexual partners and sexually transmitted diseases, it became clear that we needed to move the abstinence message outside the counseling room, and especially into the schools, to counter Planned Parenthood's dangerous sex advocacy. All over the country, entrepreneurial center volunteers who had a heart for prevention began to give classroom presentations and inspirational assemblies. Abstinence curricula and speakers began to proliferate, and many centers started abstinence education programs in schools and in the community and consider "prevention" a major part of their mission.[16]

A boon came in the early '80s when a small amount of federal dollars was appropriated through Title XX in the Department of Health and Human Services to develop national "model prevention programs" based on abstinence. During the current Bush administration, federal funding has grown for abstinence-until-marriage education through Title V, the welfare reform bill, and SPRANS grants (Special Programs of Regional and National Significance). As a result, tax-funded abstinence-education programs, including at least thirty based within pregnancy centers, have expanded dramatically and have reached more and more schools and communities (and teen pregnancy and sexual activity rates have declined!). Federal funding for programs that do not "proselytize" has helped participating centers "grow up" quickly and develop stronger infrastructures. Some centers, on the other hand, have refused all federal funding, either because they are afraid of "strings" or because they believe it will weaken testimony that the church, not the government (in the form of tax-supported programs), is ultimately responsible for turning the tide on abortion and sexual promiscuity.

The Marriage Vision

We have not ignored the growing evidence, placed before our eyes in the person of our client, that the deterioration of marriage in our culture over the past thirty years has led to a dangerous situation for single mothers and their children. The evidence overwhelmingly shows that children raised with both biological (or adoptive) parents do best in terms of economics, education, physical and mental health, and many other factors related to security and happiness. Children overall (statistically) do poorly in all these areas when raised by single mothers.

While we have always upheld the value of adoption and marriage, many of our centers fell, through the years, into complacency about promoting them, being happy, at least, that a client chose not to abort her baby. The result is that few of our clients choose marriage or adoption. A recent study by Family Research Council, *Adoption: The Missing Piece*, has challenged pregnancy centers to examine our attitudes about adoption (only about 1–2 percent of our clients choose infant adoption, about the same as in the general population). We are just now starting to examine how we can encourage adoption and marriage among our clients. For many of them, raised in an era in which divorce is rampant and co-habitation is common, marriage and the two-parent family are foreign concepts.

Many centers are also now experimenting with programs to get fathers involved, but these are "baby steps" at this point. Still, they are vital for turning the tide back toward marriage and greater security for children, and their mothers.

The Future Vision

What is the future of the alternatives to abortion movement?

In some ways, our growth over the past thirty years is the bad news. High numbers of abortions, its devastating effects, and a sexual culture that wounds women and children – all have forced us to respond. Our pregnancy centers deal with more and more of these casualties, which means that the pro-life movement has been unsuccessful in winning the war against abortion-on-demand.

The service branch has almost always considered itself "separate" from the political and educational branches of the movement. But at this point in history, we must find ways to work with each other; for if each branch continues to function independently, without a unified strategy, we will continue to win some skirmishes but lose the war, and the carnage will grow.

We should remain diverse, entrepreneurial, and, therefore, creative. We have constantly reinvented ourselves to respond to new challenges. Centers in the future may be anywhere on the continuum of woman-centered, baby-centered, medical-centered, healing-centered, prevention-centered, evangelization-centered, or family-centered. But we must guard our developing unity. We should share statistics and research, and bring all centers under one or more "umbrellas" so that we can stay "on the cutting edge" and protect ourselves from outside efforts to close us down.

Government funding is a blessing and a temptation. We should learn how to benefit from new government funds that are becoming ever more available to faith-based organizations, but we must be careful to use them wisely, only for the social service and public school portions of our mission, so we can be free to truly minister and share the Gospel in other programs. Let us not become like some of the early faith-based organizations that now cannot be distinguished from secular ones (like the Red Cross) or that have even become leaders in secularizing our culture (does anyone remember that Harvard University was founded by Christians?).

I see our movement beginning a "paradigm shift." Our prime service has been the free pregnancy test. With home tests and now abortion by pill, some wonder if we may become irrelevant. But, we have constantly responded to challenges, and we will continue to do so. Our medical clinics have the potential to transcend the abortion and family planning clinics of Planned Parenthood and to become true centers of women's holistic health. We are adding services such as pap smears and well-baby care to our STD testing, prenatal care, natural family planning, abuse recovery, and post-abortion programs. Medical services may combine with counseling and spiritual healing in certain centers, or we may have stronger networks of centers, each having a specialized mission (some medical, some counseling, some support, some healing, some spiritual). We also can work to influence academic coursework and professional continuing education programs, sharing what we see in the lives of our clients and the devastating effects of casual sex.[17]

Finally, the alternatives-to-abortion movement, with all its varied members and pregnancy centers, is woven together by one thing: the consensus that sexual integrity is the key to ending abortion. God's plan is that sex, unconditional love, marriage between a man and a woman, children, and God – all go together. If we try to remove one of these from the equation, we have almost all the modern social ills (abortion, but also rampant divorce, co-habitation, fatherlessness, a gay sub-culture, STDs, loveless marriages, promiscuity, child abuse, and more). Pregnancy centers work on prevention, so sexual integrity is protected; intervention, when crisis occurs because sexual integrity is not being lived out; and healing, so sexual integrity can be restored. If and when our society observes the right to life for the unborn, the elderly, and the sick, our centers will still be needed to help preserve and restore sexual integrity in our culture.

But unity, worldly wisdom, and professionalism will not, in and of themselves, suffice. We need to pray for God's continued protection of our work. We must acknowledge that we are fundamentally Christian (although some centers still describe themselves as "non-denominational and non-sectarian" and sometimes think of that as "secular"). We must acknowledge that we are being used mightily, at the beginning of this millennium, in the struggle of good vs. evil that has existed since sin entered the world.

Margaret (Peggy) Hartshorn, Ph.D., President of Heartbeat International (formerly Alternatives to Abortion International), became active in the pro-life movement immediately after Roe v. Wade; *she is a wife, mother, grandmother, and former college English and Humanities Professor.*

Endnotes

1   Heartbeat International, formerly Alternatives to Abortion International (AAI), has published an annual directory of life-affirming service providers since 1971, to help those in need find services and to facilitate networking worldwide. The directory is available from Heartbeat International, Columbus, OH, 1-888-550-7577, and on the web at www.heartbeatinternational.org.

2   Baptists for Life, Grand Rapids, MI; Birthright, Atlanta, GA; Care Net, Sterling, VA; Christian Life Resources, Milwaukee, WI; Heartbeat International, Columbus, OH; International Life Services, Los Angeles, CA; National Institute of Family and Life Advocates, Fredericksburg, VA; National Life Center, Woodbury, NJ; and Save-a-Life, Birmingham, AL.

3   For example, in the early years, we commonly provided girls in crisis with host homes (my husband and I housed twelve girls between 1974 and 1985); but today it is almost impossible to put our clients in private homes because their dysfunction (alcoholism, drug abuse, displaced anger) is too disruptive for the family. Instead, an entrepreneurial network of small, Christian group homes with intensive educational and healing programs has emerged to replace the host homes (and large agency-based maternity homes of the '50s and '60s).

4   Birthright was founded by the late Louise Summerhill in Toronto, Canada. The Birthright USA central office is located in Atlanta, Georgia.

5   AAI was founded in Toledo, Ohio, by the late John Hillabrand, M.D., an obstetrician/gynecologist, and Mrs. Lore Maier from Germany, who had served as a court reporter at the Nuremburg Trials following World War II. Now called Heartbeat International, the central office is in Columbus, Ohio.

6   For research on the decline of the family and marriage, with attendant social problems, see a variety of papers by The Heritage Foundation, Washington, DC, www.heritage.org. For statistics on the rise of sexually transmitted diseases and AIDS, see studies by The Medical Institute, Austin, TX, www.medinstitute.org.

7   Later, the yellow pages listed "abortion alternatives" ahead of "abortion services" in phone books.

8   A manual, written by Bob Pearson over twenty years ago, which

promoted this baby-centered vision, is still quoted extensively by NARAL on its web-site to discredit pregnancy centers, even though most people in the movement today have never even seen the manual.

9   See "The Making of a Controversy: The History of the Conspiracy Against Pregnancy-Help Centers," a Special Report (vol. iii, no. 3) by Life Decisions International, Washington, DC. Also available on their web site at www.interlife.org.

10 Thomas Glessner, J.D. (chairman of the Board of the Seattle pregnancy center, victimized by the Planned Parenthood smear campaign of the 1980s) founded and still leads NIFLA, which has also published newsletters detailing the court cases brought against pregnancy centers.

11 The NARAL kit was advertised on their web site www.naral.org, in December of 2000.

12 Birthright declined to sign because they do not participate in coalitions. A copy of *Our Commitment of Care* is available from any of the affiliating organizations.

13 CAC was founded by a number of concerned Christians, including Dr. and Mrs. Harold O.J. Brown and Dr. C. Everett Koop, with the encouragement of the late Dr. Francis A. Schaeffer.

14 Within the Catholic Church, there are a variety of diocesan post-abortion programs, loosely called "Project Rachel." This list is available in the web site of the National Conference of Catholic Bishops, www.usccb.org. Post-abortion programs that have their roots in pregnancy centers include those published and available from Care Net and Heartbeat International. National organizations that specialize in post-abortion training and programs include Ramah International, Englewood, FL; PAM (Post Abortion Ministries), Memphis, TN; Rachel's Vineyard, Bridgeport, PA; National Memorial for the Unborn, Chattanooga, TN; National Office of Post Abortion Reconciliation and Healing, Milwaukee, WI; and Hope Alive USA, Bella Vista, AR.

15 The pioneer in "negative test counseling" is Sister Paula Vandegaer, one of the founders of AAI, now President of International Life Services. In the 1970s, before we became fully aware of the proliferation of sexually transmitted diseases including AIDS, early pregnancy centers focused their approach on the emotional and spiritual damage caused by sexual relationships outside the marriage bond, a

"heroic" stand given the strength of feminism at the time. Physical health became the major focus of negative test counseling during the '80s, but we are returning to a more holistic approach focusing on "sexual integrity."

16   For example, Abstinence Clearinghouse, the only national organization that tracks and evaluates all abstinence-until-marriage programs (and also publishes a directory of these programs and holds annual conferences for abstinence education providers) was founded in 1997 by Leslee Unruh, also founder of the pregnancy center in Sioux Falls, SD.

17   Heartbeat International is beginning this effort with a distance learning program through the Heartbeat Institute, designed to reach those "in the field," as well as those in colleges and universities. Our mission also includes helping pregnancy centers develop around the world, especially in Africa and Eastern Europe, with the Christian model. We hope to form strong networks around the world that mirror the kinds of organizations we have in the U.S.: faith based, life-affirming resource centers, medical clinics, maternity homes, and adoption agencies. We must share resources even more generously with centers overseas and work with them to end abortion in their countries. (While abortions number about 1.2 million per year in the U.S., an estimated 55–60 million abortions occur annually worldwide.)

Part III
Politics and the Movement

For Better or Worse
Jack Willke, M.D.

An attempt to describe the leadership of the American pro-life movement in anything less than an entire book is a daunting undertaking. Clearly, it will be possible to name but a fraction of the movement's leaders. Accordingly, this essay will mention those who represent many others. Of necessity, this passes over literally hundreds who should be so honored by the mention. But let's get on with it.

The Early Years

In the early years (1967 through 1972), Colorado, California, and New York led the way in legalizing abortion. A dozen other smaller states also legalized abortion prior to the 1973 *Roe v. Wade* decision, but, in almost every case, these changes were highly restrictive.[1] The activity in California and New York was obviously most important.

At that time, the leaders of the movement included: Professor Robert Byrn from Fordham University; Dr. Eugene Diamond and Dennis Horan from Chicago; Joseph Whitherspoon in Texas; Dr. Matthew Bulfin in Florida; and Dr. Joseph Stanton in Massachusetts. These were a few of the very early pioneers. They wrote, lectured, and helped to get the pro-life engine started.

Organizationally, the Knights of Columbus, a Catholic fraternal and insurance group, warrant special mention. With approximately a million members, they were able to publish and circulate educational literature as no other organization could. Their many local branches provided invaluable ground troops at the start.

In 1971 and 1972, Mrs. Willke and I published the *Handbook on Abortion* and the *Life or Death* brochure, respectively.[2] These were the first two universally distributed, major educational pieces. They provided the margin of victory for the referenda victories in North Dakota and Michigan in the fall of 1972. (These measures would have legalized abortion up to twenty weeks. The referendum in North Dakota was defeated by 78 percent, the one in Michigan by 63 percent.)

Then Came Roe

Before the dust of the January 1973 *Roe v. Wade* decision had settled, a number of us met to examine the arguments that had proven convincing to the U.S. Supreme Court. There were two major ones. First and most central was the Court's refusal to recognize prenatal life as fully human life. This was not a baby – at least not yet – to the Court. Second was the finding that abortion was only a religious issue. In 1973, this meant the issue was "Catholic," which meant, in turn, imposed by the American Catholic Bishops.

To address the first finding of the Court, we devised a methodology of teaching the pro-life story. It was quite simple. First, using slides of fetal development, we presented the scientific case that human life began at fertilization. We then explained that the issue was broader than religious belief; it was, in fact, a matter of human rights. We noted the comparison with slavery and the then-current drive for passing civil rights legislation to give equal status in the U.S. to people of color. Since the racial human rights issue could be addressed by corrective legislation, we argued that the fetal human rights issue could as well.

One early worry concerned the limited time-frame during which we thought *Roe* had to be reversed. As the number of abortions rose to 1.5 million annually, so did the number of individuals with a vested interest in justifying abortion and maintaining its legal status. Each pregnant woman involves a man, and the woman seeking an abortion typically consults two other people in her abortion decision: a mother, a sister, a girlfriend, etc. Thus, four times 1.5 million would equal 6 million people a year added to the roster of those with an interest in legal abortion. In ten years, that number could reach 60 million people – almost as many as vote in a general election.

But now, after thirty years, we can look back and see that we had some, but certainly not an overwhelming, reason to be worried. We assumed that the great majority of those involved in abortion would be partisan supporters of it. Instead, their *silence* has been deafening. Men and women have suffered, not benefited, by abortion, with both psychological devastation and physical injury. We have seen that abortion contains within itself the seeds of its own destruction. To our surprise and delight, we are now seeing a generation of young people who have only known legal abortion in their lifetimes, but who are now providing strong leadership to stop it some day.

Even so, *abortion* has infected everything it has touched. Our entire culture has been changed.

The 1980s

As we approached the '80s, things really began to happen. The first major legislative accomplishment was the Hyde Amendment (1976), which stopped federal funding of elective abortions. Congressman Henry Hyde (R-IL) became a hero of the movement and remains so. We could name many in the U.S. House and Senate who deserve the title of heroic leadership, but let's pick out three pioneers: In addition to Congressman Hyde is Congressman Chris Smith of New Jersey, and Senator Jesse Helms of North Carolina. These three men were rock solid, never deviated from the pro-life movement and have simply been invaluable.

The year 1980 was a milestone. First, Ronald Reagan was elected President, which meant that pro-life leaders worked both with and within the administration. Reverend Jerry Falwell of the Moral Majority became a national figure with the help and influence of Paul Weyrich, an important and influential conservative and pro-lifer.

In evangelical circles, two figures came to the fore: Francis Schaeffer, a Protestant theologian, and Dr. C. Everett Koop, then of the Children's Hospital in Philadelphia and later President Reagan's Surgeon General. Both wrote and lectured around the country with a stirring message. They warned that the country was losing its Christian moorings and that Christians should therefore come out of their churches and participate in political and public life. They encouraged evangelicals to work with other pro-lifers, especially Roman Catholics and members of other faiths. Evangelicals responded, becoming a major political force, giving rise to the Christian Coalition and other activist groups.

One excellent example of evangelical influence and industry is the National Religious Broadcasters network. Overseas observers are astonished to find out that the almost 2,000 evangelical stations in the United States are, without exception, 100 percent pro-life. These stations have 60 million or more listeners every week and are a major reason why the pro-abortion media conglomerates in the U.S. have not completely dominated and changed the culture here. Individuals such as the Reverend T. James Kennedy of Coral Ridge Ministries, Marlin Maddoux of Point of View, Chuck Colson of Prison Fellowship, and of course Dr. James Dobson of Focus on the Family, are just a few of the radio personalities who have inspired pro-life activism. Dr. Dobson, in particular, is a modern phenomenon. Without question, he is the most significant, most respected, and most influential evangelical spokesperson in the United States – perhaps even in the world. His position is 100 percent pro-life, his approach is totally professional, and his impact on our culture has been simply beyond measuring.[3]

At the same time, Mrs. Phyllis Schlafly rose to prominence by founding the Eagle Forum and almost single-handedly defeated the Equal Rights Amendment (proposed in 1972 and finally buried in 1987), which would have inserted abortion-on-demand into the Constitution as an amendment, rather than by the Supreme Court decision of *Roe v. Wade*.

In the District of Columbia, other pro-life, activist groups were forming, including the Christian Action Council, the Ad-Hoc

Committee in Defense of Life, and the March for Life. Americans United for Life, a pro-life public-interest law firm, had begun in Chicago and was a major player, as was the National Right to Life Committee, which had been formed in 1973 and was where I served as President, 1980–1991.

In the 1970s, the aforementioned organizations were more or less co-equal. During the 1980s, however, the National Right to Life Committee became dominant. From 1980 to 1991, it grew from five to fifty employees, and went from $400,000 annual cash flow to $15 million. With its fifty state affiliates, it was clearly the leading pro-life force.

Happily, other groups arose, grew, and prospered. They matured alongside NRLC to a co-equal status, so that now there are a number of major national organizations fluctuating in terms of specific leadership. Gary Bauer, President of the Family Research Council from 1980–1998, became the prime pro-life spokesman in the Nation's Capital during the 1990s, for example. The Christian Coalition had spokesman Ralph Reed; Concerned Women for America was led by Beverly LaHaye (and now Sandy Rios). Richard Land's Southern Baptist's Christian Life Commission as well as Phyllis Schlafly's Eagle Forum have become significant players in Washington politics, along with the more recent Christian Medical Association under Dr. Dave Stephens. The United States Catholic Conference, also in D.C., has always been a strong and influential pro-life presence.

The Split

During the early 1980s, these groups argued vigorously among themselves, privately and publicly, about strategy. In Congress, both a Human Life Amendment to the Constitution and a Human Life Bill were introduced. Different groups favored different constitutional amendments, however: The Helms Amendment (sponsored by Senator Jesse Helms) would have guaranteed legal protection to all living human beings from fertilization onward. The Hatch Amendment (sponsored by Senator Orrin Hatch of Utah) would have returned abortion to its status before *Roe* as an issue to

be addressed by each individual state. Ultimately, it was acknowledged that the Human Life Bill would have been struck down by
the Supreme Court as unconstitutional. The Hatch Amendment
was voted on and defeated in June of 1983; the Helms Amendment
never came to a vote. After this, the movement settled down, focusing on less sweeping legislative goals as well as pro-life education,
which would produce the political strength necessary to pass this
kind of crucial pro-life legislation through Congress.

To this day, however, the movement's leadership is split. A
committed, vocal, and sincere minority feel that we should settle
for nothing less than a Helms type constitutional amendment to
settle the abortion controversy in one stroke. Most notable in this
camp has been Miss Nellie Gray, who sponsors the annual January
22nd Washington March for Life, and Mrs. Judi Brown, head of the
American Life League. The vast majority of pro-life leadership
today, however, sees such a single step as an impossible task, that,
if pursued relentlessly, would bear no fruit except full defeat and
therefore the continuation of abortion-on-demand. This majority
believes that the battle can only be won by incremental victories,
which will slowly change the mind of our nation and ultimately
make it possible to reach that goal of a sweeping federal amendment.

Women's Help Centers

A major factor blossoming slowly over the years has been the
women's help centers. Louise Summerhill began this dimension of
the movement with the founding of Birthright in Toronto, Canada,
some thirty years ago. Birthright is an organization dedicated to
helping women in unexpected pregnancies, and its success has
inspired the creation of almost 4,000 such centers in the U.S. The
first American leaders in the 1970s were Mrs. Laurie Maier and Dr.
John Hillenbrand. Still active are Mrs. Denise Coccilone in New
Jersey, Bob Pearson in Arkansas, Sister Paula Vandergar in Los
Angeles, and Tom Glessner in Virginia. The current *de facto* head of
the movement, both here and abroad, is Dr. Margaret Hartshorn,

President of Heartbeat International in Columbus, Ohio. These centers have become increasingly sophisticated over the years, many now employing medical professionals and using sophisticated medical equipment, including ultrasound machines. Staffed almost entirely by females, these centers are the heart of the movement and live the founding principle of the pro-life cause, "Love Them Both."

Grassroots Movement

The pro-life movement is not a Washington-based, top-down operation; it is emphatically a grassroots effort, with local towns, counties, cities, and states providing effective, homegrown leadership. Because they had the first changes in abortion laws, California, Colorado, and New York produced early leaders. Then Minnesota gave us Dr. David Osteen and Mrs. Darla St. Martin. From Michigan came Jane Muldoon; from Ohio, Peggy Lehner and your author; from Massachusetts, Dr. Mildred Jefferson; and from Indiana, Mrs. Mary Hunt. Consistently, the largest, most efficient, most effective pro-life state has been Michigan, currently under the leadership of Barbara Listing.

The movement is composed of single and multi-issue groups, with NRLC and its state right-to-life affiliates comprising the former. They focus on the life issues only (abortion, infanticide, euthanasia). Multi-issue groups are commonly religious-based, usually Christian, and concern themselves with additional issues, including such things as prayer in school, posting the Ten Commandments, pornography, etc. Examples of these, in addition to those mentioned, could include Don Wildmon of the American Family Association, Reverend Lou Sheldon of the Traditional Values Coalition, Morton Blackwell of the Leadership Institute, and many others.

Some national organizations have had an international reach. The premier example is Human Life International under the Reverend Paul Marx, who has lectured in over ninety countries, making him the most traveled pro-life person. Coming up second

are your author, who is the founder and President of the
International Right to Life Federation, and his wife Barbara, with
sixty-five countries traveled to for pro-life lectures.[4]

Pursuing a different approach has been Life Dynamics, under
Mark Crutcher. Acting aggressively, it has exposed the illicit practices of many abortion doctors, the scandal of selling baby parts,
and, more recently, the sexual predator activity of abortion
providers. Life Dynamics works to defeat abortion providers
through *litigation*.

Violent or Peaceful?

A word about violence in the movement. This has been, from the
very beginning, an incredibly peaceful, prayerful movement. We
have gone through a phase called RESCUE, when there was con-
scious breaking of the law by peaceful sit-ins and blockage of
entrances. In response to this, the abortion industry was able to
convince the U.S. Congress to pass several draconian laws and
today RESCUE is but a memory.[5]

Outside of the one thousand or more American abortion facilities, however, you still find sidewalk counselors. These protesters,
who are largely women and often with their own children, are
peaceful and prayerful. They offer help, pro-life literature, and
information to women seeking abortions. Through their efforts, literally hundreds of thousands of children live today. The suggestion
that these are violent people who shoot abortionists or burn down
clinics is preposterous. For the record, no pro-life leader has ever
been involved with, much less convicted of, acts such as burning
down a clinic.

But what of the shootings? To date, five people have been killed
– but not by members of legitimate pro-life groups. The United
States has over one thousand abortion facilities, with pro-life protesters in front of them several days a week, for over thirty years
now. The man- and woman-hours number in the hundreds of millions, and the work is nerve-racking, heart-breaking and intensely
emotional. The amazing news is not that there have been five abortionists and attendants shot, but rather that there haven't been

thousands. Leaders such as Joe Scheidler in Chicago, the Reverand Flip Benham, Reverend Pat Mahoney, and Randall Terry can be proud to have overseen one of the most extraordinary, peaceful, and prayerful social movements in the history of this nation.[6]

Church Leadership

What of church leadership? In the evangelical movement, leadership is almost ubiquitous: Christian radio stations; innumerable preachers and pastors; the multi-issue Christian leaders mentioned above — Dobson, LaHaye, Falwell, etc.

But what of the Roman Catholic sector? Certainly the U.S. bishops have presented, as dogma, a united front. Pope John Paul II has been a world leader and truly a rock on this issue. There has therefore been no dearth of leadership in the Catholic Church. If we mention one name in the U.S. Catholic hierarchy, it clearly must be Cardinal John O'Connor, the Archbishop of New York of fond memory. Another notable is Mother Angelica, with her international radio and TV apostolate on the Eternal Word Television Network (EWTN).

But Catholic clergy share with many other denominations one major deficit: Few preach on this subject. What brought slavery to an end, to a significant extent, was the fiery preaching from pulpits all over the North. Sadly, that has happened only in individual congregations in our movement. If, in fact, such widespread preaching had been part of the anti-abortion movement from the beginning, it may well be that abortion would not be legal today.

Successes and Failures

Let us now review both the failures and successes.

Failures

First, of course, we have failed to stop abortion. The roadblock, obviously, is the U.S. Supreme Court, which has permitted legislation in limited areas, which we have used (parental involvement laws, informed consent provisions, etc.). But abortion continues.

We have lost the National Democrat Party leadership. While incremental over the years, this development is now undeniable and unfortunate.

We have not influenced the secular media. Publications such as the *New York Times*, the *Washington Post*, along with all the major networks have been bulwarks for the abortion movement from the beginning, and remain so.

We have not been able to penetrate the near unanimous Jewish support of abortion-on-demand (recognizing, of course, that Orthodox Jewry, a very small minority, is strongly pro-life).

We have not been able to affect the pro-abortion policies of many of the mainline Protestant churches, though these policies are weakening by themselves in churches like the United Methodist and the Presbyterian Church U.S.A. Significantly, these Protestant churches are seeing rapidly declining membership, as contrasted with the growth of the Southern Baptists and of other evangelical and fundamentalist churches that are pro-life.

We have failed to penetrate the African American leadership in the U.S. Without question, polls show most black Americans as consistently more pro-life than whites. Nevertheless, their leadership, with very few exceptions, remains aggressively pro-abortion.

Leadership quarrels of the early 1980s set us back. Happily, those days are long gone, and the top leadership of all of the organizations now routinely work together warmly.

We failed to convince pastors and clergymen to preach aggressively against abortion.

Finally, we have failed to counter, adequately, the one remaining argument of the abortion lobby: That a woman has a *right* to choose.

Successes

We can be proud of what we have done right, however:

Abortion remains *the* central social issue of our time – even after thirty years.

Abortion in the U.S. is still a dirty word. An abortionist in the U.S. is still an outcast, especially within the medical profession.

This is not true in many other nations, and it is an important deterrent to abortion in this country.

Few U.S. hospitals still do abortions, which are largely confined to freestanding facilities staffed by abortionists, who are, again, not part of the respected medical community.

Is this a baby? This is no longer a question. Ultrasound and other medical advances have been incredibly important in this, but the pro-life movement was of central importance in teaching the nation, beyond any question of scientific doubt, that human life begins at fertilization.

The pro-life movement has changed the way religious groups view each other and has encouraged them to work together. The prejudice and bigotry that divided denominations, Christian and other, are gone, as any sidewalk counselor will attest. We've learned and lived the old saw, "If you don't hang together, you'll end up hanging separately."

Our religious radio, a shining triumph in the U.S., is the envy of pro-life movements around the world. This industry is totally pro-life.

Our movement has not just survived, but grown in the face of a militant, dedicated, and powerful pro-abortion media and academia. It has grown, too, in spite of the much greater financial resources of the abortion industry.[7]

The U.S. has developed far and away the largest, best-organized and most effective pro-life movement in the international arena.

Most Americans are still opposed to most abortions done in this country. *Roe* and its progeny created a policy and practice of abortion-on-demand that remain radically far from the wishes and convictions of the average American citizen, who would permit it only for three months, and only for a fairly narrow set of circumstances.

We have refuted most of the arguments of the abortion lobby. Space doesn't permit, but their myths include: back-alley abortions; unwanted pregnancy equals unwanted child and child abuse; it's only a religious issue; we need it to control overpopulation; rape pregnancies are common and must be aborted; and fetal handicap is an absolute indication for abortion.

We have had prominent converts to the cause, including Dr. Bernard Nathanson, founding member of the National Abortion and Reproductive Rights Action League (NARRAL), and Norma McCorvey, the "Roe" of *Roe v. Wade*. They have become important leaders in the movement.

Finally, young people are a vigorous component of the movement. They are addressing not just abortion but also teen abstinence, a movement that, if it continues, will have a major impact.

The Future

There are many question marks.

The battle over abortion is slowly being won, but it is tied closely to the issue of family life. We have seen in the last several decades the deterioration and fragmentation of the family. Divorce is rampant, pre-marital co-habitation is common, illegitimacy, in some areas, is almost the norm. In the last few years we've seen hopeful signs of this beginning to plateau and, in some cases, turn around. It is difficult to imagine that we could effectively stop abortion unless we first return more stability to family life.

Pornography is a related issue. It is out of control and is terribly damaging.

Bioethical questions, with new ones arising every month, will influence the direction of the movement. Today we kill babies *inside* the womb to get her unpregnant. Tomorrow will we be killing babies *outside* of the womb, and again for choice?

What influence will the web have? Certainly it will be profound, for good or for evil.

And now demographics, to many people's surprise, enters the world stage with an unexpected impact: Overpopulation will soon become underpopulation, with nations aggressively campaigning for more babies rather than fewer.

Conclusion

In the end, it will be the commitment and dedication of those within the pro-life movement that carry the day. Their devotion and perseverance are far beyond those within the pro-abortion movement. Without the media, the government and money, the pro-abortion movement collapses. Their strength is a mile wide but only a yard deep.

Leadership during the 1970s was often lonely. More than once, Barbara and I and others wondered if a mutual disaster took us out, would the pro-life movement continue? But today its base is broad, dedicated, and informed. If one leader or organization stumbles, others pick up the flag and charge on. This movement will not go away.

Finally, while religious belief and practice are not *the* reason to oppose abortion in this secular nation, these factors are prime motivators. As this nation slowly returns to its religious base, the high number of God-fearing, ordinary citizens will yet turn this thing around.

I may not live to see the end of abortion, but I am convinced my children will.

John C. Willke, M.D., is a physician, author, and lecturer. He served for ten years as President of the National Right to Life Committee and is currently President of the International Right to Life Federation (est. 1984) and The Life Issues Institute. He practiced medicine in Cincinnati, Ohio, for forty years, where he was on the senior attending staff of the Providence and Good Samaritan hospitals.

Endnotes

1   These first laws permitted abortion for life of the mother, rape, incest pregnancies, and some for fetal handicap.

2   The handbook was an inexpensive ($0.95) paperback, in question-answer format. It covered the scientific facts of fetal development and of abortion in a simple, usable manner. *Handbook On Abortion* and its successors, as of this writing, are in twenty-two languages and probably 2 million copies worldwide. The *Life or Death* brochure is a colored pamphlet depicting developing and aborted babies. It is still available in twenty languages and has been printed in untold millions worldwide.

3   Your author has had a five-minute pro-life daily commentary on 300 or more stations for eighteen years and a one-minute pro-life

comment on almost 1,000 stations for six years, demonstrating the near total support by evangelical stations of the pro-life message.

4   As far as publications in multi-languages are concerned, the Willkes are probably the most traveled authors in the pro-life movement, with 146 separate publications in thirty languages, in uncounted millions of copies.

5   The FACE (Freedom of Access to Clinics Act) made sit-ins a federal felony. The Supreme Court ruled that the RICO (Racketeer Influenced Corruption Act) did apply to such activity.

6   Comparison with the black civil rights movement is interesting. While the Rev. Martin Luther King and others preached peaceful actions, the Black Panthers, seeking the same goals, were violent and at times killed people.

7   Planned Parenthood, the largest abortion provider, has an annual income of $700 million (2001); only six of the state right-to-life organizations have incomes over 1 million dollars annually. See *Stopp International, the Ryan Report,* April 2001.

An Honest Evaluation
Paul M. Weyrich

A few years ago, I wrote a letter that created a good deal of controversy because it was wrongly interpreted by many as urging cultural conservatives, including many pro-life activists, to retreat
from politics.

Do not get ready to hoist up the white flag of surrender to a secular humanist America just yet; I am just as much in the fight for
the conservative cause now as I was twenty years ago when I
helped to bring evangelicals and other cultural conservatives into
politics. And I hope that the good people who have been in the
trenches for as long as three decades for the right-to-life cause will
remain in the fight.

Our Nation Has Changed

As I worked over the years to organize social, economic, and
pro-defense conservatives, quite frequently I found myself working with the leaders of the pro-life movement. I feel fortunate to
have done so; their passion is energizing and their commitment to
the sanctity of life is absolute and inspiring. But that commitment
to principle should not blind us to the realities of how our nation
has changed.

Just as a football coach in the early years of the last century had
to change his defense to fend off the newly developed forward
pass, our conservative movement must drastically revise its play-

book to account for changes in the cultural and political terrain of modern, secular-humanist America.

In my letter of February 16, 1999, I specifically stressed that movement conservatives needed to rethink what we could expect out of politics. The movement was at low ebb. The 1998 elections had gone badly, the House Republicans were in disarray with the unexpected departure of Newt Gingrich (R-GA), and the attempt to drive Bill Clinton from office had failed.

What I then realized, painfully, was that a nation is not just a government presiding over a set of families and businesses. It is also a culture – a pervasive climate of attitudes and opinions – in which political efforts either resonate or die. And ours were dying.

In the letter, I specifically noted that the failed efforts to pass referenda banning partial-birth abortion in Washington State and Colorado represented one reason why the right-to-life movement had to face up to the unpleasant fact that no longer were cultural conservatives a "moral majority" in this country. And, as the person who coined the term, it is still very hard for me to admit that we are not even a "moral majority" in some of the religious denominations that once constituted the nation's very moral fiber.

The thirtieth anniversary of the *Roe v. Wade* decision, which decision proved very important in galvanizing conservatives, and was obviously instrumental in giving rise to the pro-life movement, is an appropriate time to stand back and take stock of our direction. We have worked together for so long and so closely that I know we share a strong mutual interest in restoring our country to the God-centered values that made it great.

What to Expect from Politics

Very little has happened in the years since my letter that could be construed as progress for the right-to-life cause. I think there are three basic questions that confront both the conservative movement at-large and the right-to-life movement in particular. First: What can and should we expect out of politics? Second: What must we do to ensure our values can survive in such a hostile climate? Third: How do we define victory?

Let's take the one about politics first. When I launched Free Congress Political Action Committee (PAC) in 1974 with the late Robert Casey and Dr. Charles Moser, it was only a year after the Supreme Court had decided *Roe v. Wade*. We were seeking issues that would serve as litmus tests to distinguish who would be "movement" conservative candidates from liberals, or even "Old Right" conservatives. (Many "Old Right" conservatives found themselves in favor of legalized abortion.) Generally, a pro-life position was essential to even be considered for support from the Free Congress PAC. Other issues, such as the Panama Canal give-away a few years after *Roe v. Wade*, were very important too, and considered by us very carefully.

At that time, the pro-life movement strategy was to elect a Congress and to elect a president that would pass a "personhood" amendment to the Constitution, declaring the unborn child a "person" under the Constitution and therefore entitled to protection under the 14th Amendment, for example. In that, the New Right was united with the pro-life movement, and we collaborated very closely in many campaigns.

The election strategy had some great payoffs at first. I specifically remember Roger Jepsen's upset of Dick Clark, the pro-abortion Senator from Iowa, in which the right-to-life movement made sure that churchgoers throughout the state learned the facts of his record on abortion. Another big win in 1978 was the election of Gordon Humphrey in New Hampshire, who became a real stalwart of the right-to-life movement and who proved himself to be politically astute. Controlling the Senate could lead to a pro-life Supreme Court – that was the plan.

Then, of course, came 1980 when Republicans actually did win control of the United States Senate and put Ronald Reagan in the White House. That was exhilarating. But where did it lead us?

Having Ronald Reagan in the White House did not bring much tangible difference. True, he would address the March for Life, and he and his administration worked to limit federal funding for abortion. But he was never really willing to stick his neck out on the issue. Remember, the first nomination he made to the Supreme

Court was Sandra Day O'Connor. It was clear in 1981 that she would not be a friend to the pro-life cause, and it remains that way today. And I say that as someone who has come to admire the leadership of Ronald Reagan, particularly when it came to dealing with the then-Soviet Union.

He did nominate Robert Bork to the Supreme Court and that 1987 fight was a very important one. If someone with the values of Robert Bork could be confirmed, then so could others who shared a commitment to constitutional principles and realized, unlike the majority of justices deciding *Roe*, that there is no constitutional right to kill unborn children. Cases like *Casey*[1] or *Webster*,[2] given a better Court, might have led to *Roe*'s reversal. But the Senate was back in Democrat hands when the Bork nomination was made, and even when Republicans had control from 1981–87 (and subsequently too from 1995 to mid-2001), it never meant that pro-lifers had control, too.

Then, there was President George H.W. Bush, who had a similar mixed record, never having been viewed as a true pro-life stalwart in the first place. He did give us Clarence Thomas, but he also gave us David Souter, who shares much the same outlook *as* Justice O'Connor on the pro-life issue. After suffering the slings and arrows of distrustful pro-lifers in his first run for the Republican presidential nomination, and then as Ronald Reagan's vice president, Bush came to realize the power that the pro-life forces exerted on the Republican Party's nominating process. He wanted their support when he would try again, and the courtship paid off. However, pro-lifers were simply one of many coalition groups in his "big tent," which was large enough to also include Republicans who held the very opposite view on abortion.

Perhaps the most important lesson that can be drawn from the experiences with Reagan and Bush is that even a committed conservative politician, a Reagan, cannot be trusted to take on a cause like abortion and gamble power and prestige to make abortion a truly national issue. It is useful to politicians, for their own purposes, to have life concerns be a niche issue of concern to Americans who adhere to the values of life. But it is unrealistic of us to expect politicians to do our work for us.

Years in politics have taught me never to put much faith in politicians to accomplish my goals. Today's friend all too easily will turn into tomorrow's foe given a bad turn in the polls or a redrawn district that removes "God and Country" rural voters, replacing them with "Swinging Urban Singles" or "Suburban Soccer Moms."

The Importance of Culture: Seeking a Moral Renewal

As I said in my 1999 letter: "I think it is fair to say that conservatives have learned to succeed in politics. That is, we got our people elected. But that did not result in the adoption of our agenda. The reason, I think, is that politics itself has failed. And politics has failed because of the collapse of the culture."

That brings us to the true ailment of our country, and to the impact it has on those of us who toil in politics: Seeking a moral renewal for our country.

When I came to Washington back in the mid-1960s, at a time when many on the left were turning on and dropping out, there were still liberals who believed in God and Church and Country. The same cannot be said of liberals now, nor even of many within the Republican Party who bill themselves as conservatives but worship the Dow rather than God.

What we see in our culture – television, radio, movies, literature – reflects the pernicious secular humanism that disparages God, His Commandments, and eternal values, and prefers a culture of convenience in which celebrities and their "rich and famous" lifestyles are the touchstones on how to live. Nothing has value for more than fifteen seconds, if even that, perhaps other than measuring the worth of a man by his mutual-fund account. In this kind of post-modern civilization, the right-to-life message will have a difficult time finding a fair hearing, much less the acceptance that it would have had automatically in times past when most people truly understood and adhered to Judeo-Christian values.

As shocking as it may seem, true believing Christians and Jews are the real counterculture in America now.

What to Do: Subcultures

It was this realization that led me to adopt a modified version of the advice offered by the 1960s radicals: turn off, tune out, drop out. I'd advise any cultural conservative who truly wants to live his values to follow suit.

First, we should "turn off." Avoid the garbage that infects our culture, including turning off the junk shows that are on television. "Tune out" by simplifying your life, making sure there is time for contemplation and reflection. Finally, we should "drop out" by making our own subcultures: find our own places to live our lives and values in the way we see fit, not the way the culture-crats of Madison Avenue and Hollywood see fit. Band together with other like-minded and like-spirited people, to share our lives and our children's lives.

What to Do: Remain Politically Active

In my letter, I never meant that we should drop out of political participation. Rather, we should change our expectations of the political process. We should realize that cultural renewal is most likely to come about by changing our culture, *not by political action.*

There is still a very vital role for cultural conservatives to play in politics: Namely, making sure that government does not capitulate even further to secular humanism. Cultural conservatives and pro-lifers must stay active to make sure that our politicians remain responsive to us on the life issues. Do not expect them to do our work for us, but be prepared in theory and in practice to connect our issue to their future. That means our grassroots must be trained in campaigning and lobbying, and organized so that we can respond massively and immediately when the need arises.

As any army needs to be drilled and practiced, so too a political army needs to be. Hence the vital importance of political efforts that, on the surface, may not "save a single life." Drilling raw recruits in Arizona doesn't save any lives, either, but when those recruits see action in Afghanistan, they survive if they did the drill.

Demanding votes on interim measures, funding measures, and amendments of various kinds – the whole incremental strategy – is the drill field that teaches the next generation of pro-life leaders the political ropes. If the next generation (and in volunteer activism, a generation is about five years long) does not know how to win elections and legislative battles, there is no future to the pro-life movement. I am concerned that so many people have dropped out of the political process that it will be hard for our movement to be politically effective in the coming decades.

I would urge that more of an effort be made to look for ways to depend less on the Republican Party, although it is quite clear that it is considered to be the pro-life and conservative party. Actually, it is both those things in name only, though some presidents and leaders are more pro-life than others. Throughout the lower ranks of the GOP, there are many Republicans in positions of power who are pro-abortion and hostile to the true tenets of cultural conservatism.

We were very insistent, particularly in the early years of the New Right, that every effort possible should be made to reach out to Democrats. At that time, there were still a number of conservative Democrats in Congress, many of whom were pro-life. But the entrenched liberals who controlled the Democratic caucuses in the House and Senate made life very uncomfortable for them when they took a pro-life stance and voted their consciences (on defense and economic issues, too). Then, there were the coffers in Hollywood, the Upper West Side, and Back Bay. Everything came together to keep the Democrats from being a truly "big tent," so those pro-life Democrats jumped to the GOP. I would like to think that we could activate a stronger following among Democrats for the pro-life cause and cultural conservatism. Realistically, though, I must admit, it would be very difficult. The left is the Democratic Party, and it is the left that is simpatico with secular humanism. There are some brave, lonely voices within the Democratic Party for life and sound cultural values, but they will remain isolated for the foreseeable future.

What to Do: Local Community Involvement

At the state and local level, direct democracy is an option that pro-lifers should consider carefully as a way to surmount the political parties by taking their case directly to the public. Not every state has the initiative process, but in those that do, the pro-life movement should take advantage of it whenever possible to advance the cause.

The right-to-life movement must decide to take an absolutely tough stance and throw its support behind a presidential candidate who is both electable and absolutely committed to the pro-life cause to the point that he will absolutely go to bat for it. I am talking about somebody who will nominate the kind of jurists for the Supreme Court who really know constitutional law, apply it faithfully, not making the law to suit their whims as occurred in the *Roe v. Wade* case. A united pro-life movement can exert a powerful influence in politics, particularly if we also work to expand our outreach and base.

And the way to do that is to also be engaged in the long fight ahead to change our culture.

Earlier, I encouraged cultural conservatives to drop out. I did not mean to retreat into a cultural castle whose moat you never cross, but having your community as a base of support from which you can reach out to change the world. Dropping out of the mainstream culture does not mean evading the true problem areas of our society. One thing I fear is that many Christians will actually stay within the confines of their own faith community, and will not get out and start working with, listening to and building trust with those who could most use their wisdom and guidance.

The people who comprise the backbone of the pro-life movement's caring ministries are almost a case study of how to strike the right balance. They have done an excellent job of putting my very ideas into action. The caring ministry stream of the pro-life movement saw a problem in the culture (the plight of desperate women, mostly young, faced with unexpected pregnancies and nowhere to turn for help except the local abortuary), and, quietly but with gentle determination, set out to address that problem.

Not only do they help young women in crisis, but the pregnancy resource center movement has become a real agent for cultural change, as abstinence and other cultural renewal efforts begin at that point. Over 4,000 crisis pregnancy centers around the country are organized, managed, and funded at the local level, by pro-life men and women who are motivated by high ideals. For the most part, these are people who have a Scriptural love for their fellow human beings, who practice their faith seriously, and who keep their own lives in order, including faithful, personal prayer. They manage to raise money for their expanding ministries *by* getting better acquainted with their local communities, and in the course of doing that, they carry the message of life to the world in a way that political action never could.

Outreach

Nor should we limit the pro-life movement to Christians. Young people from secular homes can profit from the wisdom that cultural conservatives and pro-lifers have to offer. Many are seeking direction in their lives, particularly those from homes afflicted by divorce and permissive parenting. Many of these find they are able to paper over the sadness of their lives because of their affluence.

Inner-city youths can also benefit from the conservative and pro-life message. Many have a religious foundation upon which to build. But more can be done both by the pressure of the community itself and the churches in it to encourage fatherhood. America's racial minorities must become leaders among their own communities for the pro-life cause.

Strong communications campaigns aimed at showing young people the sanctity of life should play an even more important part in the right-to-life movement of the future. Religious schools have done this for years. The trick is to develop campaigns that will appeal to young people who may be divorced from religious traditions, but who may still be open to learning about protecting the unborn. Social marketing is a discipline that our opponents often use effectively; we should use the same sophisticated research and communications techniques to advance our pro-life principles.

What Is Victory?

That leads us to defining victory. Victory will be an America in which the Judeo-Christian values that guided our forefathers are once again respected and obeyed throughout the land. There will not be the glorification of promiscuous sex or alternative lifestyles in Hollywood or real life. Gone will be the celebration of youth and allowing children to do their "own thing."

Admittedly, this day is far off. The events of 9/11 presented a brief hope that this newfound sense of purpose and of God might take hold once more. It has not come to pass. But the secular-humanist society and the lifestyles that it encourages are built on lies, just as the old Soviet Union was based on lies. Hard as it was for American Cold Warriors to see, the Soviet Union was collapsing from within because the lies could no longer sustain themselves. The same will hold true when it comes to our post-modern society.

My letter of 1999 was anything but a call for conservatives to retreat from fighting our nation's real cultural ills. But placing all the chips on politics is a losing strategy as the frustrations of the last two decades have shown. We must remain active in politics. But a new battle of promoting cultural change by shunning the mainstream, and re-creating a true Judeo-Christian *society*, beckons. Change the culture, and the politics of this country will follow.

Paul M. Weyrich is President of the Free Congress Foundation, a conservative research and education foundation located in Washington, D.C. He is a former TV and radio news reporter and anchor who served as an aide to two United States senators. Weyrich had served as the first president of the Heritage Foundation before forming the Free Congress Foundation in 1977.

Endnotes

1   *Planned Parenthood v. Casey*, 505 U.S. 833 (1992) (Supreme Court decision evaluating Pennsylvania's Abortion Control Act and preserving the central holding of *Roe* that a constitutional liberty interest in abortion exists.)

2   *Webster v. Reproductive Health Services*, 492 U.S. 490 (1989) (Supreme Court decision evaluating Missouri's abortion law and allowing states more room to regulate abortion but not reversing *Roe v. Wade*.)

GOP Must Do More

Congressman Christopher H. Smith

The good news: the Republican Party is, at its core, pro-life, pro-family, and wedded to traditional values. At the grass-roots level, virtually every poll shows that Republicans strongly embrace policies that seek to cherish, protect, and enhance the precious lives of unborn children, their mothers, and others who are similarly vulnerable or at risk. Recent data from an ABC NEWS/Belief-net poll in June 2001 make this abundantly clear and comport with observable trends that span decades. By a whopping 58 percent, Republicans side with the defenseless unborn while Democrats lag at 37 percent and Independents at 36 percent.

The often disheartening news, however, is that the GOP often empowers – even encourages – pro-abortion activists within its ranks, who have undue influence relative to their numbers, and gives them plum, strategic positions where policy is hatched and implemented. As a result of this self-defeating design – or perhaps plain incompetence – pro-life initiatives suffer creeping paralysis, mismanagement, and unnecessary setbacks. As a Republican Congressman for twenty-two years, I can attest to the fact that progress on protecting life has been severely undermined over the years by the battle within, appeasement, and accommodation. The big tent is just another way of saying a house divided. Moreover, because the party fumbles the ball year after year, the pro-life grassroots constituency is left to wonder if we are indeed serious about ending this holocaust.

Is saving the lives of innocent children and mothers a priority? Do we really get it? Do we really understand how many children have been savaged and how many mothers have been irreparably harmed, and how many more children will die an excruciatingly painful death if we fail to act now? Honesty compels me to admit that we at least appear – and perhaps even are at times – lukewarm. If I have learned one lesson over thirty years in the pro-life movement it is this: Overcoming gross social injustice is not for the timid or conflicted. It takes vision, moral courage, disciplined tactics, and an unbridled willingness to engage. Even politicians should know that being liked and popular just is not important or relevant when it comes to defending lives. Do the right thing, and let the political chips fall where they may.

By contrast, the Democrat Party has sold its soul to an insatiable, radical feminist minority, and in the process has become a wholly owned subsidiary of the abortion industry. Once upon a time, even Dick Gephardt and Al Gore were strongly pro-life. Now, with powerful enablers in Hollywood and the news media, the Democrats make no apologies whatsoever for being the party of abortion. They want abortion-on-demand at home and overseas, subsidized to the max by taxpayer funding. Amazingly, they are proud of it, apparently missing the ugly truth that abortion is grotesque violence against little children. Surely dismembering or chemically poisoning babies is child abuse and poses significant physical, psychological, and emotional risk to the mother. By calling murder "choice," they try to make all the ugliness go away.

It is important to note that not all Democrats tout the party line. In the House of Representatives, for example, more than three dozen courageous and principled pro-life Democrats routinely buck the prevailing pressure in their party and are often the key to victory on crucial votes. For this they pay a dear and under-appreciated price. These brave souls, however, are the exception.

Party Platform: The Mission Statement

Both parties have staked out a position on the right to life in their platforms, which are covenants to a party's members. Platforms articulate the values and ideals of the people who band together. A party's deeds do not always match its words, but its words are a good starting point.

Every Republican Party platform since 1976 has recognized the right to life of unborn boys and girls. That means that every Republican platform since *Roe v. Wade* has challenged that Supreme Court decision. The 2000 platform says:

> As a country, we must keep our pledge to the first guarantee of the Declaration of Independence. That is why we say the unborn child has a fundamental individual right to life which cannot be infringed. We support a human life amendment to the Constitution and we endorse legislation to make clear that the Fourteenth Amendment's protections apply to unborn children. Our purpose is to have legislative and judicial protection of that right against those who perform abortions. We oppose using public revenues for abortion and will not fund organizations which advocate it. We support the appointment of judges who respect traditional family values and the sanctity of innocent human life.
>
> We oppose the non-consensual withholding of care or treatment because of disability, age, or infirmity, just as we oppose euthanasia and assisted suicide, which endanger especially the poor and those on the margins of society.

The Democrat Party platform is diametrically opposed to protecting unborn children from violence. Under the banner of "choice," the 2000 Democrat Party platform says the following:
CHOICE

> The Democratic Party stands behind the right of every woman to choose, consistent with *Roe v. Wade,* and regardless of ability to pay. We believe it is a fundamental constitutional liberty that individual Americans – not government – can best take responsibility for making the most difficult and intensely personal decisions regarding reproduction. This year's Supreme Court rulings show to us all that eliminating a woman's right

to choose is only one justice away. That's why the stakes in this election are as high as ever. Our goal is to make abortion less necessary and more rare, not more difficult and more dangerous.

The "Choice" section of the Democrat Party Platform, while shying away from the word abortion, explicitly endorses *Roe v. Wade*, stands behind abortion for any reason, says the government should pay for abortion, and even calls abortion a necessity.

The contrast is clear. The Republican Party says the slaughter of more than 42 million innocent boys and girls and the victimization of women through abortion are wrong and should be stopped; the Democrat Party has drawn a line in the sand, saying that it will not only defend the continuation of that victimization and slaughter, but also fund it. On paper, the parties are diametrically opposed to each other on the issue of abortion, but for those of us who are passionate about defending life, and who mourn each day that more unborn boys and girls are killed through abortion, words are not enough.

Record: 107th Congress

Actions speak louder than words, and the critical question is whether the words in each party's platforms are matched by the actions of that party's elected representatives. The best way to do that is to review the legislative record, starting with the current Congress, which represents the 29th and most of the 30th legislative year since *Roe v. Wade*. The House of Representatives has a Republican majority and the Senate has a Democrat majority, so the 107th Congress provides a good picture of how differently the parties' actions are regarding the sanctity of life.

As of September 2002, the Republican House of Representatives passed the following pro-life pieces of legislation:

– H.R. 4965, the Partial Birth Abortion Ban Act, which would criminalize one of the many barbaric abortion procedures;
– H.R. 503, the Unborn Victims of Violence Act, which would recognize unborn children as crime victims by allow-

ing those who commit crimes against pregnant women to be prosecuted for harm done to the unborn child as well as to the woman;

– H.R. 476, the Child Custody Protection Act, which would make it a Federal crime to transport a minor across a state line in order to circumvent state parental involvement abortion laws;

– H.R. 2505, the Human Cloning Prohibition Act, which would prohibit cloning to be used to manufacture a new human life; and

– H.R. 2175, the Born-Alive Infants Protection Act, which provides that an infant born alive, at any stage of development, is a human being entitled to legal protection, even if a doctor had intended him or her to be killed by abortion.

In addition, the Republican House of Representatives voted: to protect President Bush's Mexico City Policy, which prevents foreign population funding from going to any organization that aborts children or lobbies for abortion; to retain the prohibition on abortion funding for prisoners; and to keep elective abortion out of military hospitals.

It is worth noting that the House of Representatives also had hearings on the following topics: (1) how embryo stem cell research destroys human life, featuring as part of the hearing children who had been adopted as embryos; (2) human cloning; (3) parental rights and the thirty-year-old Title X family planning program; (4) hospitals being forced to do abortions against their will; and (5) United Nations Population Fund's (UNFPA) support of the Chinese population-control program that uses forced abortion. The hearing on the UNFPA and China's program led to a decision by the Bush Administration to deny funding for the UNFPA.

In contrast, as of September 2002, the Democrat Senate has had one recorded abortion-related vote in this two-year Congressional session. On June 21, 2002, the Senate voted to allow elective abortion at military facilities in the United States and abroad. The only House sponsored pro-life bill the Senate approved was H.R. 2175, the Born-Alive Infants Protection Act, which they passed only after all the pro-abortion organizations removed their opposition to the bill. Once those groups signed off, the Senate deemed the bill eligible to be sent to the President, who signed it into law. One reason the Senate has only voted once on anything related to the sanctity of life is that they have been promoting abortion in their committees instead of on the Senate Floor.

The Democrat Senate added language to their spending bills that would have: (1) funded abortion for prisoners; (2) *repealed* President Bush's Mexico City Policy and allowed tax dollars to go to abortion providers and lobbyists overseas; (3) required the President to give millions of dollars to the United Nations Population Fund (UNFPA); (4) eviscerated the prohibition against funding organizations that support programs of forced abortion and forced sterilization; and (5) repealed the ban on funding of abortions through the Federal Employee Health Benefits (FEHB) program.

The Senate also has had hearings in favor of embryo stem cell research and human cloning, against the President's Mexico City Policy and has passed to the Senate Floor the United Nations Convention for the Elimination of All Forms of Discrimination Against Women (CEDAW). While CEDAW's name sounds good, this treaty, which would supersede United States law, has been interpreted to condemn any limits on abortion, effectively imposing abortion-on-demand by international law.

Most importantly, the Democrat Senate has created a litmus test for judicial nominees that disqualify candidates unless they say they will uphold *Roe v. Wade*. In the words of Senator Ted Kennedy (D-MA), "there's going to be an additional test, and that is a commitment to the core values of the Constitution. And the core values of the Constitution now include . . . a woman's right to choose." Probably more than any other issue, the Democrat Senate is screening out nominated judges based on their position on abortion.

Words and Actions – Do They Match?

How do the actions of the parties in the 107th Congress match up with their platform rhetoric?

For the Democrat Senate, the actions match up quite well, which is an accurate snapshot of how committed the Democrat Party is to abortion-on-demand. The Democrat Party has gone beyond simply supporting abortion through legislation and judicial nominations. They have marginalized pro-life Democrats in their midst by also applying the abortion litmus test to their own elected officials. There are numerous examples of Democrat elected officials who had to choose between their pro-life convictions and advancement in the party, or higher office. Some abandoned their convictions in order to rise in the Democrat Party, while others chose their convictions over temporal gain. Those Democrats who stuck to their pro-life convictions are some of my heroes because they made a strong moral choice at great sacrifice to their careers and their standing in their own party. None of the pro-life accomplishments in this Congress, and many of the previous Congresses, would have happened without the remnant of pro-life Democrats in the House of Representatives. For this, they have paid the greatest professional price. This makes clear that the Democrat Party has acted consistently with their disgusting platform position on abortion.

The Republican Party regrettably cannot claim the same. One of the greatest frustrations and heartbreaks for pro-life Republicans is that the Republican Party has missed so many opportunities to protect unborn girls and boys. There is no excuse whatsoever for missed opportunities, and no one should try to make excuses for the Republican Party. Instead of making excuses, the shortcomings should be remembered and lessons should be learned.

Supreme Court nominations are the glaring example of missed opportunities for the Republican Party. Half of the pro-abortion Justices of the Supreme Court (Justices O'Connor, Kennedy, and Souter) were appointed by Republican Presidents. Only half of the Republican-appointed Justices on the Court vote pro-life, which is a terrible percentage with terrible consequences. Two Republican appointments, Justices O'Connor and Souter, even decided that an abortionist must be allowed to use the partial-birth abortion method if he believes that it is the method which has the lowest risk of side-effects for any particular woman. These judicial appointments are a far cry from the Republican Party Platform pledge that says, "We support the appointment of judges who respect traditional family values and the sanctity of innocent human life." Judicial nominations are the best examples of missed opportunities because the nominations are made by the President, one elected official who belongs to one Party, but the missed opportunities by the Republican Party extend to Congress and other elected officials as well.

Republicans in Congress continue to increase funding for abortion providers – including Planned Parenthood, the country's foremost pro-abortion organization – through the Title X program. Last year Planned Parenthood killed 197,070 unborn babies and from 1977 to 2000 they aborted a total of 2,805,951 unborn children. There is no excuse for Congressional support for Planned Parenthood. We also have not done enough to support crisis pregnancy centers, promote *ethical* stem cell research, protect conscience, protect parental rights, and educate the public on abortion's terrible impact on women, including huge increases in the incidence of breast cancer.

The fact is that it is hardly ever convenient to fight for unborn children just as it is rarely convenient to fight for any human rights. There are always excuses in the Republican Party to not do something pro-life. The "I agree with you, but not now – this is not a good time" excuse is one I have been hearing since my election in 1980. But those feeble excuses are wrong because while it may not be a convenient time, it is always a good and necessary time to speak out for the boys and girls who are being slaughtered each day. The abortionists do not let up in their execution of the innocents, so we should never put advocacy for life on hold.

Stick with the Republican Party – and Demand More

The pro-life movement's frustration with parties and lukewarm action puts us in good historical company. Peaceful abolitionists in the United States were also accused of rocking the boat and even causing hatred and violence. The Democrat and Whig parties refused to take a stand on slavery or talk about it because they did not want to alienate the supporters of slavery. Even evangelical churches split, North and South, instead of tackling the scourge of slavery head-on. William Wilberforce, the great champion for the elimination of slavery in the United Kingdom, had to work against the political parties of his time, and he relied on members of the Whig party more often than the support of his own Tory party. At least current-day pro-life advocates have a party willing to publicly take a stand in favor of life.

The temptation is to be more angry at the pro-life Republican Party when it lets us down than the pro-abortion Democrat Party that consistently opposes us, or to reject the Republican Party altogether. Both actions would be a mistake. The stated position of the Republican Party on the issue of sanctity of life is clearly superior to the stated position of the Democrat Party. Even though the Republican Party at times disappoints, there is also a clear and tangible pro-life advantage to the actions of the Republican Party versus the actions of the Democrat Party. This is true on a day-to-day and year-to-year basis, as represented by the actions of the 107th Congress.

No matter how tempting, it would also be a huge mistake to abandon the more pro-life of the two political parties in favor of a third party or to retreat to apolitical endeavors only. We live under a two-party political system. Unlike a parliamentary system where multiple parties can flourish and obtain representation, our winner-take-all system, with few historical exceptions, confines the political battles into two parties that then compete against each other. In order to keep the pro-life plank in the Republican Party Platform, create and seize opportunities to promote the sanctity of life and change the hearts and minds of those who embrace abortion, those who are pro-life must be more active and more articulate in the Republican Party, not less.

This is especially true now that the pro-life movement has been compelled by conscience to oppose the biotechnology lobby on the bioethics issues of embryo stem cell research and human cloning. This is the first time that a mainstream industry with a sophisticated lobby, predominantly associated with Republicans, has decided to make destroying and manufacturing human life a centerpiece of their lobbying efforts. The stakes are high because human cloning will usher in a massive destruction of human embryos, as well as eugenics programs, and the manufacture of human beings as products for design and sale. Pro-life activity in the Republican Party is just as critical now, thirty years after *Roe v. Wade*, as ever.

The Republican Party is a pro-life party that needs more pressure from those who are pro-life, not less. Don't settle for crumbs and half-way measures and by no means allow the cause of life to be managed or manipulated. Demand more. Demand much, much more. There is no doubt that, like our forbearers in the abolitionist movement, we will continue to be criticized by people in all parties, including the pro-life Republican Party, for rocking the boat when we speak out for those who have no voice and no power. If we allow the fear of criticism to paralyze our actions, we put millions of innocent lives at risk. Often I ask myself – have I done all I can do to end abortion? In my heart of hearts I know the answer is, no. So I – we – need to protest loudly and effectively within our party when it threatens to wander from its core pro-life stand. We need to be constant, consistent, and courageous. We should heed the words of Abraham Lincoln when he said, "To sin by silence when they should protest makes cowards of men."

The Republican Party has given those who support the sanctity of all human life a good platform and an awesome responsibility – it would be a terrible mistake if we squandered those away.

Christopher H. Smith has been a Republican Member of Congress from New Jersey since 1980.

The Republican "Lesser Evil"

Joseph Sobran

After I gave a talk in Cleveland to a Catholic pro-life group during the 2000 presidential campaign, a woman in the audience approached me in honest and righteous anger. She said that my call for Catholics, conservatives, and other pro-lifers to leave the Republican Party could have only one result: to elect Al Gore and therefore to continue the policies of Bill Clinton, particularly the promotion of abortion. If Gore won, she pointed out, he would choose the next few U.S. Supreme Court justices.

She had a serious point. I heard it often that year. And I agreed that between Al Gore and George W. Bush, Bush was the lesser evil. If elected, he would at least have no eagerness to increase the evils associated with abortion, as Gore would.

On the other hand, Bush didn't want to fight to protect the unborn. He would take no measures to reverse legal abortion; at most, he would leave things as they were. The status quo was all right with him. And anyone who was willing to accept the status quo might want to support him – except that the status quo wouldn't remain stable. Its inherent tendency is to keep shifting leftward, dragging the Republican Party along.

Suppose Gore had been elected. Even if the Republicans had maintained control of the Senate, what would they have done? Would they oppose his nominees to the Court? No. When Robert Bork and Clarence Thomas were appointed by Republican presidents, the Democrats knew that principles were at stake, and they immediately abandoned the polite custom of confirming whoever a sitting President happens to want on the court. They fought with everything they had to block both men, and they succeeded in denying Bork's confirmation.

But when Clinton was elected, the Republicans reverted to the deferential custom of letting the President have his way. They voted, with few dissents, to confirm both Stephen Breyer and Ruth Bader Ginsburg, both of whom were openly pro-abortion. Only three or four Republicans voted against Mrs. Ginsburg, and Orrin Hatch – the pro-life Utah Mormon – positively fawned over her. I forget the numbers on Breyer, but his old pal Bob Dole – another alleged pro-lifer – gave Breyer his fervent support.

This is what we can expect of the Republican Party, whether in power or in opposition. Two members of Bush's cabinet – Colin Powell and Christine Todd Whitman – are outspoken abortion advocates. The GOP fields, endorses, and funds pro-abortion candidates for office; several Republican governors, including George Pataki of New York, are pro-abortion. Every four years, abortion foes have to fight to keep the pro-life plank in the party's platform, against ever-growing Republican efforts, in league with the major media, to delete it.

The party doesn't put up serious resistance to pro-abortion Democrats. It wants the abortion issue to go away, and it counts on pro-lifers, whom it regards as an annoyance, to feel that they have no choice but to vote Republican – just as the woman I met in Cleveland did.

It isn't just abortion. The Republicans accept the whole post-New Deal regime as legitimate, though that regime is profoundly opposed to constitutional law. It is a capital mistake for the pro-life movement to treat abortion as an isolated issue, a single blunder by the judiciary, or even as a long (though egregious) usurpation of power that could be remedied by a few personnel changes in the high court. It belongs to a more general assault, by the entire Federal Government, on the principle of federalism – the division of power that ensures self-government to the states.

The Constitution allots to the Federal Government only those powers that are clearly enumerated, reserving all others to the states and the people. The Tenth Amendment makes this principle explicit; yet the Federal Government has made a habit of ignoring and trivializing it, especially since the New Deal. Many other Federal usurpations paved the way for *Roe v. Wade*, which will never be reversed until our original constitutional philosophy is reasserted and at least partially restored.

But the Republicans also accept as legitimate all the usurpations of the Federal judiciary, including *Roe v. Wade*, in which the U.S. Supreme Court made the astonishing assertion that the states have no power to perform the most basic duty of any state, namely, to protect innocent life from violence. If that is true, federalism is meaningless. *Roe v. Wade* was no honest mistake, no innocent misapplication of the court's task of "interpreting" the Constitution. It was, as Justice Byron White said in his dissent, an act of "raw judicial power," a crime against constitutional law itself. It merited impeachment of the seven justices who committed it. Yet almost nobody – even in the pro-life movement, let alone the Republican Party – proposed this obvious remedy.

If the Republicans faced a party that offered to restore constitutional government, we would of course have no hesitation in voting against them. But because they oppose a party that intends to compound all existing evils aggressively, they seem slightly preferable. So the two-party system presents us with a dilemma, and most of us have let the Republicans have our votes as the lesser evil. But as we keep choosing evil, the dilemma only gets worse with each election. As the Democrats move leftward, the Republicans don't move rightward – they move leftward too, though not quite as far.

At some point we have to stop and tell the Republicans that the lesser evil isn't good enough, that they don't represent us and don't deserve our votes. I don't mean that we should refuse to support each and every Republican candidate for any office; some Republicans are real reformers and would restore a Christian social order if they had the opportunity.

But the Republican Party as a whole has forfeited our backing, and Bush is proof. So is New York's former mayor Rudolph

Giuliani, an advocate of sodomite rights and partial-birth abortion. No serious pro-lifer wanted to see Al Gore in the White House or Hillary Clinton in the Senate, but if we vote for Republicans who are only superficially different from the Democrats we not only gain nothing, we also ensure that the Republican Party will move further and further from good principles.

Two year ago New York's Conservative Party was willing to endorse Giuliani for the U.S. Senate if only he would renounce partial-birth abortion; regular old abortion, the party had decided, would be acceptable. But Giuliani refused even this concession. No wonder our choices get worse and worse.

So a vote for Bush, though he was nominally anti-abortion, was actually a vote for making both major parties pro-abortion in the future, just as both major parties now support the socialist programs of the New Deal and the Great Society. The lesser evil gets more and more evil.

Such is the Republican dilemma. There is no corresponding Democratic dilemma. The Democrats keep the left satisfied. The left doesn't have to agonize over whether to vote Democratic, because it knows it will eventually get everything it wants from the Democrats. Charles Rangel and Maxine Waters are right at home in the Democratic Party. They tolerate no dissent on gay rights and abortion and the rest of the leftist agenda; the party's Castroites could even attack Gore for breaking with them on the repatriation of Elian Gonzalez, and Gore wobbled.

The Democratic left forms the core of American politics, and the Republican Party is a sort of reluctant satellite of the Democrats, trying to hold its own constituencies while appeasing the left. Only when pro-lifers and other social conservatives break out of this orbit will they become a serious force again.

We now have another slender option: the Constitution Party. But there is something ironic about this. For a long time, *all* parties were Constitution parties. Everyone agreed that the Federal Government should never exceed its assigned powers. Today demanding constitutional government makes you marginal, eccentric, "extremist." The mess we have now is the long-term result of people deciding to be "realistic" and settling for the lesser evil instead of insisting on what they knew to be right. That kind of "realism" is a bad habit we must break, and the sooner the better. Such bogus "realism" can only ensure that future Republican candidates will be to the left of Al Gore and Hillary Clinton – just as Rudolph Giuliani is to the left of the Democrats of yesteryear.

The "war on terrorism" has rescued the Republicans from having to deal with abortion for the time being. The terrorist attack on the World Trade Center and the Pentagon profoundly shocked all Americans, of course, and nearly everyone agreed that the Federal Government must respond.

President Bush welcomed the opportunity to act as a wartime leader, and few could blame him. Yet one can't help being struck by the difference between his attitudes toward terrorism and abortion. The horror of terrorism, which killed 3,000 Americans in a few minutes, appalled him; he has given no sign that he regards abortion with anything like the same horror, though it claims 4,000 lives *every day*. He spoke of terrorism as "evil" and promised swift action to combat it; he had never called abortion "evil" or treated it as an urgent problem. He called terrorism a threat to our way of life; abortion has already debased and corrupted our way of life for nearly thirty years.

Nobody is surprised by this. By now it is tacitly understood that for Republicans, abortion is an issue that belongs on the back burner. Of course we all understand that the events we now refer to simply as "9/11" were so dramatic, as well as evil, that they commanded top priority. But this also underlines what a low priority Republicans have given to abortion.

Surely part of the reason for this contrast is that responding to 9/11, unlike fighting abortion, enjoyed virtually unanimous support, even in the media. Republicans, unlike Democrats, have a marked preference for "bipartisan" causes, as opposed to those that excite controversy and carry political costs. Going beyond the standard platitudes about the "Judeo-Christian tradition," Mr. Bush even praised Islam as a "religion of peace," so as to avoid offending Muslims in this country. Yet while tentatively asserting his own

Christian faith, he has never cited Muslim abhorrence of abortion to strengthen the case against it.

Enough time has passed for us to see the obvious. Republicans have no more excuses for their failure to oppose abortion with a will; pro-lifers have no more excuses for supporting them. A vote for the Republican Party is only a vote for lip service.

Joe Sobran is a writer, columnist and lecturer who speaks frequently on the life issues, the Constitution, and Shakespeare. His most recent book is Hustler: The Clinton Legacy (Griffin Communications, 2000).

Principle or Pragmatism?
Abortion Politics in the
Twenty-First Century
Phyllis Schlafly

"If you keep doing what you've been doing,
you'll keep getting what you've been getting."

Pro-life political activists, most of whom can currently be found in the Republican Party, may do well to reflect on that expression as we enter the thirtieth year post-*Roe v. Wade*.

Consider the goal of the pro-life movement during the 1970s and early 1980s. How successfully have we, as a movement, advanced that goal? Is the right to life more or less respected than the Supreme Court in 1973 ruled it should be? Is our political clout stronger or weaker than in the past? How effectively are we structuring Congress in order to move our ball down the field in the legislative arena? How are we going to spend our time, energy, and money in the future? Will we tread water, creating a ripple here and there, or will we strive to win the race?

The right-to-life cause is noble, and its importance cannot be overstated. Faced now and in the future, not only with abortion-on-demand, but with: the creation of life outside the womb through in-vitro fertilization, the existence of human embryos abandoned by their parents to a life suspended in liquid nitrogen, human embryo experimentation, the creation of artificial wombs, the potential creation of human beings through cloning, infanticide, assisted suicide, and euthanasia – are we going to keep doing what we have been doing?

In the Beginning

When the Supreme Court handed down the *Roe v. Wade* decision, millions of us emerged from the stunning realization that such a thing not only *could*, but *had*, happened in America. We thought it was simply a matter of time to re-establish the right to life. During the first few years, pro-life organizations sprang up in every community in every state, made up of people who simply believed that, if we could help people understand the reality of abortion – if we could educate them – the tide would turn.

We soon learned that education was not enough. The laws must be changed and, in order to accomplish that, we had to elect pro-life lawmakers. Prior to *Roe*, most pro-life activists had never been involved in politics. However, beginning in 1972 when the process of ratification of the Equal Rights Amendment to the Constitution was underway in the states, thousands of women, most of them Christians, were mobilized within the Stop ERA movement and began to get their feet wet in partisan politics. Because ratification of the ERA would have made us a sex-neutral society in which denial of the right to kill one's baby would be considered "sex discrimination," thereby cementing abortion into law in every state in the Union, the right-to-life and Stop ERA forces joined hands, especially within the Republican Party, where there was at least some receptivity to our values and views.

In the mid-to-late 1970s, the Republican Party was in the minority and the Democrats were largely in control. Conservative ideas were beginning to gain traction, and Ronald Reagan was becoming recognized by many in our party as a gifted leader who analyzed the issues, wrote his own speeches, and articulated the conservative message in language that everybody could understand. As pro-lifers became party activists, working to elect pro-life candidates and becoming Delegates to local, state and national conventions, the hold that Republican liberals and "moderates" had on the party began to weaken. Reagan challenged President Gerald

Ford in 1976 and conservatives, energized and committed, came into the party in droves to support him. Although Reagan lost, an army was growing, fueled by his decision to support the pro-life cause. In 1980, in the historic clash between Reagan and George H. W. Bush for the Republican presidential nomination, grassroots political activists delivered the nomination to Reagan. We were ecstatic! We believed we were on the way to changing the judiciary and passing a pro-life constitutional amendment that would end abortion. We thought it was only a matter of time.

During the 1980s, the Republican Party enjoyed unprecedented growth. Scores of pro-life candidates were elected to office, although sadly, many were found to be only nominally so. But participation in the party continued to grow with the emergence of many Christian groups. Hopes were high that someday soon, we would achieve our pro-life goals.

The virtual media blackout of the truth about abortion in America almost stifled our cause as far as the vast majority of Americans were concerned. It was the tension within the Republican Party and the debates that took place in hundreds of conventions across the country that gained publicity for our cause. Constituents began to demand that candidates for office say where they stood on the right to life, and those confrontations were newsworthy. Public understanding of the reality and consequences of abortion was greatly enhanced by the debates within the Republican Party.

The leadership of the Democratic Party, its presidential candidates and its party platform, consistently promoted legal abortion, taxpayer-funded abortions, and "a woman's right to choose." Democratic candidates are generally required to march in lock-step with the party line. This marked a major difference between pro-life Republicans and pro-abortion Democrats, and the Republican Party's growth, especially in the South, was a direct result.

The Era of Political Pragmatism

In describing the election of George Bush to the presidency in 1988, Peggy Noonan said that we thought we were electing Ronald

Reagan to a third term. While Bush had never agreed with Reagan on the right to life, he moved a bit closer by declaring that he opposed abortion except in cases of rape, incest, and life of the mother. While that was a far superior position to that of his Democrat opponent Michael Dukakis, it failed to promise legal protection for unborn babies. Instead of pointing out that under the circumstances, supporting Bush was better for the pro-life cause, movement leaders proclaimed him unequivocally pro-life. Perhaps without realizing it, they made it difficult for us to demand a solid pro-life commitment from other candidates down the line.

We subsequently began to see pro-life groups and political action committees supporting Republican candidates who justify abortion for one reason or another. In some cases, candidates gained the support of pro-lifers *and* establishment liberals in the party who understood that a candidate with exceptions was not serious about ending legal abortion. Over the years, pro-life grass-roots Republicans put millions of dollars into the coffers of the Republican National Committee, the National Republican Congressional Committee, and the National Republican Senatorial Committee only to find their hard-earned money going to support the campaigns of men and women who would join hands with pro-abortion Democrats to fight the pro-life cause in Congress and elsewhere.

Somewhere along the way in the mid-to-late '80s, the goal of achieving a human life amendment to the Constitution was lost, except for a few congressional stalwarts who re-introduced it from time to time. Progress was made in the judiciary, but the defeat of Robert Bork and the betrayal by David Souter left conservatives still shy of the five votes necessary to reverse *Roe v. Wade*. The turnover of seven justices on the Supreme Court since the election of Ronald Reagan has moved the Court toward upholding some abortion restrictions, and rejecting physician-assisted suicide, which is analogous to abortion. Abortions in America have declined somewhat, but not ended. Pro-lifers seemed to be resigned to a minimalist approach involving the regulation and restriction of the practice of abortion. The question must be asked:

What is the goal of the pro-life movement now? Is it to end legal abortion or to accept the status-quo?

The Exception Makes the Rule

When you promote candidates for public office who do not share your desire to reach the ultimate target of your cause, you can't expect to see the ball moved down the field toward your goal line. A spirit of compromise exists among some pro-life leaders who are willing to forgo restoring legal protection of the right to life, and instead, have chosen to work on regulatory issues such as taxpayer funding of abortion, funding of abortion providers overseas, a ban on partial-birth abortions (a problematic piece of legislation that contains a troublesome loophole) and the Born-Alive Infants Protection Act, the need for which clearly demonstrates our country's decline into acceptance of infanticide. Along the way, candidates were endorsed who justify abortion in certain circumstances, despite the fact that the exception makes the rule. Those who justify abortion for any reason ensure that abortion will remain legal.

The ultimate implications for humanity of in-vitro fertilization were virtually ignored by the pro-life movement for years. The fact that human embryos were being engendered in petri dishes and implanted into their mothers, while freezing those who are "left over," seemed to escape much notice until these practices became commonplace in the United States. The fact that we are today faced with bioethical problems of monumental proportions, that involve the fate of embryonic human beings, goes to the heart of what the pro-life movement should be all about, namely, that the inherent God-given right to life attaches at the moment of conception when the sperm and the egg are joined to create a single-cell human being. If protection of that fundamental right were restored via a human life amendment to the Constitution or by a statute based on the overturning of *Roe v. Wade*, killing human embryos for their stem cells or for any other reason would be illegal.

The Party or the Cause?

Most Republican candidates call themselves "pro-life" because they believe they must in order to win in a Republican primary. Every four years at the Republican National Convention, there is a battle over the pro-life platform plank. Pro-life conservatives work through the convention process to become national delegates and secure a coveted position on the platform committee. The noisy pro-abortion crowd, featuring Republicans for Choice and the National Republican Coalition for Choice, lobby hard for removal of the plank, assisted by prominent pro-abortion senators, governors, and members of Congress. The Republican National Coalition for Life, together with Christian Coalition, Family Research Council, Concerned Women for America, Pat Buchanan and his followers, and many others have successfully organized overwhelming support for the pro-life plank and won, every four years.

It's a beautiful plank! It says that "the unborn child has a fundamental right to life which cannot be infringed." It calls for adoption of a human life amendment to the Constitution and the extension of Fourteenth Amendment protection to the unborn child. It opposes taxpayer funding of abortions and organizations that promote abortion. It calls for the appointment of judges who respect the sanctity of human life. The platform fully reflects the nobility of our cause. But, in the end, far too many Republican candidates ignore it, and some say they have never read it. Many pro-life Republicans, who *should* condition their support of a candidate on adherence to those principles, fail to do so.

We should be about electing lawmakers who agree that the right to life is sacred and should be protected by law. So often we hear the question, "Well, he may not be perfect but he's better than liberal candidate X." While that may be the case, it is incumbent on the pro-life leadership to make known to its followers the truth about candidates so they have the proper expectations of their performance once elected to office. We must strive for 100 percent pro-life candidates, no exceptions, no compromise. When we have such a candidate, we should declare it loud and clear with public endorsements and financial contributions.

In the case of a candidate who receives the Republican nomination but who justifies abortion for any reason, we have choices. We can stay out of the contest. Or, in the case of a Democrat opponent who is Clintonesque in advocacy of legal abortion, we can make it known if the Republican has made commitments to the advancement of pro-life legislation and commend him for that. We can say we prefer him to the pro-abortion Democrat. But the pro-life mantle should not be bestowed on someone who has not earned it. The Republican Party has established a high standard that must not be undermined by self-described pro-lifers whose desire to curry favor with "big tent" Republicans has overtaken their desire to restore respect for human life.

Will We Keep On Doing What We've Been Doing?

If we keep on doing what we've been doing, we will continue to keep on getting what we've been getting. Are we willing to spend the next decade, or two, or three, chipping away at the edges of the pro-life cause? Even if that were our chosen course, we haven't that much time. Decisions are being made right now regarding the fate of the human embryo that will affect the fate of humanity. Pro-life-with-exceptions members of the U.S. House and Senate are joining with pro abortion Democrats in support of embryonic stem-cell research and cloning. Why should anyone be surprised? They weren't committed to the pro-life cause in the first place.

Political parties exist in order that citizens can organize to promote their philosophy of government and public policy objectives. After *Roe*, pro-life Americans learned how to use the system to advance our cause. Over the years, it appeared to grow in the minds of some that it is more important to be a loyal Republican than to restore the right to life. While the years of debate over abortion within the Republican Party and between Republican and Democrat candidates helped to educate millions about the truth of abortion, our population is still where it was in 1973, with 60 percent tolerating abortion, 20 percent opposing it entirely, and 20 percent firmly supporting it.

Our cause is greater than abortion alone. We must establish once and for all that our objective is to restore respect and protection to each and every human life from conception, or in the case of a human clone, from inception. In a March 14, 2002, speech in Buffalo, New York, Supreme Court Justice Antonin Scalia dismissed the notion that abortion is a constitutionally protected right, but he also said the Constitution doesn't explicitly prohibit abortions, either. He indicated that the issue should be ultimately decided by a constitutional amendment.

Legal protection for all human life, without exceptions or compromise, must rise again to the forefront of the pro-life agenda. This goal could be reached by a no-exceptions amendment to the United States Constitution. This goal could be approached by the appointment of constitutionalist justices to the U.S. Supreme Court. A giant step toward the realization of this goal could be achieved by Congressional legislation. For example, Congress should forbid the appropriation of any Medicaid funds to any state that finances abortions or assisted suicide, or to any hospital that trains doctors to perform abortions, or to any university or laboratory that uses any of its facilities for practice or research that involves the destruction of human life. The constitutionality of Congressional conditions on the appropriation of federal money has been repeatedly upheld by the U.S. Supreme Court, even by the *Roe* court, which upheld a ban on the use of taxpayer funds for abortions (*Harris v. McRae*). Congress thus has the power, through Medicaid appropriations, to stop Oregon's assisted suicide law and to stop New York City Mayor Bloomberg's plan to coerce all doctors trained in New York City hospitals (one-seventh of all doctors) to be trained to perform abortions.

U. S. Senators who call themselves pro-life must refuse confirmation of justices who believe the killing of innocent human life is acceptable. We can't tolerate any more David Souters appointed by Republican Presidents.

Candidates who do not agree with these goals should not receive our support. All candidates representing whatever political party, whether Republican, Democrat, Libertarian, Constitution,

Green, or any other, should be required by pro-life voters to say publicly whether or not they support these goals. If pro-life Catholics had done that, Bill Clinton and Al Gore would not have received such a high percentage of the Catholic vote. If pro-life and pro-family leaders had done that, George Bush would have been required to make some concrete commitments to advance the pro-life agenda in return for the pro-life support he received. Instead, the pro-life mantle was bestowed upon him even though he promised almost nothing.

Pro-life leaders and Republican politicians who continue to allow political pragmatism to trump the principled pro-life expectations of the grassroots are taking a grave risk. Let's not forget that an estimated 4 million pro-life Christian voters stayed home from the polls in the 2000 election.

Colleen Parro has served the pro-life cause at the local, state and federal levels since 1973. Along with its national chairman Phyllis Schlafly, she helped found the Republican National Coalition for Life, and has directed the organization since 1990.

Phyllis Schlafly has been a national leader of the conservative movement since the 1960s and is best known for her victory over the principal legislative goal of the radical feminists – the Equal Rights Amendment. She now heads the national pro-family organization Eagle Forum, continues her thirty-five-year-old monthly newsetter called "The Phyllis Schlafly Report," and pens a syndicated column which appears in 100 newspapers.

Casey's Heirs and the Fall of Pro-Life Democrats

Raymond L. Flynn and Mark Stricherz

Just off the corner of Connecticut Avenue and S Street in downtown Washington, D.C., there is a small mural of John F. Kennedy on a fence, his hands clasped and face somber. The surrounding DuPont Circle neighborhood practically announces itself as Democrat territory, but a brief walk around suggests that this is not exactly the Democrat Party of President Kennedy, Lyndon Johnson, or Boss Daley. Down the street are the gay-run Lambda Rising Bookstore and Human Rights Campaign Action Center. A few blocks away is Thaiphoon, a trendy Thai restaurant. Next door is The Princeton Review, or perhaps just a building whose maroon awning bears its logo.

On the third floor of this building, in room #302, is another outpost of the Democrat Party, though it feels like it belongs more in Fort Worth or Baton Rouge than in D.C.'s hip DuPont Circle. As you enter the narrow hallway, you are surrounded by cardboard boxes piled six-feet high. A few feet to the left is the office, maybe 10 by 12 feet, stuffed with dark file cabinets. Inside are an intern, a youngish-looking woman, her baby son, and a navy blue stroller. Kristen Day, who's 33, brought her eight-month-old son, Jack, to the office today, though she sometimes works out of her home in northern Virginia. Her title is Executive Director but she took a 50 percent pay-cut from her previous job as Chief of Staff to Michigan Democratic Rep. James Barcia.

This office is the headquarters of Democrats for Life of America, Inc. The organization, largely moribund until it moved to D.C. in April 2002, aims to challenge the party's commitment to abortion rights. "I think we [Democrats] say that we should help the underdogs who don't have a voice. It just seems natural we would want to help unborn children," says Day.

Good luck. Like the group's office, pro-life Democrats occupy a tiny, threadbare spot in the nation's elite. They get no favorable national media, no millionaire donors, and their numbers are dwindling within Congress. Their interest groups are puny and poor: Day's group, for example, has 400 members and a $100,000 annual budget, while groups such as the National Organization for Women (NOW) and the National Reproductive Rights Action League (NARAL) have multi-million dollar budgets and hundreds of thousands of members. And their politicians can't really seek national office, because most of the party's delegates are pro-choice.

The only real clout pro-life Democrat politicians have is among the masses, with Joe Six-Pack. As Louisiana Senator John Breaux said this January, if one of their candidates ever got past the Democrat primaries and got the party's presidential nomination bid, he could feasibly win the general election. (Indeed, according to exit polls taken by the *Los Angeles Times* after the 1996 and 2000 elections, the abortion issue, in presidential elections, *favored* Republicans: Of the 9 to 14 percent of all voters who named abortion as their top concern, 2.5 million more voted for the pro-life candidate than the pro-choice one.)

But that's not about to happen, because Joe Six-Pack no longer runs the party. Look at what happened to former Governor Robert Casey of Pennsylvania in 1992. He wanted to change the party's abortion-rights stance – and was denied a speaking slot at that year's convention for his efforts. Casey was excluded largely because of a quota, which was drawn up after the party's disastrous 1968 convention in Chicago. This quota rule didn't exist when Lyndon Johnson and Boss Daley controlled the party. Yet its existence today, along with the lack of money, organization, and political courage, helps explain the Casey conundrum.

One of the widespread beliefs among today's pro-life Democrats is that some day the party will abandon its pro-choice stance – that the current position is merely temporary. "There are alternatives [within the party to the pro-choice position]," said William Pierce, a board member of Democrats for Life of America. "We're calling party leaders to their conscience." Pierce doesn't discount the difficulty of changing the party's position, and the group has sensible goals, such as lobbying labor unions not to send checks to groups like NARAL and Emily's List, a political action committee which donates exclusively to pro-choice Democrat, woman candidates. But even this wildly understates the case.

In reality, pro-life Democrats are a dying breed. Their own party barely tolerates them, while Republicans take them for granted. They have no firebrands among their ranks – nobody like, say, Representative Barney Frank on gay marriage; nor do they have any real leaders, like Robert Casey. None of them has offered any plans to dramatically reduce the 1.3 million abortions performed every year in this country. They include popular, honorable politicians – but not overly courageous ones.

Today's Democrat party is much different from its New-Deal predecessor (1928–1968). It has a different governing class, a different organization, and a different set of rules. Call it, as political writer John Judis has, the McGovern-plus coalition. And it bears about as much similarity to the New-Deal coalition of the 1930s as the New-Deal coalition did to the Southern-controlled Democratic Party of 1832 to 1928 – which is to say, not much.

The Party's Over: From FDR to McGovern

To grasp why pro-life Democrats face bleak prospects, it's important to understand how the party was run during its New Deal-phase. Back then, the party was almost entirely blue collar. Catholics and white ethnics were heavily represented, but most of its base worked in manual labor and belonged to unions. During the 1930s, when birth-control pioneer Margaret Sanger tried to have the federal government subsidize contraception, President Roosevelt refused to go along. "His core base was the inner city, urban Catholic areas where the Italian or Irish or Polish or whatever lived, and he said, 'There's no way I'm going to offend those groups,'" said Alex Sanger, who wrote his college thesis at Princeton on his grandmother, and who is now President of the International Planned Parenthood Federation. At that time, the Republican Party was the home of contemporary feminism. (In 1940, the GOP, then made up exclusively of white-collar workers, endorsed the Equal Rights Amendment [ERA], becoming the first party to do so.) The Democrat Party's base, by contrast, was pro-life.

And so were its leaders: the political bosses. Think of Mayor Richard J. Daley of Chicago or James Michael Curley of Boston. Their basis of power was patronage: They delivered services to constituents in exchange for votes. But there were elements of fairness in their rule too. These men tended to be religious, and they tended to look, quite naturally and practically, to the local Catholic Church for support. But their Achilles heel was parochialism. Blacks and women were given their separate spheres of control, while young people had to wait to enter the ranks. This state of affairs had endured since the mid-nineteenth century, but it crumbled during the social upheaval of the 1960s and '70s.

The bosses' swan song turned out to be the 1968 Democratic Convention in Chicago. With students battling police on national TV, the Convention's delegates voted for a change in the party's membership. Students, formerly without a voice, would now have a voice. "All state Democratic parties," the rule read, "must give all Democratic voters a full, meaningful, and timely opportunity to participate in the selection of delegates." To that end, the rule created a Commission on Party Structure and Delegate Selection, later known as the McGovern-Fraser Commission (1969–1971).

The rule was never intended to change the party's support of the war in Vietnam, but that's what happened, because of the commission's twenty-something staff, who deeply opposed the war. Key to their goal was the involvement of students and women. "It was well known at the time that most women opposed the war," says Ken Bode, the commission's then-thirty-year-old research director. The commission's staff therefore drafted soft quotas for delegates. Women, minorities, and those thirty years of age and younger would have to be appointed, rather than elected, in reasonable proportion to their numbers in the population.

The McGovern-Fraser Commission isn't remembered as a defining event in the history of American politics, but it was, because it helped realign the two parties along *cultural* rather than *class* lines. For Democrats, it spelled the end of the bosses' reign. Most union workers would remain in the party, but the party's new leaders hailed from white-collar America: specifically, the college-educated or meritocratic elite. At the time, they were the public faces of the New Left. They opposed the war but favored everything else – forced busing, the environment, black power, and above all, the sexual revolution. In effect, loyal blue-collar Democrats were replaced by social-liberal activists, and a party largely financed by big unions became a party largely financed by elite interests.

The quota rule went into effect during the '72 presidential race and made an immediate impact. At the party's convention that year, 43 percent of the party's delegates were women, compared to only 13 percent in 1968. This internal party change occurred just as the Twenty-Sixth Amendment, giving 18-year-olds the right to vote, was being ratified by the states. And, even more significant, it coincided with the rise of the feminist movement. A generation of college-educated and single women now realized they could take leadership roles in the evolving party. Hillary Clinton, for example, switched from a Goldwater Republican in 1964 to a McGovern Democrat by 1972.

Pro-life women might have been able to exploit the rules in their favor to fill the party's leadership posts, but the historic moment dictated otherwise. Ray Flynn notes that a combination of economic and social factors hastened pro-lifers' demise. "No one wanted to be active in their communities anymore. Most young mothers now work because they want to work to help pay for the extraordinary cost of housing, along with education and taxes and everything else. They don't want to (come home from work) to go to a political meeting and listen to some windbag. They want to be with their family and children." For feminists, however, things were different. Alex Sanger, a twenty-one-year-old staff member on the commission at the time, explains that feminists "were active with the various movements, and they were seeking to change laws and society," he says. "Pro-life women had the law on their side. They didn't have to do anything."

Or so they thought. Today, of the fifty-two Democrat women in Congress, every single one supports abortion rights. They, like most of the party's leaders, would feel perfectly at home in restaurants like Thaiphoon, or paying thousands of dollars to enroll their Ivy-League aspiring youngsters in programs like The Princeton Review. They are the base of the McGovern-plus coalition.

The Platform

The women's rights plank of the 1972 Democrat convention actually made no mention of abortion, even though a handful of states had, by that time, repealed their abortion laws. The platform, instead, said that birth control should be available to all.

In 1974, resurgent labor groups were able to remove the Commission's quotas. As a result, the party's platform on abortion that year was only a muted one-sentence endorsement of *Roe v. Wade*. "We feel," it read, "that it is undesirable to attempt to amend the U.S. Constitution to overturn the Supreme Court decision in this area."

But by 1980, the power of the McGovern-Fraser Commission's quotas on delegates reasserted itself. In fact, pro-choice feminists turned the commission's soft quota on women into a *hard* quota. With President Carter reeling from stagflation and the Iran hostage crisis, Gloria Steinem, Bella Abzug, and others forced the party to adopt a 50-50 quota on male-to-female delegates. As a result, the Democrats at their 1980 Convention in New York openly supported abortion rights: "We . . . recognize the belief of many Americans that a woman has a right to choose whether and when to have a child. The Democratic Party supports the 1973 Supreme Court decision on abortion rights as the law of the land and opposes any constitutional amendment to restrict or overturn that decision." What's more, the party platform came out for government funding of abortion, which is a requirement of groups like NARAL and NOW.

As this incident reveals, the Democrat party, by 1980, had completely embraced the abortion industry and pro-choice feminists. They had effectively kicked out religious voters, which helps explain the rise of the "New Right" (or the Christian Coalition) among Republicans in the late 1970s. Today, the party platform is a full-throated endorsement of abortion: "We believe it is a fundamental constitutional liberty that individual Americans – not government – can best take responsibility for making the most difficult and intensely personal decisions regarding reproduction."

The "Skunk at the Garden Party"

In 1996, pro-life Democrat representatives did pass a conscience clause on abortion: "We respect the individual conscience of each American on this difficult issue, and we welcome all our members to participate at every level of our party," it reads. But while the former may be true, the latter essentially isn't. Pro-life Democrats are not welcome in any real way by the Party.

Consider the Democratic National Committee. Democrats for Life of America, Inc., isn't even listed on the DNC website, though Day says she's been asking for this for months. Senator Robert Torricelli, former head of the Democratic Senatorial Campaign Committee, referred in January to pro-life Democrats as "anti-choice."

Party donors don't welcome them either. "About as much as a skunk in a garden party," says ex-Congressman Ron Klink of Pennsylvania, who ran for the Senate two years ago. He says his problem wasn't a lack of support from party leaders in Congress, who generously contributed time and money to his campaign. His problem was that Democrat donors, once they learned of his pro-life, pro-gun, and pro-union stands, wanted nothing to do with him. "It happened every day, many times a day," Klink says of donors' rejection. "It was on the phone, in person and to my face." By the end of the race, that lack of support cost Klink. His campaign raised a mere $3.6 million, while GOP Senator Rick Santorum raked in nearly $13 million, according to the Center for Responsive Politics. Yet Klink lost by only a 45 to 53 margin. Compare Klink's fundraising to pro-choice Senate candidates that year, and the gap becomes starker. Representative Deborah Stabenow of Michigan pulled in $477,000 from Emily's List alone, enabling her to eke out a narrow victory.

Of course, pro-life Democrats are not disfavored officially. Congressional party leaders often recruit pro-life candidates for agricultural and blue-collar districts. Yet they have only done so since 1998, when they realized pro-lifers were needed to help them regain the majority they lost in Congress in 1994.

Even if Klink had won, he would have only been the third or fourth Democrat in the Senate to oppose abortion rights. And when he served in the House, he was one of only thirty-five to forty pro-life Democrats. This is a dramatic change: It wasn't too long ago that pro-life Democrats made up about 60 percent of the party's congressional ranks. In June of 1976, for example, the vote on the Hyde Amendment, which barred federal Medicaid funds for abortion, included support from 113 House Democrats and 20 Democrat Senators. Those numbers are unthinkable now. In 1997, the last time the House voted on the Hyde amendment, only fifty-eight Democrats favored it – an almost 50 percent drop.

The Future

There is little reason to think that the ranks of pro-life Democrats will grow, either. One major roadblock is that, while they can join the rank and file, they really can't rise to positions of power – whether to the Senate, or to the party's leadership posts – and much less to the party's presidential nomination. Nevada Senator Harry Reid is the only pro-life Democrat in a leadership position in the party, but his anti-abortion credentials are doubted by Kristen Day. No pro-life cabinet members were in the Clinton administration. And while pro-life Democrats can join some powerful congressional committees, such as Appropriations, they cannot hold power on the ones that threaten abortion.

Given this dramatic decline of pro-life Democrats, it's tempting to conclude that anti-abortion voters should never support them.

Yet pro-life Democrats are still a presence in Congress, and include able and honorable politicians like Congressmen Bart Stupak of Michigan and James Oberstar of Minnesota. In working-class districts, pro-life Democrats force Republican candidates to emphasize their pro-life credentials. If all pro-life Democrats became Republicans, the GOP could take pro-life voters and politicians for granted.

Pro-life Democrats could – and should – also become more of a swing vote – just as much as soccer moms, and influence both parties accordingly. In the 2000 Presidential election, for example, Ray Flynn endorsed George W. Bush. "When I spoke to the Knights of Columbus or in union halls in Missouri, Michigan, and Illinois and Pennsylvania, the message I gave them was that it's more important to be a good American and a good Catholic than a good Democrat," he says in his Boston accent. "And that message, wherever I went, got the biggest applause."

Of course, no one speaks of "Bush Democrats," the way they did of "Reagan Democrats." Nor should they, given that the Bush administration has appointed no pro-life Democrat to a high-profile, cabinet-level job. The administration's one Democrat is Transportation Secretary Norm Mineta, who is pro-choice. And many top Republicans, from Environmental Secretary Christie Todd Whitman to Senator Arlen Specter of Pennsylvania, to Congressman Thomas Davis of Virginia, are as well.

There is no doubt that pro-life Democrats could and should do much more. Every political movement – whether for civil rights, for the labor movement, or for the right to life – needs *leaders* as well as grass-roots supporters. But pro-life Democrat politicians aren't leaders now.

And unless they get a mixture of money, media, organization, favorable party rules, and courage – they never will be.

Raymond L. Flynn, the former Mayor of Boston and former ambassador to the Vatican with the Clinton administration, is the President of the Catholic Alliance. Mark Stricherz, who worked for the Jesuit Volunteer Corps in Baton Rouge, LA., after college, is a writer living in Washington, D.C.

Time for Constitutional Fidelity
The Constitution Party
Howard Phillips

Since the *Roe v. Wade* decision on January 22, 1973, leaders of the pro-life movement have, almost without exception, based their anti-abortion political strategies on unwavering support for the presidential and vice-presidential nominees of the Republican Party, and have rested their legislative hopes on the election of Republicans to the U.S. Senate and House of Representatives.

This strategy of blind partisan loyalty has completely failed, if one presupposes that the goal of pro-lifers should be to restrict the practice of abortion. The simple truth is that not even one abortion of an unborn child has been prevented by pro-life political support for Gerald Ford in 1976, Ronald Reagan in 1980 and 1984, George Bush, the elder, in 1988 and 1992, Bob Dole in 1996, or George Bush, the lesser, in the Year 2000.[1]

Indeed, during the roughly thirty years since *Roe v. Wade* was decided, an estimated 40 million babies have been intentionally killed in the United States. Republican Party strategists have put pro-life votes in their pocket and failed to do that which was always within their power to accomplish to restrict abortions.

It is not that Republican presidents, senators, and representatives have lacked the authority – or even the ability – to end legal abortion, they simply have not possessed the wit or the will to pursue and attain that objective. It is a watchword of the Constitution Party that "to achieve victory, first you must seek it." The GOP has not achieved victory over abortion, because they have not sought it.

It is not the objective of the Republican Party, or its leaders, to end abortion. Even when GOP proselytes make anti-abortion pronouncements, these are accompanied by codicils, conditions, and caveats concerning which the fine print is either unread or ignored by eager pro-life activists, whose love of political pragmatism makes them blind to political truth.

George Bush says he opposes abortion – with exceptions. Acceptance of exceptions (allowing the killing of innocents fathered by rapists or close family members) surrenders the core principle that the first duty of civil government is to prevent the shedding of innocent blood. Is the child conceived by rape not as innocent as any other unborn child? God does not enable us to give birth to "exceptions" – only to little boys and girls, none of whom may justly be executed in the wombs of their mothers.

Indeed, the Fifth Amendment to the Constitution of the United States stipulates that *"No person shall be . . . deprived of life . . . without due process of law."* Similar language (restricting state governments) may be found in the Fourteenth Amendment.

If the unborn child is in fact a human person, as all sincere pro-lifers would agree, then, before that child may, within Constitutional limits, be executed, he or she must first be indicted for a capital offense, brought to trial before a jury of his or her peers, convicted on the testimony of two witnesses, sentenced to death, defeated on appeal, and scheduled for execution.

So far as I am aware, no abortion has been preceded by any such procedural niceties.

What Good Is the Platform?

Here's what Republican national platforms have postulated at the GOP's presidential nominating conventions, beginning in 1984 (emphasis added):

1984: "The unborn child has a fundamental individual right to life which cannot be infringed. We therefore reaffirm our support for a human life amendment to the Constitution, and we endorse legislation to make clear that the Fourteenth Amendment's protections apply to unborn children. We oppose the use of public revenues for abortion and will eliminate funding for organizations which advocate or support abortion. We commend the efforts of those individuals and religious and private organizations that are providing positive alternatives to abortion by meeting the physical, emotional, and financial needs of pregnant women and offering adoption services where needed."

1988: "Deep in our hearts, we do believe . . . that the unborn child has a fundamental individual right to life which cannot be infringed. We therefore reaffirm our support for a human life amendment to the Constitution, and we endorse legislation to make clear that the Fourteenth Amendment's protections apply to unborn children. We oppose the use of public revenues for abortion and will eliminate funding for organizations which advocate or support abortion. . . ."[2]

1992: "We believe the unborn child has a fundamental individual right to life that cannot be infringed. . . . We oppose using public revenues for abortion and will not fund organizations that advocate it. . . . We reaffirm our support for appointment of judges who respect traditional family values and the sanctity of innocent human life."

1996: "The unborn child has a fundamental individual right to life which cannot be infringed. . . . Our purpose is to have legislative and judicial protection of that right against those who perform abortions. We oppose using public revenues for abortion and will not fund organizations which advocate it. . . ."

2000: "As a country, we must keep our pledge to the first guarantee of the Declaration of Independence. That is why we say the unborn child has a fundamental individual right to life which cannot be infringed. We support a human life amendment to the Constitution and we endorse legislation to make clear that the Fourteenth Amendment's protections apply to unborn children. Our purpose is to have legislative and judicial protection of that right against those who perform abortions. We oppose using public revenues for abortion and will not fund organizations which

advocate it. We support the appointment of judges who respect traditional family values and the sanctity of innocent human life."

In office, Republicans have failed to act on the principles first
enunciated in the 1984 platform. Personhood has not been proclaimed as official policy by GOP presidents or congressional
majorities – and Republicans elected to office, in the White House
and on Capitol Hill, have, since 1984, sent many billions of dollars
to "organizations which advocate or support abortion," despite
pledges of personhood and non-funding in the party's platforms.

Oddly, pro-life leaders, who should know better, have bought
into the Republican lie that "we are doing the best we can" and that
the only realistic strategy for ending abortion is to secure some
form of constitutional amendment. No constitutional amendment
is necessary to end the use of public revenues going to organizations which advocate abortion!

Of course, even there, they reject amendments which would
safeguard all innocent life, positing that such a "purist" approach
is even more politically unrealistic than the idea of securing ratification of a watered-down amendment. If the political evidence is to
be believed, pro-lifers do not have the votes of two-thirds of the
members of the House and Senate needed to approve a constitutional amendment (assuming pro-life advocates could agree on the
wording of any such amendment), nor majorities in three-fourths
of the fifty states to ratify any such amendment which might be
sent them. Accordingly, the constitutional-amendment strategy for
opposing abortion is as politically unrealistic as it is unnecessary.
Of course, even if ratification of a constitutional amendment were
politically feasible, it would be constitutionally superfluous, given
the already existing provisions in the Fifth and Fourteenth
Amendments to the Constitution stipulating that no person may be
deprived of life without due process of law.[3]

Personhood and Judicial Appointments

In his January 22, 1973 *Roe v. Wade* opinion, even arch pro-abortion
Justice Harry Blackmun, writing for the majority, acknowledged in
a footnote that if the fetus were determined to be a human person,

abortion would be comprehensively unconstitutional: *"If this suggestion of personhood is established, the appellant's case, of course, collapses, for the fetus' right to life would then be guaranteed specifically by the [Fourteenth] Amendment,"* Blackmun observed.

Commitment to "personhood" has not ever been a prerequisite for nominees of Republican presidents to federal judicial positions. Of the seven justices who supported the *Roe v. Wade* decision, five were Republican Supreme Court nominees: Harry Blackmun (Richard Nixon), William J. Brennan (Dwight Eisenhower), Warren E. Burger (Richard Nixon), Lewis F. Powell, Jr. (Richard Nixon), and Potter Stewart (Dwight Eisenhower). William O. Douglas (Franklin Roosevelt) and Thurgood Marshall (Lyndon Johnson) also supported the decision. Only William H. Rehnquist (Richard Nixon) and Byron R. White (John Kennedy) dissented.

After *Roe*, Ronald Reagan named Sandra Day O'Connor to the U.S. Supreme Court, despite her consistent pro-abortion voting record as a member of the Arizona State Senate and her participation in the leadership of Planned Parenthood. Not one member of the U.S. Senate voted against her confirmation.

George Bush, the elder, named David Souter to the U.S. Supreme Court. He did so despite the following: (a) pro-abortion U.S. Senator Warren Rudman was one of Souter's prime political sponsors; (b) as a Harvard proctor, Souter had counseled a student couple to procure an abortion, even at a time when abortion was statutorily illegal in Massachusetts; and (c) as a trustee of both Concord Memorial and Dartmouth Hitchcock hospitals in New Hampshire, Souter had pushed for, and succeeded in obtaining, a shift in hospital policy from zero abortion to convenience abortion.[4]

Despite these hard, cold facts, not a single Republican Senator voted against confirmation of David Souter.[5]

Bill Clinton proposed two comprehensively pro-abortion nominees for the U.S. Supreme Court – Ruth Bader Ginsburg and Stephen Breyer. Only nine Republican Senators voted against Breyer: Frank Murkowski – Alaska; Paul Coverdell – Georgia; Dan Coats and Richard Lugar – Indiana; Trent Lott – Mississippi; Conrad Burns – Montana; Bob Smith – New Hampshire; Jesse

Helms – North Carolina; and Don Nickles – Oklahoma.[6] Only three Republican Senators opposed Ginsburg: Bob Smith – New Hampshire; Jesse Helms – North Carolina; and Don Nickles – Oklahoma.[7] Indeed, the leading Republican on the Senate Judiciary Committee, Orrin Hatch, was a cheerleader for both Breyer and Ginsburg.[8] The pro-life rhetoric of other GOP politicians counted for nothing.

When George Bush, the younger, had his opportunity to name federal judges, the first two names he sent up to the Senate were Roger Gregory and Barrington Parker, each of them a pro-abortion liberal. His attempt to curry favor with Democrats on the Senate Judiciary Committee was comprehensively unrequited and unappreciated, although I am sure it gave Senators Tom Daschle and Patrick Leahy a few good chuckles.[9]

Government Subsidies

Nor ought we ignore the Republican Party's consistent support for federal subsidies to Planned Parenthood and other pro-abortion organizations, whether through the Legal Services Corporation, the United Nations, Title X, or other elements of the federal budget.

President George Walker Bush's great-grandmother, Dorothy Walker Bush, was a long-time supporter of Planned Parenthood, and Bush's father, George H. W. Bush, during his single term in the U.S. House of Representatives (1967–69), was given the nickname by House Ways and Means Committee Chairman Wilbur Mills of "rubbers" Bush because of Bush I's early support for Federal provision of contraceptives. Running for President in 1988, GHWB would often proclaim, "I'm against abortion, but for family planning" – and pro-life leaders found that acceptable.

The federal Legal Services program, through its "law reform," "group representation," and "community education" activities, and by reason of the membership composition of many of the boards of directors of its 325-plus grantees, has, since the early 1960s, been a mainstay and a key element of the abortion arsenal. Its "back-up center," the National Health and Environmental Law Project (initially based at the University of California in Los

Angeles), launched many of the test cases which preceded and culminated in *Roe v. Wade*.

And, of course, the role of the United Nations in promoting
"population control," very often including abortion, is legendary.

Other Life Issues

There are, of course, other life-related issues. Despite the president
having spoken against most fetal tissue research, the Bush
Administration funds it. As the Republican National Coalition for
Life (RNCL) explains:

> President Bush has named the executive vice-dean of the radi-
> ology department at Johns Hopkins University School of
> Medicine to head the National Institutes of Health which
> funds more than 43,000 biomedical projects in the United
> States that employ more than 10,000 people. . . . President
> Bush also nominated Dr. Richard Carmona of Tucson, AZ, to
> fill the position of U.S. Surgeon General. When asked if both
> nominees share Bush's ethical opposition to human cloning
> and embryonic stem cell research, White House press secre-
> tary Ari Fleischer told reporters, "Suffice it to say that these are
> administration appointees. They serve the president; they
> serve his policies and I don't think you would expect the pres-
> ident to appoint people who hold wildly different views than
> he does."

To which RNCL responded:

> What is troubling is Bush's own morally unacceptable posi-
> tion. He does not support experiments on human embryos,
> *unless they were killed prior to October 10, 2001*. What's the dif-
> ference *when* a developing baby is killed for his stem cells?
> He's still very dead. The line has been crossed.

The RNCL continued:

> Now we have learned that the NIH has invited "applications
> for grants to develop, conduct, evaluate, and disseminate

short-term courses on laboratory research techniques for human embryonic stem cell lines. The courses should include hands-on experience to improve the knowledge and skills of biomedical researchers to maintain, characterize, and utilize human embryonic stem cells in basic research studies and be made available to investigators in research areas of interest to all of the institutes and centers of the NIH."

WHY? Why is the Bush administration using our tax dollars to build a cadre of researchers who will become experts at human embryonic stem cell research and share their knowledge with their colleagues? This doesn't look like a project that has an end in sight. This looks just like what we said it was when the President announced his support of "limited' research on stem cell lines taken from tiny humans who had already been killed – a beginning – an opening of the door to a world we hoped we would never see.

We invite you to take a look at the grant proposal yourself and see how the federal government is becoming complicit in developing 'better methods' of dissecting these tiny humans.[10]

Similarly, the Bush administration played a key role in blocking anti-cloning legislation in the U.S. Senate. As the Family Research Council, a pro-life and pro-family organization in Washington, D.C., explained:

This morning the Senate invoked "cloture" on the terrorism insurance bill, effectively foreclosing a vote on an amendment proposed by Sen. Brownback, which would have prevented the patenting of cloned human beings. The vote on the Brownback amendment would likely have been the most significant pro-life vote this session of Congress. Consequently, Family Research Council notified members of the Senate Monday that their vote would be 'scored' on FRC's congressional scorecard. The votes were 'there' to pass the Brownback amendment. White House lobbyists, however, were anxious to avoid a vote on the Brownback amendment and wanted a 'clean' bill. They gathered near the Senate floor, and in an effort to scuttle the Brownback amendment, assured some senators that family groups would not score the bill. Relying on that misrepresentation, several senators changed their votes and helped fashion a 60-vote majority for cloture, effectively killing Sen. Brownback's amendment. In the legal arena, material misrepresentations of fact are called 'fraud.' In Washington, such misrepresentations are called "politics. . . ." (emphasis added)

The White House had an opportunity to lead on an issue of critical importance to pro-family/pro-life groups, but instead chose to dissemble. Such tactics are reminiscent of the previous administration and are not worthy of this one.[11]

The Constitution: What We Can Do Now

The Preamble to the Constitution asserts that "We, the People of the United States, in Order to form a more perfect Union, establish Justice, insure domestic Tranquility, provide for the common defence, promote the general Welfare, and secure the Blessings of Liberty to ourselves and our Posterity, do ordain and establish this Constitution for the United States of America." Our posterity resides in the wombs of American mothers.

Let us now review some of the remedies which the Constitution provides for those who are serious about ending abortion.

1   Article I, Section 1, of the U.S. Constitution requires that *"All legislative Powers herein granted shall be vested in a Congress of the United States, which shall consist of a Senate and House of Representatives."* Accordingly, it is unconstitutional for Congress to assign policy-setting functions, including the disposition of financial resources, to any other entity. No civil service bureaucrat, no federal department or agency head, no federal regulator, no federally subsidized private organization, no international bureaucracy, and no judge has the con-

stitutional authority to legislate or disburse funds with respect to abortion. Support should be withheld from any and all candidates for federal office – executive, legislative, or judicial – who fail to manifest understanding of and commitment to enforcement of this basic constitutional requirement.

2   Article I, Section 7, provides that *"Every bill which shall have passed the House of Representatives and the Senate, shall, before it becomes a Law, be presented to the President of the United States; If he approve he shall sign it, but if not he shall return it, with his Objections to that House in which it shall have originated, who shall enter the Objections at large on their Journal, and proceed to reconsider it. If after such Reconsideration two thirds of that House shall agree to pass the Bill, it shall be sent, together with the Objections, to the other House, by which it shall likewise be reconsidered, and if approved by two thirds of that House, it shall become a Law."* Accordingly, if either 34 of 100 senators, or 145 out of 435 representatives, object to overriding a presidential veto of funds to entities which promote "population control," in any form, that veto shall stand, and no funds may be disbursed or policies established in contravention of same.

3   Article I, Section 8, begins with the following language: *"The Congress shall have Power To lay and collect Taxes, Duties, Imposts and Excises, to pay the Debts and provide for the common Defence and general Welfare of the United States."* It therefore follows that revenues secured by the federal government may not be used for any purpose except those enunciated above and enumerated in Article I, Section 8.

4   Article I, Section 8, also provides that the Congress shall have power *"To constitute Tribunals inferior to the supreme Court."* Congress may not abolish the Supreme Court, although it is free to alter its size and composition within constitutional limits. All other Federal courts are statutory creations. If Congress is unhappy with any federal district, or appellate court, it may either use its power of the purse to withhold funds from any such court, or enact legislation to abolish said court.

5   In the same vein, a president may veto funds or authority

for a court with whose activities and pronouncements he is in disagreement. He has not only the power of veto, but also the power of impoundment, which has been used by U.S. presidents beginning with George Washington.

6   Concerning abortion in the District of Columbia, this can be simply barred by resort to that provision of Article I, Section 8, which assigns Congress power *"To exercise exclusive Legislation in all Cases whatsoever, over such District."*

7   Other restrictions on the disbursement of funds to promote or provide abortion can be found in that provision of Article I, Section 9, which makes clear that *"No Money shall be drawn from the Treasury, but in Consequence of Appropriations made by Law."*

8   Article II, Section 2, says that *"The President shall have Power to fill up all Vacancies that may happen during the Recess of the Senate, by granting Commissions which shall expire at the End of their next Session."* Accordingly, if the Senate refuses to confirm anti-abortion judicial nominees, the president may secure their appointment for a limited period of time, during which period of time they may fully enforce constitutional prohibitions against abortion.

9   Furthermore, the president may, by means of recess appointment, nominate United States attorneys whose number one priority shall be to prosecute abortuaries and abortionists for violations of federal law, as well as of the Constitution itself. These U.S. attorneys may, for example, prosecute violators of such federal laws such as the Americans with Disabilities Act, and those administered by OSHA, the EEOC, and other federal regulatory programs – thereby causing abortionists to feel some of the pain they inflict on unborn children and their mothers.

10   Article III, Section 1 says *"The judicial Power of the United States, shall be vested in one supreme Court, and in such inferior Courts as the Congress may from time to time ordain and establish. The Judges, both of the supreme and inferior Courts, shall hold their Offices during good Behaviour."* If "good Behaviour" is to be defined as, *inter alia*, fidelity to the plain text of the

Constitution, we have much work ahead of us in seeking to remove, by impeachment and by other lawful means, those judges whose behavior is anything but good.

11 Article III, Section 2, makes clear that *"The judicial Power shall extend to all Cases, in Law and Equity, arising under this Constitution, the Laws of the United States, and Treaties made, or which shall be made, under their Authority; to all Cases affecting Ambassadors, other public Ministers and Consuls; – to all Cases of admiralty and maritime Jurisdiction; – to Controversies between two or more States; – [between a State and Citizens of another State; –]* between Citizens of different States, – between Citizens of the same State claiming Lands under Grants of different States, [and between a State, or the Citizens thereof, and foreign States, Citizens or Subjects.]* "**

The key provision Section 2 stipulates that: *"in all the other cases before mentioned, the Supreme Court shall have appellate jurisdiction both as to law and fact, with such exceptions and under such regulations as the Congress shall make."*

This language is very clear. It gives Congress, by simple majority vote, the power to limit the appellate jurisdiction of the Supreme Court – whether the issue is abortion or some other.

12 Article IV, Section 4, says *"The United States shall guarantee to every State in this Union a Republican Form of Government"*. That which distinguishes a republic from a democracy is that, in a republic, one's right to life, liberty, and property may not be extinguished by simple majority vote in any manner except by due process of law.

Again, this is reinforced by the pro-life provisions of the Fifth and Fourteenth Amendments to the Constitution.

The Politics of Subtraction and The Constitution Party

Clearly, the pro-life movement needs to switch from a strategy of partisan loyalty to one of constitutional fidelity. To those who say the success of such a strategy is impossible, my response is to say the Republican loyalty strategy hasn't worked. It's time to try something new.

We may not have the votes to score electoral victories in the context of a strategy of multiplication or addition, but we can accomplish a great deal through the politics of subtraction: We may not have three-quarters of the population opposed to abortion – or even 51 percent, or perhaps not even 34 percent. But, unquestionably, we live in a society where there remain 1, 2, 3, 4, 5 percent, or more who oppose the killing of innocent unborn children and who know that abortion is an abomination in the sight of God.

If we can persuade some significant number of those in the pro-life "minority" to withhold their votes from any and all candidates who fail to commit themselves to acknowledgement of the person-hood of the unborn, and to full use of Constitutional authority to safeguard the lives of the unborn, then we will begin to make some political progress.

Indeed, a pre-condition of support for any legislative candidate ought to be willingness to co-sponsor and support legislation affirming the personhood of the unborn. No presidential candidate is entitled to pro-life support unless he publicly pledges to affirm his commitment to the personhood principle and his readiness to act constitutionally in a manner consistent with that principle.

If abortion is the number one issue, then pro-lifers must reject "the lesser of two evils" strategy and pursue a strategy of subtraction. The "lesser of two evils" strategy hasn't persuaded its beneficiaries to stop abortion. *However, if Republicans are confronted with electoral defeat in close elections, they may decide to act against abortion – or to be replaced by candidates who will, who make and act on constitutional pro-life commitments.*

Our movement is capable of providing (or withholding) the margin of difference – if you will, the "balance of power" – between the two major parties. We must first become "the opposition," committed to action on principle. Then we can look forward to becoming "the alternative" to one or both of the major parties, and ultimately to having our cause assume power in its own right.

For those who argue that we ought vote for "the lesser" of two evils, the best answer is "why?" What has been accomplished by such a course of action? Again, not a single baby's life has been protected from the abortionist's knife by the election of Republicans to the White House or to the Congress.

To those who rejoice in the election of George Bush over Al Gore, I would posit that a good case can be made that, under a Democratic Party president, conservative Republicans would oppose measures which they now support (including pro-abortion judicial appointments) under their partisan comrade, George W. Bush. For evidence, I would point to the increased funding which has been enacted under President Bush for the United Nations, for the federal Department of Education, for Planned Parenthood, for the National Endowment for the Arts, for the Legal Services Corporation, for most-favored-nation status for Communist China, for World Bank subsidies to Communist China, for fetal tissue research – and for so much more.

It's time for the pro-life movement to consider and act upon a "strategy of subtraction." In doing so, I urge pro-life leaders to consider the Constitution Party, whose platform reads:

> The pre-born child, whose life begins at fertilization, is a human being created in God's image. The first duty of the law is to prevent the shedding of innocent blood. It is, therefore, the duty of all civil governments to secure and to safeguard the lives of the pre-born.[12]

How many more abortions must there be before pro-life leaders look unemotionally at the evidence and conclude that their strategy of supporting the supposed "lesser of two evils" has been a consistent failure, which has resulted in ever more abortions day-after-day, week-after-week, month-after-month, year-after-year, election-after-election.

Whenever you vote against what you believe to be right and know to be necessary because the "right" and the "necessary" seem to be "politically unrealistic," you are voting against yourself and voting to assure a continuation of policies which contradict your most fundamental convictions.

Howard Phillips is the Chairman of The Conservative Caucus in Vienna, Virginia.

Appendix A

Ending Legal Abortion
(Excerpts)

Herb W. Titus

Since *Roe v. Wade*, pro-life strategies have been based upon the premise that the Supreme Court's opinion in that case is the Supreme Law of the Land. Therefore, short of a constitutional amendment or Court reversal, it has been assumed that federal, state and local officials – executive, legislative and judicial, must conform their actions concerning abortion to rules handed down by the courts.

This working premise is erroneous. It is both unwise and unconstitutional.

Article VI of the United States Constitution states that three things are the Supreme Law of the Land: "This Constitution . . . the laws of the United States . . . made in pursuance thereof; and all treaties . . . made under the authority of the United States." Conspicuously absent from this list is a court opinion.

At the time that the Constitution was written, it was universally understood that court opinions were not laws. Therefore, under no circumstances could it be contended that federal court opinions are "the laws of the United States" within the meaning of Article VI. . . .

[W]hen Article VI of the Constitution states that all federal, state and local officials executive, legislative and judicial, "shall be bound by oath or affirmation to support this Constitution," it means that those officials are duty bound to support the Constitution as it is written, not as it has been construed by the United States Supreme Court.

This does not mean that a civil government official may defy a court order rendered by the United States Supreme Court in a case in which that official was a party. It does mean, however, that a state or local official who is not a party has the duty and the power to act according to the constitutional text, even when the action taken is inconsistent with a court opinion interpreting that text. . . .

[I]n the early 1980's, the United States Senate had before it "The Human Life Bill." . . .

[T]hey went behind the constitutional text to the common law as reflected in the nation's founding charter, the Declaration of Independence.

That law, the Report [proposing the Human Life Bill] stated, established that all human beings are legally equal. Furthermore, the Report continued, the very purpose of the Equal Protection Clause of the Fourteenth Amendment was to enforce that equality rule upon the States. Such a rule of equivalent value of all human life, the Report concluded, demanded that abortion be outlawed. . . .

Even though the Report drew this conclusion, it did not incorporate it into the text of the Human Life Act. Instead, it left it to the discretion of every State to decide whether to prohibit abortions, and if so, by what rules. . . .

By leaving it to the States to decide whether a child in the womb of the mother is a human being deserving the full protection of the law, the Report chose not to embrace the common law definition of personhood. That decision has plagued the pro-life movement to this day and in two distinct ways.

First, it tacitly conceded that state and local legislatures may define legal personhood in any way that they choose, notwithstanding the life principle embraced by the nation's charter. Second, it assumed that Congress has no authority to protect innocent human life in the womb of a mother if the States choose not to provide such protection. Neither [one] of these assumptions [is] true.

As for Congress, the very purpose of the Equal Protection Clause was to deny to the States any power to withhold from any class of human beings the benefits and protections of the common law. . . .

The Equal Protection Clause was designed to guarantee such common law protection by denying to the States any power to classify or treat any human being as anything but a legally recognized person. That is exactly what states are doing when they follow the Supreme Court's ruling in *Roe v. Wade* – denying to a class of human beings the protection of the common law solely on the ground that pre-born children are not persons.

Following the adoption of the Fourteenth Amendment, Congress enacted a number of criminal statutes designed to outlaw such practices. One of these statutes protects "any inhabitant" from acts "under color of any law, statute, ordinance, regulation or custom" that "willfully" deprive him "of any rights, privileges, or immunities secured or protected by the Constitution" or of "full and equal benefit of all laws and proceedings for the security of persons and property as is enjoyed by white citizens." 18 U.S.C. Section 242.

This law should be enforced by a President of the United States against abortion providers and women seeking such services, especially when those services are funded by state law or otherwise given special encouragement or protection by that law. . . .

In addition to the enforcement of existing or future criminal statutes, the President may instruct the Attorney General to bring civil suits seeking injunctions against abortion clinics and abortion doctors on the grounds that they are public nuisances. . . .

The President may also, under his constitutional authority to "take care that the laws be faithfully executed," refuse to spend any money appropriated by Congress for the purpose of supporting any activity that facilitates or promotes abortion. This means that the President may cut off all federal funds to such abortion promoting organizations as Planned Parenthood and to such abortion facilitating activities as fetal tissue research.

This power is available to the President even if Congress should mandate that the funds that it has appropriated must be spent. Such a mandate violates the constitutional vesting of all of the executive power in the office of the President because the very essence of executive power is the discretion not to enforce a law. See *Marbury v. Madison*, supra.

Finally, the President has the power to appoint only judges to the federal bench, including the United States Supreme Court, who have clearly and consistently affirmed the legal personhood of the pre-born. Indeed, his constitutional oath of office to "preserve, protect and defend the Constitution of the United States" requires him to exercise his appointment power consistent with his understanding of the Constitution, independent of either the judicial or the legislative branches. . . .

As the nation's chief constitutional officer, the president has the duty and authority to issue a Presidential Proclamation affirming the right to life of the pre-born child and to call upon state governments to protect that right with all deliberate speed and appropriate means. . . .

In many states, statutes prohibiting abortion remain unrepealed and available to local prosecutors to bring criminal actions against abortion providers. While such laws may very well provide for an exception to protect the life of the mother, they afford statutory authority to a prosecutor who takes seriously his duty to "support" the Constitution's high regard for the right to life.

The problem today is that state prosecutors assume that their duty to support the Constitution means obedience to Supreme Court opinions even when they were never parties to the cases. Rightfully understood, their duty is to interpose their office between *Roe v. Wade*, a constitutionally erroneous opinion, and the people whose rights they are duty bound to protect.

Even in States where the statutes have been changed to conform to the *Roe* formula, a prosecutor may still have ample authority under the state's law and constitution to bring criminal actions against abortion promoters and providers.

In Virginia, for example, producing an abortion, except to preserve the life of a mother, remains a felony. . . .

In addition, *Roe v. Wade* can be avoided by any state legislature that challenges its factual underpinnings. The *Roe* decision is based upon a number of factual assumptions that, if true in 1973, are no longer true today.

The major factual premise of *Roe* is that a medically safe abortion poses no significant health risks to the mother. Numerous studies since *Roe* have proved that assumption false. Physiological complications, including uterine perforations, excessive bleeding and endotoxic shock, attend even the normal abortion process. Other physiological complications, such as cervical and ovarian cancer, placenta previa, pelvic inflammatory disease, appear after an abortion and are causally linked to it.

And there are numerous psychological and emotional side effects. Among the significant emotional risks are guilt and depression, suicidal ideation and sexual dysfunction. . . . These emotional and psychological traumas contribute to a variety of sociological impairments, including psychic numbing, substance abuse and relationship instability. This, in turn, adversely impacts family and other intimate associations.

None of this came before the Court in *Roe v. Wade*. Nor did the Court have before it evidence that the medical profession does not adequately protect the interests of women who obtain abortions in clinics. Nor did it have before it the threat that permitting abortion poses to the sanctity of life generally or to the economy.

Given these glaring factual omissions, *Roe v. Wade* is no longer a binding legal precedent for, as the High Court itself has observed, changes in the facts upon which a court ruling rests is sufficient reason not to follow that ruling. *Planned Parenthood v. Casey*, 505 U.S.833 120 L Ed 2d 674, 703–6 (1992).

It is time for a new pro-life strategy, one based squarely upon the principle that the taking of innocent life is never justified. Such a strategy would seize the moral and constitutional high ground in the abortion debate and has a realistic chance to succeed.

These excerpts are from a 1997 study prepared for The Conservative Caucus Foundation by former Regent Law School Dean Herb Titus, a 1962 cum laude graduate of the Harvard Law School. Mr. Titus worked in the U.S. Department of Justice, and served as a professor of law at the state universities of Oklahoma, Colorado, and Oregon. In July 1993, he established The Forecast, a monthly journal on law and public policy, which provides a Biblical and Constitutional analysis to current issues. A recognized constitutional and common law scholar, he is the author of numerous articles and a book entitled *God, Man and Law: The Biblical Principles.*

Endnotes

1   If restrictions on partial-birth abortion are enacted by Congress, it is possible that there will be a reduction of some small percentage in the number of killings permitted. This remains to be seen, depending on ways in which the White House and the Justice Department respond to potential judicial hostility.

2   1988: "Deep in our hearts, we do believe . . . that the unborn child has a fundamental individual right to life which cannot be infringed. We therefore reaffirm our support for a human life amendment to the Constitution, and we endorse legislation to make clear that the Fourteenth Amendment's protections apply to unborn children. *We oppose the use of public revenues for abortion and will eliminate funding for organizations which advocate or support abortion.* . . . We commend the efforts of those individuals and religious and private organizations that are providing positive alternatives to abortion by meeting the physical, emotional, and financial needs of pregnant women and offering adoption services where needed."

1992: "We believe the unborn child has a fundamental individual right to life that cannot be infringed. We therefore reaffirm our support for a human life amendment to the Constitution, and we endorse legislation to make clear that the 14th Amendment's protections apply to unborn children. *We oppose using public revenues for abortion and will not fund organizations that advocate it.* We commend those who provide alternatives to abortion by meeting the needs of mothers and offering adoption services. We reaffirm our support for appointment of judges who respect traditional family values and the sanctity of innocent human life."

1996: "The unborn child has a fundamental individual right to life which cannot be infringed. We support a human life amendment to the Constitution and we endorse legislation to make clear that the Fourteenth Amendment's protections apply to unborn children. Our purpose is to have legislative and judicial protection of that right against those who perform abortions. *We oppose using public revenues for abortion and will not fund organizations which advocate it.* We support the appointment of judges who respect traditional family values and the sanctity of innocent human life."

2000: "As a country, we must keep our pledge to the first guarantee of the Declaration of Independence. That is why we say the unborn child has a fundamental individual right to life which cannot be infringed. We support a human life amendment to the Constitution and we endorse legislation to make clear that the Fourteenth Amendment's protections apply to unborn children. Our purpose is to have legislative and judicial protection of that right against those who perform abortions. *We oppose using public revenues for abortion and will not fund organizations which advocate it.* We support the appointment of judges who respect traditional family values and the sanctity of innocent human life."

3   See Appendix A, reproducing parts of a study prepared for The Conservative Caucus Foundation by former Regent Law School Dean Herb Titus in which he disputes the presumption, held by most in the pro-life movement, that a constitutional amendment or a court reversal of *Roe* is legally necessary to protect the unborn.

4   Testimony of Howard Phillips in Opposition to the Confirmation of David H. Souter to be a Justice of the United States Supreme Court, before the Committee on the Judiciary, United States Senate, September 19, 1990.

5   Senate Roll Call no. 259, 10/2/90, confirmed 90-9 – Republicans 44-0, Democrats 46-9.

6   Senate Roll Call no. 242, 7/29/94, confirmed 87-9 – Republicans 33-9, Democrats 54-0.

7   Senate Roll Call no. 232, 8/3/93, confirmed 96-3 – Republicans 41-3, Democrats 55-0.

8   See also Testimony concerning the nomination of Ruth Bader Ginsburg to be Justice of the U.S. Supreme Court by Howard Phillips, Chairman, Conservative Caucus, before the U.S. Senate Judiciary Committee, July 23, 1993.

9   *The Legal Times* of May 14, 2001 profiled President GWB's judicial nominees at page 14: Miguel Estrada, one of two nominees to the U.S. Court of Appeals for the D.C. Circuit – "If Bush has the opportunity to name the first Latino Supreme Court justice, many are placing their bets with *Estrada*. . . . *Estrada* was largely groomed in the Clinton Justice Department, where he served as assistant solicitor general from 1992 until 1997 under Drew Days III and Acting SG Walter Dellinger. . . ." "Barrington Parker Jr., President George W. Bush's pick for the U.S. Court of Appeals for the 2nd Circuit, actually has deep Washington roots. . . . He was appointed to the U.S.

District Court for the Southern District of New York by former President Bill Clinton in 1994. Parker, 56, would fill a slot on the New York-based 2nd Circuit vacated by Judge Ralph Winter, a Ronald Reagan appointee who took senior status. . ."

"For a number of years, *he was* the president of the board of the Harlem School of the Arts, as well as *vice president of the NAACP Legal Defense and Education Fund Inc.* He continues to serve on the boards of the New School University in New York City and the South Africa Legal Services and Education Project. *He is also a member of the Council on Foreign Relations. . . . "It has been five months since then-President Bill Clinton angered conservatives with his last-minute recess appointment of Virginia litigator Roger Gregory to the U.S. Court of Appeals for the 4th Circuit. . . . Now, President George W. Bush has nominated him for a permanent appointment to the bench. . . ."* (emphasis added) "Before his appointment, Gregory was a partner in Richmond, Va.'s Wilder & Gregory with former Democratic Virginia Gov. L. Douglas Wilder. Wilder had been his political science and constitutional law professor in classes at Virginia State University. . . ." HPISB#670, 5/31/01.

10   Read it at: http://grants1.nih.gov/grants/guide/pa-files/PA-02-054.html" Source: Republican National Coalition For Life *FaxNotes*, April 2, 2002 *HPISB#692, 4/30/02.*

11   Source: Ken Connor, Family Research Council's *Washington Update*, 6/18/02, HPISB#696, 6/30/02.

12   The Platform continues:

To that end, the Constitution of the United States was ordained and established for 'ourselves and our posterity.' Under no circumstances may the federal government fund or otherwise support any state or local government or any organization or entity, foreign or domestic, which advocates, encourages or participates in the practice of abortion. We also oppose the distribution and use of all abortifacients.

As to matters of rape and incest, it is unconscionable to take the life of an innocent child for the crimes of his father.

In addition, Article IV of the Constitution guarantees to each state a republican form of government. In a republic, the taking of innocent life, including the life of the pre-born, may not be declared lawful by any institution of state or local government – legislative, judicial or executive. The right to life should not be made dependent upon a vote of a majority of any legislative body.

Moreover, this right should never depend upon a majority of justices on any court, including the United States Supreme Court. Therefore, although a Supreme Court opinion is binding on the parties to the controversy as to the particulars of the case, it is not a political rule for the nation. *Roe v Wade* is illegitimate, contrary to the law of the nation's Charter and Constitution. It must be resisted by all civil government officials, federal, state, and local, and by all branches of the government – legislative, executive, and judicial.

In office, we shall only appoint to the federal judiciary, and to other positions of federal authority, qualified individuals who publicly acknowledge and commit themselves to the legal personhood of the pre-born child. In addition, we will do all that is within our power to encourage federal, state, and local government officials to protect the sanctity of the life of the pre-born through legislation, executive action, and judicial enforcement of the law of the land.

In addition, we condemn the misuse of anti-racketeering and other federal laws against pro-life demonstrators, and strongly urge the repeal of the RICO and FACE Acts as unconstitutional expansions of federal power into areas reserved to the states by the Tenth Amendment.

Finally, we also oppose all government 'legalization' of euthanasia, infanticide and suicide.

For more information on the Constitution Party, visit http://www.constitutionparty.com.

Letter to the Troops
The Grassroots of the Pro-Life Movement
James C. Dobson

What were you doing in January of 1973? Some of us were young professionals, climbing the corporate ladder, or in my case, immersed in academia. Others were raising small children or were perhaps children themselves, while a percentage were not yet born. Few Americans were any more than marginally aware of the two U.S. Supreme Court decisions handed down that month which would tragically alter the moral, medical, and legal landscape of our nation. But despite our inability to foresee their magnitude at the time, the court rulings issued on January 22, 1973 – *Roe v. Wade* and *Doe v. Bolton* – would profoundly change our lives and our nation.

As the ramifications of those decisions became clear in the months that followed, public reaction ran the gamut from praise to condemnation. Amidst the social upheaval that ensued in the wake of legalized abortion, there emerged a growing, organized voice of dissension – a voice we recognize today as the grassroots pro-life movement. But what *is* "the grassroots pro-life movement," and who count themselves among its numbers?

Who We Are

We are men, women, boys, and girls who may have been touched by abortion at some point – either through personal experience or through the experience of family and friends. Many of us are evangelicals or Catholics whose convictions are formed by the biblical truth that each of us is created in the image of God and that *every* life – no matter how small or seemingly insignificant – holds inestimable worth in His sight. Because this is true, we know that the extermination of a baby in the womb – a human life at its most helpless and vulnerable – is an act of unspeakable evil that grieves our Creator. We have faced discouragement and disillusionment in recent years as this same evil act has come to be celebrated by the cultural elite as a noble and fundamental right.

Our hearts break at the realization that abortion not only kills an innocent baby, but that it also maims his or her mother physically, psychologically, and spiritually. In the face of such inhumanity toward mother and child, feelings of sadness will inevitably give way to a sense of righteous indignation. We feel a swell of anger in our chests when we are reminded of the lives that have been destroyed by abortion. And so we are compelled to act in opposition to this grievous social injustice, marching in the streets, writing letters to our congressmen, and volunteering at pregnancy resource centers. From the bumper stickers on our automobiles to our voting records, we are proudly pro-life. We give our money to pro-life organizations and our time to pro-life campaigns. We spend cold Saturday mornings silently praying outside abortion clinics. We sacrifice our comfort and convenience to demonstrate our care for the abandoned and forgotten.

Now, as the clock ticks past January 22, 2003, we look back on the thirty dark years that have comprised the *Roe v. Wade* era. How can we begin to put our feelings into words as the U.S. commemorates three decades of legalized abortion? Terms like "frustration," "discouragement," and "heartache" come to mind. In light of our nation's abortion policy and the death toll that now reaches more than 40 million, we almost feel ashamed to call ourselves Americans.

Active Citizens

But we *are* Americans, and as children, we were taught that in our democratic form of government, every voice counts. We were encouraged to be good citizens by voting and participating in the electoral process. The opportunity for civic involvement implies that we can, indeed, effect a change in the direction of our nation. It's a lesson that many of us take to heart and attempt to implement in our lives.

When it comes to the issue of abortion, however, many Americans feel that the promise of civic-driven change rings hollow. Fewer and fewer political candidates can describe themselves as truly "pro-life." The lifetime appointments of pro-abortion federal judges leave precious few democratic options for reversing abortion-centered court rulings, and long-term solutions to judicial tyranny are elusive. Even post-1973 Supreme Court decisions on abortion swing between the hope of *Webster* and the dismay of *Casey*. And as we saw in 1992, the election of *one* pro-abortion president can single-handedly reverse years of pro-life policy, leaving many Americans disenchanted with the prospect of ever achieving lasting results in the battle to defend life. But the law remains a teacher, whether we are disenchanted or not. Court rulings and public policies that enshrine legalized abortion *must* be dismantled – if not by us, then by those who follow us.

Looking back on thirty years, we are also painfully aware that our efforts have not sufficiently convinced our neighbors and co-workers that abortion is an evil worth fighting. Opinion polls tell us that Americans remain divided on this issue – virtually split down the middle into pro-life and pro-abortion camps. Of course, it is also true that the majority of Americans oppose most abortions and want to see fewer of them. Unfortunately, that view has not, as of yet, been translated into national policy.

Nevertheless, our commitment to effecting lasting change remains firm, even while our feelings fluctuate between hope and despair. Through the years, I have asked friends and supporters of Focus on the Family to rank the issues that should, in their view, be given priority in our ministry. Abortion consistently tops the list. Millions of grassroots Americans care deeply about preborn children, their right to life and the needs of their mothers. Yes, we have faced many discouraging moments during the past three decades of state-sanctioned abortion, but that is neither the whole story, nor the end of it.

What We Have Done Right

Looking back on this era of legalized abortion, there is much the pro-life movement has done right. Most notably, the community has demonstrated a faithful determination to speak out on behalf of those who cannot speak for themselves. Like the prophets of old, we hold the trumpet of truth to our collective lips, decrying the immorality and injustice of abortion. This is no small accomplishment in a culture that often endeavors to ignore or silence our cries. Considering the influence of abortion advocates among the cultural elite, it's amazing that the practice has not gained more widespread acceptance in this country. Certainly, promoters of abortion thought it would be a "done deal" years ago. The fact that Americans are still divided on abortion three decades after its across-the-board legalization is a testament to the commitment and tenacity of the grassroots pro-life movement. In its 1992 *Casey* decision, some members of the Supreme Court admonished pro-lifers to give up the fight and accept legalized abortion – a charge to which we've responded in unison with a hearty – "Never!" The abortion question is far from being answered in the affirmative, and that in itself is reason for hope.

As we all know, defending the preborn child targeted for abortion is only possible if at the same time we reach out to his or her mother with life-affirming alternatives. I greatly admire the community-based pregnancy-resource centers and maternity homes that provide tangible love and support for women facing unexpected pregnancies. Without these facilities, the pro-life movement would be lacking in love – much like, as Scripture says, "a resounding gong or a clanging cymbal." At Focus on the Family, we believe so strongly in the work of these organizations that we have created a ministry devoted to supporting them through conferences, pro-life materials, and a host of additional resources. While Planned Parenthood and other abortion providers reap enormous profits and receive governmental support to boot, these pro-life groups sacrificially and benevolently donate services while receiving little, if any, public assistance.

The pro-life movement has also raised awareness of the plight of millions of women who have been hurt psychologically, injured physically, and even killed, as the result of a legal abortion. Their stories are recounted, their wounds healed, and their lives remembered through our message that abortion will always be a risky and dangerous venture for women.

Although we have done an admirable job of "getting the word out" about the evil of abortion, there is still room for improvement. After all, each and every one of us has been touched by abortion in some way. There are many who, as mothers, fathers, and grandparents of aborted children, have deeply personal testimonies to share. These stories need to be heard, because it is as we speak and hear the truth that healing occurs. Not everyone with an abortion testimony will – or should – speak publicly. However, those who do will bear witness to the hope that can arise from the ashes of abortion's aftermath. Out of their healing, others who have experienced similar pain can find comfort.

It has also become increasingly important that we make every endeavor to highlight the diversity within our ranks. Too often, the pro-life movement is unfairly and untruthfully – characterized as being dominated by white males who don't fully understand the issues at hand. In reality it is women, from a rich array of ethnic backgrounds, who represent the heart and soul of our efforts, and we must make sure their voices are heard. Because of unfair media bias and influence from radical feminists, much of the public inaccurately views the pro-life movement as being insensitive to the needs of women. The perspectives and voices of pro-life women can forcefully counter this misconception.

The Challenges

One of our movement's greatest challenges is to continue to take full advantage of the legal latitude afforded to the pro-life cause by the Supreme Court. Since 1973, the court has issued thirty abortion-related rulings. While none have reversed the damage of *Roe* and

Doe, the court *has* recognized the wisdom of allowing states to regulate abortion. Thankfully, many states have enacted court-approved measures such as parental involvement laws, informed consent, and reflection periods that protect the rights of teenagers and their parents, as well as other women seeking abortions. Other states, however, have not. The pro-life movement must continue to push for passage of these incremental measures in *all* states. Legislatures should also pass laws ensuring that abortion clinics meet minimal health standards as well as establishing separate criminal penalties when preborn children are injured or killed as a result of violent acts against their mothers.

Incrementalism

On a related note, I recognize that this incremental strategy is not universally embraced in the pro-life movement. Certainly, we all pray for a time when abortion is neither desired nor accepted by society. Our goal must always be to bring about a decisive end to this evil practice, with public policy that matches public sentiment. However, that time has not yet come, and so we must take advantage of the limited opportunities available to us. If we hold out for only the purest legislative approach, we will be left in the dust. An "all-or-nothing" mentality is neither practical nor feasible at this point. We need to wisely incorporate the court-approved, common-sense restrictions that are already in place in many states, even as we look ahead to our ultimate goal of eliminating abortion altogether.

While the issue of "incremental gains" has been one of the most hotly debated controversies among the pro-life ranks, disagreements have arisen on a host of other topics as well. But regardless of the issue, pro-life groups need to do a better job of keeping their disagreements private in the years to come. After all, leaders of pro-abortion organizations rarely quarrel in front of an audience. They may argue to the point of bloodletting behind closed doors, but when they walk out to the lights and cameras of the public eye, they're all singing the same song. We can learn from their example!

The Future

With these thoughts in mind, we now must ask, what lies ahead? How should the movement's strategy for the next few years take shape? There are others better equipped to answer those questions in detail, but I would like to offer a few general observations.

First and foremost, we must commit every decision and every new endeavor to earnest prayer. The pro-life movement was born out of the deep faith and Christian conviction of men and women who saw legalized abortion as the affront to Almighty God that it is. There is no question that we are in a battle, and while many of our "opponents" take the physical form of activist groups and pro-abortion politicians, this is ultimately a spiritual struggle. Now, more than ever, we must ask our Heavenly Father to make us "as shrewd as snakes and as innocent as doves" (Matthew 10:16) as we seek to demolish the dark spiritual stronghold of legalized abortion.

There are a number of strategic goals to keep in mind for the coming years as well. For example, the election of pro-life candidates to office must remain a priority. Likewise, the composition of the U.S. Supreme Court will change in the near future, as several justices near retirement. Future appointments to the high court *must* be pro-life judges who understand the limits of the Constitution and will not legislate from the bench. Of course, our opponents in the pro-abortion camp will do everything within their power to ensure that only the most liberal justices are appointed. This will be a brutal battle, and we must be prepared to devote our full energies and resources to supporting those Supreme Court nominees who are willing to defend the sanctity of human life.

Finally, it is up to parents and churches to educate young people about the relationship between the sanctity of human life and appropriate sexuality within the context of marriage. In many ways, the Supreme Court's infamous 1973 decisions were a logical consequence of the sexual revolution. Statistically, unmarried women constitute the vast majority of those who seek abortions; married women are more likely to embrace motherhood. If we can train the next generation of young people to remain sexually pure until marriage, we will go far in eliminating the market for abortion.

The role of the church, however, does not stop there. Abortion is fundamentally a moral issue that must be addressed more vocally by church leaders. Where is the thunderous voice of righteousness erupting from pastors and other clergy as they denounce the premeditated slaughter of preborn children in the womb? One sermon each January commemorating Sanctity of Human Life Sunday is not enough to combat the evil of abortion or its influence in our culture. I cannot help but believe that God expects more from those who are called to lead His people and be a voice of truth to the nation.

Let me close with a few words to the young people in the grassroots pro-life movement. Every generation has its life-and-death issues. Although we would have hoped that our society would have settled the question of the preborn child's value long before now, that has, sadly, not been the case. Therefore, the responsibility for defending the preborn child from the horror of abortion begins to fall upon your shoulders.

This is a noble struggle. You follow countless men and women throughout the centuries who sacrificed to care for the weak and vulnerable. These brave individuals stood fast to defend abandoned infants, Nazi prison camp victims, and African-American slaves. Dedicating one's life to the protection of the "least of these" (Matthew 25:40) was a grand act of character then, as it is now. Just as we are inspired by the stories of abolitionists who fought slavery in previous generations, we can only hope that one day those who follow our path will be encouraged by our courageous acts.

May our passion to protect all innocent human life be an inheritance to you that ignites your own hearts. May you learn from our mistakes and succeed in reaching your peers. New challenges have already arisen as biotechnology races toward genetic engineering, cloning, and so much more. Remember that the truth is the same with every new development: human life is sacred and worthy of our protection.

We are not the first generation to stand between the innocent and the indiscriminate forces of death. We will not be the last. We are, however, called to stand <u>now</u> and to believe that what we do, even thirty years after *Roe*, makes a difference. And while some in our ranks have been lost to fatigue and exhaustion, many new recruits have taken up the cause. Won't you join us as we catch a second wind and ask God to strengthen us for the next leg of the race?

James C. Dobson, Ph.D., is the President and Founder of Focus on the Family. Dr. Dobson earned his Ph.D. from the University of Southern California (1967) in the field of child development and holds fifteen honorary doctoral degrees.

There's More to Abortion than Abortion

Nat Hentoff [1]

I've involved myself in many controversies through the years, but by far the most fiercely controversial position I have ever been identified with was my decision to be pro-life. It was a decision that surprised me at the time. Until then, in the early 1980s, it had never occurred to me that there was a rational secular position in opposing abortion. What little I knew personally of pro-lifers indicated they were all committed Christians. And I am an atheist.

In any case, having spent my first twenty-eight years in Boston, I had known during that period only one pro-lifer. She was the wife of a jazz bass player, and she was Catholic. I liked her a lot – she was one of the most honest people I've ever known – but I ascribed her views on abortion solely to her having been brought up Catholic. All my other friends – students, musicians, journalists, labor organizers, professors – were unconditionally pro-abortion.

The father of that jazz bass player was an eminent physician in a suburb of Boston who decided, when he was in his fifties, that he could no longer bear the suffering of women who desperately wanted an abortion and had no way to get one. (There was a legendary doctor in rural Pennsylvania who performed abortions for a small fee, but he was getting old.) So this physician in Massachusetts started to perform abortions – at no fee. It was a matter of conscience, he said, and there should be no price tag on that. Somehow the police found him out, and he was sentenced to prison for ten years and stripped of his right to practice medicine.

That story stayed with me. From the time I came to New York in 1953, I did not stray from the pro-choice creed. I was on the board of the New York Civil Liberties Union when it was a key factor in the successful struggle to make abortion legal in New York State – before the Supreme Court's 1973 *Roe v. Wade* decision. My wife, Margot, is, and was then, a ferocious defender of a woman's right to end a pregnancy, but within limitations.

The Company You Keep

It was in 1983 that I entered on the path of pariahdom among most of my friends and colleagues. An infant, initially known as Baby Jane Doe, had been born on Long Island with spina bifida. This is a lesion in the spinal column, and if it is not repaired quickly through surgery, there is danger of infection that can lead to permanent brain damage. Usually there is an accumulation of spinal fluid in the skull. As soon as possible, a shunt should be inserted to drain the fluid. Otherwise the pressure on the brain often leads to mental retardation.

The parents of Baby Jane Doe decided, however, that she would not have the operation, nor would a shunt be inserted. She was to get only "conservative treatment" – antibiotics, for instance, until she died.

All the press – print and broadcast, including the CBS newsmagazine *60 Minutes* – vigorously supported the parents. They listened to the parents' lawyer and printed the alleged facts – without checking – that the infant would, in any case, not live long, would be in intractable pain for all of her brief life, and would never recognize her parents. It was an act of compassion to let the child slip into eternity.

When the press – print and broadcast – are unanimous on anything, I get suspicious. Nothing is that simple. I found the names of the three leading pediatric neurosurgeons in this country, and called them. They were aware of the infant's condition, and the particular location of the lesion in her spine. Each of them told me that if an operation was performed very soon to close the lesion in the spine, and if a shunt was inserted in the skull, the child would – at worst – have to walk with braces as she grew up. She would *not* be retarded; she would *not* be in intractable pain; and she certainly would recognize her parents.

So I began writing – some eight columns – in opposition to the parents, their lawyer, and the press. Just about everybody in the newsroom at the *Village Voice* thought I was balmy. This was a damaged kid who would die soon. Why waste all this space on her? Besides, it was pro-lifers who were supporting her right to aggressive treatment. Be careful about the company you keep, I was warned.

On the other hand, I was becoming uncomfortable with the company I *had* been keeping for years. I heard Janet Benshoof, then head of the Reproductive Freedom Rights unit of the American Civil Liberties Union (ACLU), say in a lecture that this case was really an extension of reproductive freedom rights – a woman's right to choose. The mother of Baby Jane Doe had every right to make any decision she wanted about the infant's condition. By that analysis, Baby Jane Doe, though born, had no rights of her own. She was her mother's property. The ACLU officially insisted that there be no interference by any governmental body in the future of Baby Jane Doe. The mother's privacy rights were at stake.

But this was not a fetus. This was a born child. And, as Harry Blackmun emphasized in *Roe v. Wade*, once you're born, you're a person under the Constitution. And that means, I wrote, that before you're killed, you have the right to due process – independent of your mother's wishes – and you have the right to equal protection of the laws.

My comrades at the ACLU thought I had taken a strange turn. Janet Benshoof told a friend that I must have become a born-again Christian. Yet I was still a Jewish atheist. To my initial surprise, people I knew – liberals and civil libertarians – including reporters, editors, and staffers in Congress, couldn't understand where I was coming from. Many of them insisted the life of Baby Jane Doe was subordinate to the priorities of the mother. To keep this damaged kid could cost a lot of money and emotional distress. It would be understandable if she was to be sent back. Not killed. Just allowed to die.

Years later it was eventually revealed that Baby Jane Doe's real first name was Keri-Lynn. She was not in pain; she laughed and played with her parents (whom she recognized) and other children. But she couldn't walk. She attended special classes; her intelligence was considered below low-normal but she was educable – as reported in *New York Newsday* by Kathleen Kerr.

The Science: The Fetus as Patient and Human Life as a Continuum

Appalled that Baby Jane had been given no rights of her own by her "protectors," I began to recognize the zealotry of the abortion-rights movement. And I also began to question their "evidence" that the unborn were not entitled to any rights. I began to read the medical textbooks that physicians in prenatal care read – not pro-life books, but such standard texts as *The Unborn Patient: Prenatal Diagnosis and Treatment* by Harrison, Golbus, and Filly, published by W. B. Saunders Company, a division of Harcourt Brace Jovanovich.

God is nowhere mentioned in the book. Its first chapter begins, "The concept that the fetus is a patient, an *individual* whose maladies are a proper subject for medical treatment as well as scientific observation, is alarmingly modern. . . . Only now are we beginning to consider the fetus seriously – medically, legally, and ethically." And I read about the growing sophistication of fetal surgery – operations of the fetus that remedy various defects. But the same fetus, the next day, can legally be killed by abortion.

I spoke to a number of physicians who do research in prenatal development, and they emphasized that human life is a *continuum* from fertilization to birth to death. Setting up divisions of this process to justify abortion, for example, is artificial. It is the life of a

developing being that is being killed. The euphemisms for an aborted fetus – "the product of conception" and "a clump of cells" – are
what George Orwell might have called Newspeak.

What particularly helped clarify the abortion question for me
was a statement in the *Journal of the American Medical Association*
(February 18, 1990) by a North Carolina physician, Dr. Joel Hylton:

> Who can deny that the fetus is alive and is a separate genetic
> entity? Its humanity also cannot be questioned scientifically. It
> is certainly of no other species. . . . That it is dependent on
> another makes it qualitatively no different from countless
> other humans outside the womb. . . . It strikes me that to argue
> one may take an innocent life to preserve the quality of life of
> another is cold and carries utilitarianism to an obscene
> extreme. Nowhere else in our society is this permitted or even
> thinkable – although abortion sets a frightening prospect.

As time went on, I began to understand that there is much more
to abortion than abortion itself. The mindset – the ability to regard
as just and necessary the killing of at least 1.3 million developing
human beings a year – helps strengthen the consistent ethic of
death in the nation – including the discounting of the Baby Jane
Does and the rise of support for "assisted suicide."

Liberal Champions of the Powerless

In 1984, a coalition of disability-rights groups and some pro-lifers
began to lobby Congress to pass a bill to extend the Child Abuse
and Treatment Act. One section would broaden the definition of
child abuse to include the denial of medically indicated treatment,
hydration, and nutrition to infants born with life-threatening conditions. Furthermore, each state, to keep getting funds for child-
abuse programs, would have to put in place a reporting system that
would be alerted whenever a handicapped infant was being
abused by denial of treatment or food. There were documented
cases around the country of that terminal form of child abuse. The
Archives of Internal Medicine, for instance, reported that some five

hundred Down Syndrome infants a year were "allowed to die" by physicians.

I covered the development of that bill as a *Washington Post* columnist. It finally passed with language that was not as strong as it ought to have been; but historically, that section of the bill was potentially a vital beginning in making it more difficult for physicians to end the life of an infant and then put on the death certificate a false report of the cause of death. In the years since, however, as *Pediatrics* magazine (January 1997) reports, many physicians have figured out ways to evade this child-protection law.

During the debate in Congress, I was most impressed with a comment by Illinois Congressman Henry Hyde, a pro-life advocate much scorned by liberals. "I suggest," he said, "that a question of life or death for a born person ought to belong to nobody, whether they are parents or not." He continued:

> The Constitution ought to protect that child. . . . Because they are handicapped, they are not to be treated differently than if they were women or Hispanics or American Indians or blacks. Their handicap may be a mental condition or a physical condition; but by God, they are human, and nobody has the right to kill them by passive starvation or anything else.

And what of the passionate *liberals* in the House – the champions of the powerless? There was a parade on the floor of ardent pro-choicers who voted against the proposed law protecting Baby Does. Among them were John Conyers, Geraldine Ferraro, Ron Dellums, Don Edwards, Robert Kastenmeier, Gerry Studds, George Crockett, David Obey, Pat Schroeder, Tom Downey, Henry Waxman, Barney Frank, Charles Rangel, Edward Markey, and the then-long-time chairman of the Judiciary Committee, a very effective liberal, Peter Rodino.

In a passionate speech on the floor, Geraldine Ferraro spoke for her pro-choice liberal colleagues in focusing on the parents' right to privacy to make life-and-death decisions for handicapped newborns – who, obviously, had no voice in the matter.

There is more to abortion than abortion.

"It Opened All the Doors"

During the 1980s I tracked nearly every final court decision on euthanasia in the individual states – withdrawing feeding tubes or respirators – and they all cited *Roe v. Wade* as a key precedent for terminating life. The privacy right to end the life of the fetus was legally extended to a surrogate to end the life of a husband, wife, or children who were incompetent – or appeared to be.

At a conference on euthanasia at Clark College in Worcester, Massachusetts, I met Derek Humphry, the angel of death of our time. (Jack Kevorkian is only the field commander.) Humphry, the founder of the Hemlock Society, is originally from England, and he told me that for some years in this country he had great difficulty getting his message across about the many-splendored doors of death: self-administered suicide, physician-assisted suicide, euthanasia.

"But then," Humphry said, "a wonderful thing happened. It opened all the doors for me."

"What was that wonderful thing?" I asked him.

"*Roe v. Wade*," Derek Humphry answered.

The Jesse Jackson Story

Twenty or so years ago, there was a man who foresaw the effects of abortion as a constitutional right on the fundamental values of the nation:

What happens to the mind of a person, and the moral fabric of a nation, that accepts the aborting of the life of a baby without a pang of conscience? What kind of a society will we have twenty years hence if life can be taken so casually?

The same man said back then,

There are those who argue that the right to privacy is of a higher order than the right of life. That was the premise of slavery. You could not protest the existence or treatment of slaves on the plantation because that was private and there-fore outside of your right to be concerned.

Also, he told of how he himself had almost been aborted. A doctor had told his mother to let him go, but she refused. "Don't let the pro-choicers convince you that a fetus isn't a human being," this survivor used to warn. "That's how the whites dehumanized us, by calling us niggers. The first step was to distort the image of us as human beings in order to justify that which they wanted to do – and not even feel they'd done anything wrong."

The pro-lifer I've been quoting is Jesse Jackson. He became pro-choice when he decided to run for President. He figured that was where more of the votes were. In 1994 I saw him on a train, and we talked for a while about habeas corpus and the death penalty. Finally I told him I'd been quoting the former pro-life Jesse Jackson because his writings on the subject were among the most compelling I knew.

He looked troubled, and I asked him if he had any second thoughts on having reversed his views on abortion. He looked even more troubled, and said, "I'll get back to you on that." I haven't heard from him since.

A Pro-Life Welcome?

On the other hand, not all pro-lifers have welcomed me into the fold or, in any case, have answered some of my questions as to their pro-life consistency. I've gotten to know the chairman of the House Judiciary Committee, Henry Hyde, who – unknown to most civil libertarians – is sometimes very strong on free-speech issues. But he is also a supporter of capital punishment, and I asked him how he can be pro-life and also pro-death.

He told me he'd get back to me on that. There has been no subsequent word from him, either.

A more dramatic division between me and some pro-lifers became vivid during the Reagan years. I was invited to speak at the annual Right to Life convention in Columbus, Ohio. I would be the novelty of the year – a Jewish atheist civil libertarian. A pro-lifer beyond any category they had ever seen. I expected to be warmly welcomed. The welcome turned out to be very warm indeed.

The event was held in a large field outside of the city. A rickety platform faced the almost entirely Catholic Republican crowd. I told them that, as pro-lifers, they ought to practice a consistent ethic of life. They ought to actively oppose capital punishment, preparations for war, and the life-diminishing poverty associated with the policies of then-President Ronald Reagan. I emphasized that he had just cut the budget for the WIC program (a federally funded supplemental food program for women, infants, and children).

Reagan and those who supported him – I said, rolling right along – gave credibility to Congressman Barney Frank's line, "Those who oppose abortion are pro-life only up to the moment of birth."

From the back of the large crowd, and then moving forward, there were growls, shouts, and table-pounding. They were not sounds of approval. At the end of my speech, a number of pro-lifers began rushing toward the platform. It was clear they didn't want my autograph. I said to the then-head of the National Right to Life Committee, Jack Willke, sitting next to me, "Jack, I hadn't quite made up my mind to give up my life for this cause." He smiled and moved his chair away from me.

It turned out that these souls on fire only wanted to tell me that I was in grievous error about Ronald Reagan, an exemplary Christian President. I was in error, they made it clear, because I had not yet found God. Later, in the mail, I received several bibles. It didn't work.

Out of Character for the Left to Neglect the Weak

At the *Village Voice*, my pro-life heresy has not been warmly received. Three editors, all women, stopped speaking to me after my first pro-life piece there. In two of the cases I didn't feel much of a loss. The third woman became the editor-in-chief for a time, and we agreed there were other things we can talk about.

In speaking to pro-choicers on the left, I have told them about a friend of mine and her priorities of choice. Having been active in the antiwar and civil-rights movements, Mary Meehan wrote an article for *The Progressive* in which she noted:

Some of us who went through the antiwar struggles of the 1960s and 1970s are now active in the right-to-life movement. We do not enjoy opposing our old friends on the abortion issue, but we feel that we have no choice. . . . It is out of character for the left to neglect the weak and helpless. The traditional mark of the left has been its protection of the underdog, the weak, and the poor. The unborn child is the most helpless form of humanity, even more in need of protection than the poor tenant farmer or the mental patient. The basic instinct of the left is to aid those who cannot aid themselves. And that instinct is absolutely sound. It's what keeps the human proposition going.

Agreeing with that instinct is Feminists for Life of America, my favorite advocacy group of any kind. Its founders, in the 1970s, also came out of the civil rights and antiwar movements. It keeps growing in numbers and impact, and its credo is, "We oppose all forms of violence, including abortion, euthanasia, and capital punishment, as they are inconsistent with the core feminist principles of justice, nonviolence, and nondiscrimination."

Its first president, Rachel McNair, was arrested at least seventeen times – for protesting against nuclear plants and weapons, and for passing out pro-life leaflets at abortion clinics, as well as for sitting in front of a clinic door. Somehow, Rachel and her colleagues are not much mentioned in the press; they don't fit the stereotype of pro-lifers as looking like Jesse Helms.

Pro-Choicers Purify the Species

By contrast, the press usually treats most pro-choicers with gentle care. But largely omitted are the views of those pro-choicers who regard abortion as an essential purifier of the species. I've met a goodly number of them.

In New York, when abortion was legalized in 1971, a staff commentator on WCBS radio celebrated the breakthrough by saying that abortion "is one sensible method of dealing with such problems as overpopulation, illegitimacy, and possible birth defects. *It is one way of fighting the rising welfare rolls and the increasing number of child abuse cases."* (Emphasis added.)

I've often heard this joyous analysis from some pro-choicers who prefer not to speak in this vein publicly, but are otherwise quite open about the extra dividends of abortions – a safer and more aesthetically pleasing society.

In 1992, Nicholas von Hoffman wrote in the *New York Observer*:

> Free, cheap abortion is a policy of social defense. To save our-selves from being murdered in our beds and raped on the streets, we should do everything possible to encourage preg-nant women who don't want the baby – and will not care for it – to get rid of the thing before it turns into a monster. . . .

> At their demonstrations, the anti-abortionists parade around with the pictures of dead and dismembered fetuses. The pro-abortionists should meet these displays with some of their own: pictures of the victims of the unaborted – murder vic-tims, rape victims, mutilation victims – pictures to remind us that the fight for abortion is but part of the larger struggle for safe homes and safe streets.

There's more to abortion than abortion.

Less like Robespierre than Nicholas von Hoffman is Brian Lehrer, who hosts an eminently civilized talk show on New York's WNYC, which is part of National Public Radio. He has said on the air that "We save a lot of money if we allow medical funding of abortions for women – a lot less [*sic*] kids will be on welfare."

What a blessing that will be for them.

Doctors Become Killers

A corollary dimension of the American culture of death was brought into the national consciousness with the court decisions on assisted suicide. Providing Derek Humphry with more pride and pleasure, Barbara Rothstein, chief judge of the federal district court in the state of Washington, became the first judge in the history of the nation to declare physician-assisted suicide constitutional. She likened the freedom of the terminally ill to end their lives to a woman's fundamental right to an abortion, and cited two abortion-rights decisions: *Roe v. Wade* and *Planned Parenthood v. Casey*.

Shortly thereafter, two United States Circuit Courts – the Ninth and Second Circuit Court of Appeals – made steeper the slippery slope of "privacy" by ruling that doctors had not only a right to assist in the suicides of terminal, mentally competent patients, but also a right to kill incompetent patients, under certain conditions. That is, doctors can engage in euthanasia on patients who cannot take the pills to kill themselves. No federal appellate court had ever before legitimized euthanasia and assisted suicide.

Both courts gave credit to the Supreme Court's abortion decisions – again, the privacy right to kill one's fetus can be a legal basis for getting help to kill oneself. Both courts, moreover, went beyond assisted suicide. They declared that there is not a clear line between physician-assisted suicide (the doctor supplying the lethal drugs to the patient but not being there when the patient takes them) and the *direct* administration by the doctor of the final potion.

The consequences of death as a treatment of choice were underlined two years before these decisions in a report by the New York State Task Force on Life and the Law (composed of bioethicists, lawyers, clergy, and state health officials), which said, in part:

> Assisted suicide and euthanasia will be practiced through the prism of social inequality that characterizes the services in all segments of society, including health care. Those who will be most vulnerable to abuse, error, or indifference are the poor, minorities, and those who are least educated and least empowered. . . . Many patients in large, overburdened facilities serving the urban and rural poor will not have the benefit of skilled pain management and comfort care.

Many physicians are not knowledgeable about ways to control and limit pain. And if pain is indeed uncontrolled, suicide is a most seductive alternative. Many physicians, moreover, are not able to diagnose clinical depression. When the bottomless hopelessness of the clinically depressed is not being treated, suicide can become irresistible. None of this was explored in the two historic federal court decisions. It started with *Roe v. Wade* and had now logically embraced patients of all ages.

Dr. Christoph Hufeland, a German physician, writer, and humanist (1762–1836), warned: "If the physician presumes to take into consideration in his work whether a life has value or not, the consequences are boundless and the physician becomes the most dangerous man in the state."

Nat Hentoff is a staff writer and columnist at the newspaper, Village Voice. *He is also a columnist for the United Media Syndicate (that column goes to 250 newspapers around the country), as well as at Legal Times and Editor & Publisher. This article first appeared in Mr. Hentoff's book,* Speaking Freely *(Knopf, 1997).*

Endnotes

1   Mr. Hentoff wants to make clear, that while he differs with many of the contributors on many social and political issues, he is pro-life.

Part IV
Religion

Where Are the Shepherds?

Jean Garton

It was a typically cold and overcast January day in Washington, D.C. Thousands of people had once again traveled to the Nation's Capital for the annual March for Life. These were men, women, and young people of all religious persuasions united in their opposition to the 1973 U.S. Supreme Court rulings on abortion. Their hand-drawn posters and large banners added color to the gray day and to their somber parade as they moved through the streets of the world's premier city of power and prestige.

Familiar slogans were on display with the hope that passersby and members of the press would recognize their inherent and common sense truth.

–   It's a Child Not a Choice
–   Abortion Stops a Beating Heart
–   Love Them Both
–   Jesus Loves the Little Children, Unborn Babies Too

At that year's March, however, there appeared a new and different banner. In large black letters it said: HERE ARE THE SHEEP! WHERE ARE THE SHEPHERDS?

Those few words capture the frustration of many religious people because of what they view as a lack of leadership on the part of leaders most responsible for proclaiming the biblical and historic pro-life witness. Where *are* the shepherds?

Media Spin Abortion as a "Catholic Issue"

Following the 1973 *Roe v. Wade* and *Doe v. Bolton* rulings by the United States Supreme Court, the most visible and vocal response came from the Roman Catholic Church. At the 1974 Senate hearings on a Constitutional Amendment designed to afford protection under the law to unborn children, an impressive panel of four cardinals gave testimony.[1]

The media spin following the hearing was to portray the abortion issue as Catholics versus Protestants. The shorthand version in most news reports was that the Catholic hierarchy was seeking to impose its religious views on the American public; that only Catholics opposed abortion while Protestants and Jews claimed no religious grounds for rejecting abortion. (This widespread myth continued until the 1980s when Evangelical leadership entered the public arena with a strong, articulate pro-life witness.)

On that day in 1974 (the first major public discussion of the abortion issue to involve religious leaders), the Cardinals were followed by a panel of representatives from Protestant and Jewish groups who favored abortion rights. Sound bites from their testimony were featured prominently in TV reports and newspaper articles. When, lastly, the third panel was called – Protestant, Jewish, and Mormon representatives who *opposed* abortion-on-demand – television cameras were unplugged, tape recorders were turned off, and reporters hurriedly left to meet deadlines.[2]

The Factors

Looking back over the roller-coaster history of abortion in America, many "sheep" continue to believe that the response of religious leaders has been weak and disappointing. Many factors have helped shape the muted and often absent voice of religious leaders, including the survey evidence that the majority of Americans no longer share in the basic values that once provided the framework for the fabric of Western culture.

    1   *The Clergy Factor*. There are more than 300,000 Protestant churches in the U.S. and 20,000 Roman Catholic churches.[3] Yet Catholic clergy and lay leaders have exerted the most influ-

ence in attempting to create what Pope John Paul has called "a culture of life."

2   *The Economic Factor.* Protestant clergy face practical realities from which their Catholic counterparts are protected, such as being removed by their congregation (as some have) if they speak in opposition to abortion.

3   *The Compassion Factor.* Many clergy justify their silence by claiming that they don't want to cause pain to aborted women in their midst. Their silence hurts women, especially those who need to hear a word of forgiveness as well as women contemplating an abortion who need God-directed counsel.

4   *The Feminist Factor.* Many religious leaders have been persuaded that abortion helps women; that it is a solution to their social, economic, and personal problems. Yet the feminist movement opposes telling women the risks of abortion and of the long-term consequences experienced by many aborted women.

5   *The Political Correctness Factor.* To be pro-abortion today is socially acceptable while being pro-life is not. PC adherents portray pro-lifers as mean-spirited, insensitive, and uncaring while they, in turn, conduct themselves with all the zealotry of a cult religion. Social and professional intimidation, with fear of being labeled part of the Radical Religious Far Right, has silenced many a church leader and lay person.

6   *The Media Factor.* A poll a few years ago revealed that 70 percent of respondents believe the media to be "fair and balanced" in reporting on the abortion issue. In the vacuum created by timid and intimidated church leaders, "the sheep" are left vulnerable to distorted and incomplete information.

7   *The Political Factor. Roe* and *Doe* cemented the idea in the American psyche that "if it's legal it must be right." Without strong, clear religious teaching to the contrary, the growing number of religious women having abortions has been called "The Church's Secret Shame."[4]

8   *The Medical Factor.* With indisputable evidence of the connection between abortion and breast cancer, the silence of the

medical profession on this and other complications from abortion is a betrayal of women. From the beginning, some clergy deferred to physicians who assured them that abortion was safe, easy, and a "blessing" for women.[5]

–   While these and other forces in the culture wars have hindered the effectiveness of religious pro-life leaders and denominational groups, observers might suggest that some hurdles have been self-imposed by the religious pro-life community itself.

–   A lack of understanding of the difference between an organization and a movement too often led to a one-size-fits-all way of "doing business." That overlooked the differences in ethnic groups and geographical location and the need for specialized approaches.

–   Most denominational groups structured themselves after secular organizations by establishing chapters, state affiliates, and a national board. A different model might have better served the work and witness of religious leaders.[6]

–   Some Catholic pro-lifers believe that the introduction of the Seamless Garment concept defused the Church's focus on the dire plight of the unborn.[7]

–   Pro-life churches and their organizations tend to focus on education and on producing print materials while neglecting to follow up their theological convictions with day-to-day ministry work of providing supportive services for pregnant women. This omission continues to fuel the charge that pro-lifers care only about the baby but not the woman.

–   Denominational pro-life groups often took on other battles within their church bodies, such as gay rights, evolution, the role of women and, thereby, diminished the single, sharp focus needed to fight abortion.

–   The strictures of various church bodies concerning ecclesiastical matters (such as joint worship and joint prayer) have limited attempts by religious leaders to present a unified public witness on a national scale.

–   Religious leaders often look to legislation as the answer in the struggle for the rights of the unborn. Columnist Cal Thomas offers the reminder that "There is no biblical mandate for reforming the world through government. The Kingdom of God is not going to arrive on Air Force One."[8]

From Horrible to Tolerable

Commentators have drawn a comparison between the acts of terrorism on September 11th, that claimed the lives of 3,000 innocent people, and the "terrorism" of abortion which daily claims an even larger number of innocent victims. While the date September 11th, 2001, will be embedded forever in the American psyche, the date of January 22nd, 1973, has never enjoyed that kind of impact. Yet, as Richard John Neuhaus has said, "Abortion isn't really about a woman's right to choose. Fundamentally, abortion is about the decline of human significance."[9]

With every passing year there is a loss of gravity for the continued legal destruction of millions of unborn children. The number of religious Americans involved in pro-life activities continues to decline as the country becomes increasingly desensitized to that destruction. Bonnie Chernin Rogoff, founder of Jews for Life, decries the propaganda that "slowly and carefully transforms something horrible into something tolerable." "People I speak to about partial-birth abortion used to recoil in horror at the description and leave the room; now they are able to discuss it over a sandwich and coffee."[10]

The Future

What will it take for religious leaders to make a difference in the future? What will that future even look like in terms of pro-life issues? At the 2002 conference of the California Medical Association a workshop was offered titled "Health Care War Stories and Solutions."[11] The physicians and medical personnel in attendance offered the following "solutions":

– What to do with the aged has not been solved. Eventually utilitarian motives, cost considerations, and a misunderstood "compassion" will result in new laws permitting both assisted suicide and euthanasia.

–   Abortion will become "medical" (chemical) rather than surgical, with patient and clinician anonymity leaving few options for protest.
–   Reproductive options will be limited, first, only by morality and the imagination; later, only by the imagination.
–   Human cloning will happen. Soon.
–   Gene manipulation and therapy will eventually become widespread, possibly leading to designer babies; possibly leading even to a form of eugenics.
–   Pre-natal testing, already mandated in many states for specific conditions, and enforced through threat of liability in other states, will expand to include hundreds of conditions.

As society and science move ever onward to what is technologically possible, many churches are too naively trusting or too preoccupied with internal battles to respond to the reality that their moral vision is steadily being reset by the cultural and scientific elite. Without exploring the question of the future of human nature, of man as commodity rather than creation, of the mounting assaults on whole classes of humans – *a key role of religion* – the value and dignity of all people will be radically undermined.

In terms of shaping the future, realistically and practically, it will need to be "the sheep" rather than the shepherds who take the initiative, as has been done effectively by groups such as the Knights of Columbus, Baptists for Life, Lutherans for Life, and many other denominational groups.

–   *Leaders* must be identified who are committed not only to moral clarity but to strategic clarity as well. In the past, the religious response generally has been to hold meetings, adopt statements, pass resolutions, quote Bible verses, and talk to themselves. Ideas in a vacuum – ideas by themselves – are basically worthless unless they are translated into action.
–   *Education* needs to occur in denominational schools and programs *beyond* the annual nod given on Life Sunday in January or during Respect Life Month in October. The principle of the sanctity of life ought be a core value in religious education.

– *Recruitment* is essential given the reality that major church bodies (and the pro-life movement) are aging more rapidly than is the general population. A concerted effort must be made to mentor, "draft, and help pro-life young people to enter culture-shaping professions such as the law, medicine, journalism, education, as well as religious service."

– *Visuals* are part of daily life, and Americans are assaulted by images and promotional pictures designed to sell us something. In "selling" others on the value of life, pro-life images too often have featured death rather than life. Expanded use of visuals that are positive and life-enhancing would diminish the number of people who are "turned off" to a pro-life message by gory photographs and violent images.[12]

– *Ethnic Diversification.* There is a staleness to the argument that "we've tried to get ethnic groups involved, but they don't respond." If the Same Old Same Old hasn't (and isn't) working, then it is time for a bold strategic shake-up as to how these constituencies might be reached.

– *Reaffirm the Value of Motherhood.* Ours is the first society in history to declare that raising children is *not* meaningful work. As long as the value of unborn children is diminished, then the value of conceiving children, carrying children, and caring for children will also be diminished.

The Truth Business

The evils of our age are not new, but the attacks on the less wanted, less perfect, and less affordable are escalating at a dizzying rate. People yearn for strong and bold religious leadership – leaders who will not cease to be outraged by the ongoing horror of over 40 million legal abortions.

Yet, many despair that such leaders can be found, but even that is not new in human history. On the eve of American independence, John Adams, in a lament to his wife, Abigail, said, "I'm afraid we have not Men fitted for the Times." As history unfolded, his fear was allayed by the leadership of his colleague, John Witherspoon, a "shepherd" in the Presbyterian Church, who helped educate hundreds of "sheep" who, in turn, profoundly shaped America's most important institutions.[13]

Since September 11th, 2001, the watchword in America has been "security." We expect to go to work and expect to return home again. We expect to receive mail and not fear touching a poisonous white powder. We expect to open our mailbox and not have a pipe bomb explode. We expect to be safe and secure in the privacy of our homes. Home safety is on everyone's mind. The unborn child deserves no less than to be secure in the place God intended to be the safest home of all.

Recent poll data suggest that a gradual shift in favor of "anti-abortion" sentiment is occurring. To nurture and expand that sentiment will require an unremitting and unflinching commitment to the truth. Because, as has been said by Father Frank Pavone, National Director of Priests for Life, "Truth has an attractive power of its own." The Church is in the truth business; in the Good News business. If current leaders don't recognize that they have good news for struggling pregnant women and for hurting aborted women, then for whom *does* the Church have good news?

Dr. Jean Garton is the founder of Lutherans For Life and author of the book, Who Broke the Baby? *She lectures on topics related to the Family, Education, Life Issues, and the Christian Life.*

Endnotes

1   U.S. Senate Subcommittee on Constitutional Amendments, March 7, 1974. Panel #1: Cardinals John Krol (Philadelphia), Timothy Manning (Los Angeles), Humberto Medeiros (Boston), John Cody (Chicago.)

2   *Id.,* Panel #3: Dr. Ralph Bohlmann, Executive Director of Commission on Theology, and Dr. Jean Garton (Lutheran Church-Missouri Synod); Rev. Robert Holbrook (Baptists for Life); Rabbi J. David Bleich (Rabbinical Council of America); Dr. David McKay (Church of Jesus Christ of Latter Day Saints.)

3   *World Almanac* (World Almanac Books, World Almanac Education Group, Inc. (2001).

4   Nancy Ellen Hird in *Christian Reader*, July/August 2002 at pages 55-56.

5   Dr. Bernard Nathanson, the director of the largest abortion clinic in the 1970s, promoted abortion at clergy gatherings across the country. Later, admitting responsibility for 60,000 abortions, Dr. Nathanson became an ardent pro-life advocate and a convert from atheism to Catholicism.

6   The National Pro-Life Religious Council attempts to link denominational groups for the purpose of sharing resources and programs. It is one of other models that ought be explored to increase effectiveness.

7   The late John Cardinal O'Connor of New York, addressing the primacy of abortion, said, "You can be hungry but alive. You can be homeless but alive. You can be handicapped but alive. But you can't be killed and be alive."

8   Quoted in *Family News from Focus on the Family by Dr. James Dobson*, May 2002.

9   Father Richard John Neuhaus, a former Lutheran pastor now a Catholic priest, was one of the first non-Catholic members of the clergy to give leadership on pro-life issues beginning in the late '60s.

10   Bonnie Chernin Rogoff, "Between Two Holocausts," *Celebrate Life*, July-August 2001.

11   March 4-7, 2002, Workshop #28.

12   Vacationers to a resort area at the New Jersey shore during the summer of 2002, protested the enlarged pictures of aborted babies that were flown low over the beaches, claiming that such graphic images traumatized their children.

13   Quoted in a letter by Alan R. Crippen II, Rector of the Witherspoon Fellowship.

LeChayim –
To Life! Judaism Is for Life
Rabbi Daniel Lapin and Adam L. Fuller

Since President George W. Bush's inauguration in 2001, many prominent Jewish groups have been fighting the president's judicial appointments because they fear that his nominees threaten "abortion rights." Supported not only by the American Jewish Congress and the Religious Action Center of Reform Judaism, the National Council of Jewish Women has been on a crusade, code-named "Benchmark," to keep the thirty-year-old *Roe v. Wade* decision preserved. *Roe*, of course, established the so-called constitutional right to abortion and the practice of abortion-on-demand.

A recent poll published in the heavily circulated Jewish newspaper, the *Forward*, reports that 90 percent of American Jews feel that "abortion should generally be available to those who want it."[1] Pro-life Jews are still scratching their heads trying to figure out this irony: Why are so many Jews pro-choice when abortion so obviously violates our most basic religious value, the sanctity of life? How is it that the most respected rabbinic authorities consider abortion a heinous crime in the eyes of God, yet so many Jews are fighting tooth and nail to keep it legal? Given that the right to life is valued just as much in the Jewish faith as it is in the Christian, why are more Jews not supporting their Christian allies in the pro-life movement?

An even bigger question is: Why are Jews so visible and prominent in liberal causes? Well-intentioned and philo-semitic

Americans, decent folk without an anti-Semitic bone in their bodies, are genuinely puzzled by this question. Why do the descendents of the people who gave the world the Ten Commandments seem more hostile to those Commandments than anyone else in America?

Abortion and Jewish Law

In Judaism, abortion for any reason other than saving the life of the mother is a reprehensible sin against God. In fact, we believe not only that the unborn child has a soul but that the child is taught the entire Torah by God while still in the womb. When the child is born, however, his Torah knowledge is erased, and he is given a lifetime to relearn it.

Rabbinic authorities take different approaches to explain why abortion is unjust and prohibited in Jewish law. Rabbi Yitzhak Breitowitz, a professor of law at the University of Maryland, eloquently highlights four different routes.[2] First, he explains that abortion, while not a full-fledged murder, i.e., not said to be punishable by death, is still in the "species of murder." Second, abortion frustrates the development of human life. Third, the Torah generally rebuffs the modern notion that human beings are free to choose what they can and cannot do with their own bodies. Abortion is a form of self-mutilation, and other than for lifesaving reasons, God has given us an injunction against that. Just as tattoos and body-piercing are not permitted, neither is abortion. Lastly, abortion provides a cop-out to accepting moral responsibilities towards developing life.

The Secularization of the Jewish Community

But many Jews do not accept any of this as God's directive. The Torah principle of *yeridah ha'dorot* explains, in part, why Jews are accepting Jewish law less and less: With every generation, the giving of the Torah at Mt. Sinai is moving further and further behind us in time, and Jews are therefore becoming less and less adherent to it. When God began to reveal the Torah to the Israelites at Mt. Sinai, the assembled Jews, in a combination of ecstasy and terror, found His voice overpowering. After He had spoken only the first two of the Ten Commandments (out of 613 total), they begged Moses to act as an intermediary. For the rest of the forty years the Jews spent in the Wilderness, the divine message would be conveyed with a human voice.

One has to know that Jewish attraction to liberalism is not new. In one form or another, many Jews have been liberals for more than three thousand years. Talmudic tradition reports that upon receiving the Ten Commandments, the Israelites wept. Their gloom was caused by the realization that the godly revelation they had just experienced now prohibited the lascivious lifestyle to which they had grown accustomed in Egypt. At that moment, liberalism was born: The eternal search for "liberation" from God's seemingly restrictive rules. There are those who will always seek – or if necessary, create – the escape hatch through which to flee God's rules. Liberalism, under many different names, has always found eager converts. As Aldous Huxley wrote with candor in *Confessions of a Professional Free Thinker*: "We were opposed to morality because it interfered with our sexual freedom."

Many non-observant Jews desperately pursue liberalism, *often unconsciously*, as a way out of their Covenant. Think of entertainers like Woody Allen to know how obsessed with God many Jews are, long after they have shrugged off any intimate relationship with Him. Most vacationing Jews who order bacon and eggs for breakfast invariably glance around guiltily as if expecting Moses, or at least their rabbi, to suddenly walk into the hotel dining room. Not every single Jewish liberal is consciously aware of trying to escape God's rules, but this underlying principle fuels all of secular liberalism's adherents. It is the true purpose of liberalism. Jews who do observe God's rules – kosher food laws, the Sabbath, and marital laws – know it is not easy. Those who do not observe these laws feel lingering guilt, and resent any suggestion that these laws are as binding today as they were on the day they were given from Mt. Sinai.

Adhering to some of God's rules suggests that the Jewish soul owes allegiance to them all. Is God your boss or isn't he? Better to reject them all than feel obligated to abide by any. Once eating lobster is normalized, eventually homosexuality and abortion are also permitted, even if it takes a few generations to get there. The more you need to rationalize eating lobster, the more you need to insist that everything else is all right too. How intoxicating and liberating the rejection of God's Law can seem for Jews! How appealing is liberalism.

This explains why non-observant Jews often lead the fight for the acceptance of homosexuality as a normative lifestyle. The only timeless stand against sodomy is the Bible's. With regard to abortion, non-observant Jews insist that only the woman should exercise veto power over the next generation because any other position concedes the existence of an external authority for our values. Modern liberalism simply means becoming "liberated" from the external authority of God. God either does not exist or He is irrelevant, so He and His ways are out-of-date, out-of-touch, and unnecessarily repressive compared to the enlightened wisdom of humankind.

Liberal Jews increasingly reject the understanding, held for millennia, that God has eternal directives, in both written and oral tradition, for the Jewish people. Some secular Jews deny their Jewish identity altogether, although this is thankfully not widespread. Most Jews call themselves "culturally Jewish," picking and choosing the beliefs that "work" for each person individually. This lets them maintain a uniquely non-Christian identity and provides an alternative to cutting Torah off entirely, while remaining partly "spiritual." Liberal Jews love "spirituality" because it assures them that they can enjoy God's presence in their lives without first submitting to His demands.

For the most part, liberal Jews embrace a uniquely American form of atheism, which applauds a lying, philandering, scandal-ridden president who leaves church with a Bible clutched under his arm only to rush across town and address a defiant, fund-raising gathering of ultra-Left Hollywood abortion activists. America's unique form of atheism enables people to arrive at their houses of worship in order to participate in a gay-pride service. This form of atheism declares, of course, that religion and God are important, but that their importance is either confined to the ethereal or that God and religion should be formed in our own image. Sure we believe in God, says the liberal. In whatever form He, She, or It may take for each individual.

People who entirely reject religious faith are rejecting the best avenue for grasping spiritual reality. They are therefore making a choice to remain in the grip of materialism. This simply means that they experience little or nothing in their daily lives that is not constrained by the natural limitations of physical matter. They have chosen not to relate to anything they cannot see, touch, eat or wear. Their life is, well, limited. This is largely why they are unable to see abortion as the heinous act that it is. They see neither the infant, nor the infant's soul.

For secular humanists, the only glimpses into a transcendent eternity are the transforming moments into and out of physical life: sex, then death. This is why Hollywood is consumed with dramatizing the two ends of life: Sex is often the act of conceiving life, and violence is often the act of bidding it farewell. Just as liberal Jews hang on to a limited sense of spirituality, everyone is captivated by sex and violence because their souls yearn for contact with the infinite. This is why it is now easier for Americans to deny the tremendous ramifications of abortion. What does life mean for them without God? The unborn child is given life – very undeveloped life – but life still, and then it is given death. In Judaism and Christianity, "living" is a wonderful God-given privilege, but what does it mean for an atheist?

The Jewish Lobby and the Pro-Choice Movement

Now, having explained why individuals of Jewish ancestry may be radically liberal, why do so many *official* voices of the Jewish community line up at the liberal end? What does protecting a woman's so-called "right to choose" have to do with the missions of Jewish groups like the Anti-Defamation League or the American Jewish Congress?

The standard answer to this question from the Jewish leadership is that Jews identify with the downtrodden because of their history of persecution. We assume liberalism to be a kinder, gentler philosophy than conservatism. Liberalism seems to be morally superior, and in fact, many warm-hearted, well-meaning Jews have been told so by their rabbis and the leadership of Jewish organizations. Each year, Jews read the words in the Passover Seder: "Remember that you were once slaves in the land of Egypt." The Egyptian experience was the first in a long sequence of oppressions. Jews have retained that feeling in our national consciousness, leading to a tendency to identify with the underdog.

But, while this may be true on an individual level, it is unconvincing when applied to the community at large. Indeed, the Jewish community does not support all underdogs. It sympathizes very selectively, picking and choosing its issues very carefully. Invariably, the majority of so-called Jewish organizations, and certainly the large nationally known ones, will line up not with the underdog but with secular liberal dogma. In the case of abortion, for example, the "little guy" is ironically not the unborn child, but the pregnant woman. And they tell themselves that they are doing the morally correct thing.

In sum, Jewish groups have redefined Judaism to mean liberalism. And, because Judaism now means liberalism, it stands to reason that opponents to liberalism – conservatives – are anti-Semitic. This is not only intellectually dishonest; it is reprehensible. Anti-Semitism is often an unfair charge because it is undefined – which leaves the accused with no way to clear himself. If he did not do something to hurt Jews, then he must have said something to offend Jews. If he cannot be proven to have said anything nasty about Jews, then maybe he thought something we Jews might find offensive, and naturally we claim to know what was in his heart. The unfounded charge of "anti-Semite" brands the victim and leaves the accuser absolved. It is time for us to recognize the charge of anti-Semitism for what it often is: A political weapon intended to bludgeon critics of liberalism into silence.

Rethinking Who Our Friends Are

The time has also come for American Jewish conservatives, be they Orthodox, Reform, Conservative, or unaffiliated, to identify themselves proudly. We should publicly distance ourselves from the

Judaism-equals-liberalism equation. We should recognize and proclaim that much of what the Jewish community decries as anti-
Semitism is really anti-liberalism. We should unite with Christians
against anti-Christian bigotry just as firmly as we stand against
anti-Semitism. Throughout Jewish history, responsible rabbinical
leadership has always questioned the wisdom of a minority Jewish
population conspicuously opposing the Jewish establishment. On
abortion, however, the official Jewish voice is anti-biblical, which
makes it nothing but the gravest folly.

We should recognize that while our theological perspectives
are different, we really do have a lot more in common with
Christians than most Jews tend to think. After all, our value systems both derive from the same testament, the Torah. Especially
when we consider that conservative political views held by many
Christians follow naturally from Jewish tradition, the message is
clear: It is time for Jewish leaders to rethink their accustomed loyalty to secular liberalism, including the commitment to "abortion
rights."

In light of what has been on the minds of Jews lately –
America's war on terrorism and Israel's national security problem,
we can certainly be optimistic that Jewish sentiments are showing
signs of change. Jews are beginning to rethink the premise that
Judaism and liberalism are one and the same, and that conservatism is another word for anti-Semitism. We have seen certain
Jewish leaders express true graciousness toward America's
Christian culture, which has done so much to ensure American
support of Israel. Gary Rosenblatt, editor of New York City's *Jewish
Week*, tells of the conversation he had with a newly enlightened
Abraham Foxman of the Anti-Defamation League, who bumped
into the Christian leader Gary Bauer and *thanked him* for his efforts
on behalf of Israel. The ADL also recently ran an advertisement in
six newspapers reprinting an article by Ralph Reed, former head of
the Christian Coalition, explaining his support for Israel. That is the
same Christian Coalition whose founder, Rev. Pat Robertson, the
ADL had slandered in its notorious 1994 report *The Religious Right:
The Assault on Tolerance and Pluralism*.

The next step is for the Jewish establishment to rethink its opposition to the Christian political leadership on issues not specific to U.S. or Israeli national security. Proud Jews need to rethink exactly what it is about being Jewish that makes them proud. Is it the Torah, or is it fear of Christians? If they believe, as Jews should, that the Jewish nation exists because of a divine revelation our ancestors experienced at Mt. Sinai with the giving of the Torah, then they will have no choice but to recognize the teaching of the Torah, to wit that God has given the unborn child a soul.

Jews must stop fighting Christians on the issue of abortion. Protecting the unborn should not be a Christian "obsession;" it is a *Judeo*-Christian responsibility. Every Jew should recognize this.

Rabbi Daniel Lapin is the author of many books and the President of Toward Tradition. Adam Fuller is a Ph.D. candidate in Political Science at the Claremont Graduate University.

Endnotes

1   "Women's Group Vows Full-Court Press In Vetting Judge Nominees on Abortion," *The Forward* (15 February 2002).
2   Speech, "The Sanctity of Life and Jewish Abortions," American Jewish Assembly meeting, The Silver Spring Jewish Center, July 9, 1995.

An Islamic View of Life Issues and the West

Dr. A. Majid Katme

My professional pro-life journey started approximately ten years ago, when I was named the Muslim Coordinator for the Society for the Protection of Unborn Children in London (SPUC), England. I represent a community of approximately 2 million British Muslims, and my work includes lobbying Members of Parliament and keeping my community informed about legal and policy developments on the life issues, especially the fact that 600 innocent and healthy babies are killed by abortion in Great Britain every day!

I have also attended several United Nations Conferences, including those on Population and Development in Cairo (September 1994), on Social Development in Copenhagen (March 1995), on Women in Beijing (September 1995), on Habitat and Housing in Istanbul (June 1996), on Food in Rome (November 1996), and on the International Criminal Court, also in Rome (June 1998). I was honored to address the international Conferences on the Family – in Prague in 1997, and in Manila in 1999.

I was and am grateful to God and to my organization, SPUC, for the opportunity to participate in these meetings, to learn what is happening internationally, to represent my people, and to share the Islamic view on matters so vitally important to the family, and therefore to society.

The Islamic View of Life Issues

I feel strongly about the pro-life movement – as a doctor, as a human being, and as a Muslim.

Islam is poorly understood, even distorted, in the West, especially in the mass media. This widespread ignorance was aggravated, of course, with the events of September 11, which were painful for all people of good will, but painful in a distinct way for peace-loving Muslims.

Complicating matters is that Muslims themselves are increasingly ignorant of Islamic teachings, and a rising number are becoming secular Muslims, influenced by – and then working with – some of the anti-life groups at the United Nations. So too are some Muslim governments turning away from Islam's teachings, succumbing to the U.N. and to the secular ways of the West. Still, an Islamic culture will persist, and the West should try to understand it, for it has shaped and will shape the Muslim people, even when many Muslims mix it with secular elements.

The Muslims of the world have primarily two sacred sources and references: First, we have the last Holy Book: *Al Qur'an*; then we have the sayings and actions of the last prophet, Muhammad (*ahadith / sunnah*) (peace be upon him). Practicing Muslims believe in God, the Creator, who is the Author of all life. We believe that human life is sacred, from the moment of its creation at conception, to its end at natural death. We also believe in the Ten Commandments, the miraculous conception of Jesus (peace be upon him) and in his Mother, the Blessed Virgin Mary. Islam has five "pillars": (1) Belief in One God and Muhammad as God's last prophet; (2) Praying five times a day; (3) Fasting in the Holy month of Ramadan; (4) Zakat, or giving to the poor; and (5) Making the pilgrimage to Makkah (Mecca), the birth place of Muhammad, once in one's life.

At the time of the life of the last prophet, Muhammad (peace be upon him), there was not a single case of abortion, and in one case of adultery, he protected the right to life of the child conceived. In addition, the Holy Book, *Al Qur'an*, has many verses which clearly forbid the taking of any child's life – indeed, of any human being's life. For example:

> In the name of God (Allah), the Most Compassionate and the Most Merciful:

> Do not *kill* or take human life which God has declared sacred . . . (Chapter 6, verse 151)

> *Do not* kill *your children for fear of poverty, it is we who shall provide sustenance for them as well as you. Killing them is certainly a great sin ... (Chapter 17, verse 31)*

> *Whoever* kills *a human being (a soul), unless it be for murder or corruption on earth, it is as though he had killed all mankind*, and whoever saves a life, *it is as though he had saved the life of all mankind . . . (Chapter 5, verse 31) (emphasis added)*

Not only these, but Islam has punishments for any one performing or assisting in abortion. Islam also has given many and varied human rights to the child not yet born (the fetus), such as good nutrition, rights of inheritance, the right to a will, and the right to lineage (to know his parents), etc. Indeed, the fetus is recognized just as a "fully born" child would be.

Muslims also believe in the sanctity of the family and sexual morality. We honor and try to protect chastity, marriage, motherhood, and responsible parenthood.

Accordingly, Islamic teachings and much of the Muslim world are decidedly against – indeed, horrified by – abortion, euthanasia, adultery and fornication, sexual promiscuity, homosexuality, population control, pornography, sex and violence in the media, designer babies, egg and sperm donation, genetic engineering, embryo research, and human cloning.

All these practices threaten the security of families and therefore the well being of both children and parents, and society at large. In the Muslim tradition, any pregnancy is a day of celebration, and any child is a gift from God, for which one should be grateful. Chastity until marriage is the norm, and marriage and family are respected and honored. Children, even many children, are encouraged, with full parental responsibility.

Islam also encourages the extended family – grandparents, uncles, aunts, brothers and sisters, as a haven for security, education and support.

The Islamic View of Women

Perhaps the most misunderstood issue of Islam, especially by Western people, is the Muslim view of women.

The world should know, first, that Islam teaches that man and woman are equal in the eyes of God. Both shall be rewarded or punished, both will enter either Heaven or Hell. They are equal. Islam also encourages education for women, just as it does for men, and protects the civil rights of women, such as the right to the vote and to free speech. In fact, the rights of Muslim women are superior to the rights of many other women in the world, for Islam also protects: the right to full financial support by the husband and by the state; the right to own property and to receive inheritances; the right to consent to marriage (Islam is against forced marriages); the right to decide on family size; and the right to be treated gently, kindly and humanely by father, husband and children with full sustenance, for the last prophet Muhammad has stated: "Heaven is under the feet of your Mother."

The problem is that many Muslim women do not know these rights and do not ask for them. In addition, cultural factors – such as men's narrow mentality in some countries – negatively affect the position and image of Muslim women.

But Islam recognizes the biological differences between men and women and how those differences matter in psychology, reproduction, and roles in life. In particular, Islam honors motherhood and encourages women to be educated and prepared for this most important job. Islam regards healthy pregnancies – including prenatal care, natural birth, and breast-feeding – as important aspects of women's health.

Islam also encourages modesty in one's appearance – to avoid problems such as male temptation, sexual harassment of women, rape, or adultery. Modesty, decency, and legitimacy are important rules in Islam for the sake of all of us. In some parts of the world, girls are genitally mutilated so that they cannot take pleasure in sexual relations. Islam has no such order or practice. On the contrary, Islam recognizes and protects a woman's right to sexual satisfaction in marriage. Muslims circumcise their sons especially for hygienic and health reasons.

Islamic View and Impressions of the West: The United Nations, the Mass Media

I have had occasion to work with many pro-life, Christian groups since my affiliation with SPUC. But one's impression of the West is not derived from these groups. On the contrary, the world has two main sources of information on the West: First and most importantly, is the impression created by the mass media, not only in news reports, but in entertainment with movies and television. The second source, especially for me, is the face put forward at international gatherings such as the aforementioned United Nations' conferences.

Muslim believers (and many Christian believers) are shocked to see the introduction and advance of so many anti-life and anti-family ideas at United Nations conferences. The radical notions in so many draft documents are clear for anyone to see, and include:

1   the assumption that abortion is a "reproductive right" or part of "reproductive health;"
2   immoral sexual behavior (such as fornication, adultery, homosexuality) characterized as sexual "rights;"
3   the distribution and imparting of explicit sexual information to children in the name of "sex ed;"
4   the complete disregard for and rejection of natural, normal, traditional marriage and family with the promotion of homosexual couplings (called "various forms of the family");
5   the undermining of parental responsibility with the creation of so-called children's "rights;"
6   the denigration of motherhood;

7   the contempt for chastity and femininity; and, most recently

8   the attempt to characterize the condition of pregnancy, if unexpected or undesired, as "forced" and therefore a crime against women and humanity.

It should be obvious that this agenda means decadence and immorality of the most de-stabilizing kind. The planet would be a mess if societies were to adopt these horrifying and destructive UN plans. Indeed, the United States, for all its admirable qualities, is now reeling from the societal effects of these very ideas and practices (divorce, abortion, abandoned children, sexual promiscuity, sexual disease, pornography, etc.) – and yet, this is what the West seems to have in mind for the rest of the world!

The UN is responsible for "family planning" clinics in many Muslim countries – these clinics are not about true family planning, where mothers and fathers welcome children, or space children, in family life. They are, instead, run by population control-minded organizations such as the IPPF (International Planned Parenthood Federation) and the UNFPA (United Nations Family Planning Association) – the same organizations which push the immoral and radical ideas mentioned above. "Family planning" is a euphemism for their anti-life and anti-family agenda, which threatens Islam. On top of that, a large number of Muslim governments are going secular, some because of promised international money, some because of ideological corruption, but the result is the same: They are going away from the teachings of Islam, to the dismay of the Muslim people, in favor of a Godless and immoral way of life that will destroy the family – and our culture – as we know it.

What we see in the mass media – both news and entertainment – simply reinforces the impressions created at the United Nations. Sex and violence, both real (in the crime reports), and made-up (in the movies and on television) are everywhere. America exports this to the rest of the world. Anti-American sentiment, at least among Muslims, has much to do with the global exportation of this immorality.[1]

Natural Compatibility with Western Pro-Life Groups

Happily, there are groups from the West who are as alarmed about these trends as we are. Muslims and western pro-life groups (and international ones), and specifically Christian believers, have formed a natural alliance with Muslims at UN meetings. We simply discovered that we talk the same language and share the same concerns. After all, we believe we have the same source of life – God, our Creator. Obviously, we have our differences, too, but these are to be respected. We Muslims are ordered in the *Qur'an* and by the last prophet, Muhammad (peace be upon him) to work with anybody on shared moral convictions, and to respect Christian, Jewish, etc., beliefs.

I am personally reaching out to many Christian organizations as the Muslim Coordinator for SPUC. This work is long overdue, because of our shared concerns, but coalitions have developed spontaneously and successfully up to this point. For the future, these coalitions could be more formal and more long-standing (at present, they exist only for short time periods).

For years I have thought to tour the U.S. to act as a catalyst for many pro-life, pro-family, Christian-Muslim conferences and meetings. Over 7 million Muslims live in America. They are a great potential resource for the pro-life movement there.

Also needed is an educational campaign about the dangers of the UN, using all communications avenues (internet, radio, TV, etc.). We should remember that fifty-six Muslim countries are members of the UN, with approximately 1.5 billion Muslims. If these nations can be informed of the immoral UN agenda, and mobilized against it, their strength and efficacy could be great.

We should remember too that abortion is in many ways a *symptom* – a natural byproduct of a culture that does not honor chastity or practice abstinence. Given this, I am not surprised to see so many pro-life organizations adding abstinence to their campaigns. If we could be successful with a message of decency and sexual morality, we would not only stop abortions, but also prevent all of the sexually transmitted diseases, which are now so numerous, along with the scourge of AIDS, which is a top killer in some countries. Many social problems would also be alleviated, including drug abuse, and the crime that so often goes with this.

It is encouraging, though, that so much data now exist – statistics on health, social science findings, psychological studies – which support the call for sexual morality.

We must also, of course, counter the population control propaganda (many Muslims believe that population control is a conspiracy to reduce the number of Muslims in the world!) and stop the pro-abortion organizations such as UNFPA and IPPF, especially in Muslim countries. For this, however, a lot of money will be needed, as these organizations are well funded, including funds by governments.

Because our values are *eternal* and of *divine origin*, they will certainly be *victorious*. We must simply open our hearts and do our homework. Because the fight for life is above all else a spiritual fight, we must also pray at all times to God for guidance and support.

Dr. A Majid Katme is the Spokesman for the Islamic Medical Association and Muslim Coordinator for the London-based Society for the Protection of Unborn Children (SPUC). He is available to speak on any aspect of this article and can be reached through SPUC. www.spuc.org.uk/index.htm or by e mail at akatme@hotmail.com.

Endnote

1   Of course, Muslims also object to U.S. support for Israel, against the Palestinian Refugees, and this contributes to anti-American sentiment as well.

Part V
The Culture

The Problem of Selling Half the Story

Barbara R. Nicolosi

There is no arena of American society that has been more consistently and squarely pro-choice than the entertainment industry. In politics, law, medicine, and religion, pro-life heroes have risen up, and have managed to keep the sanctity of life-flame flickering. This is not the case in the world of mainstream entertainment. Everybody with any real power in movies and television is either hysterically pro-choice, or else indignantly pro-choice, or else so completely engulfed in the abortion mentality that questioning it strikes them as annoyingly bizarre, like questioning the morality of dental floss or Belgian waffles.

But thirty years into this total domination of the culture of entertainment, polls continue to show the American public ambivalent about abortion. And strangely, despite the passionate consensus about the glory of the pro-choice cause among entertainment artists and executives, there has not been the full-scale onslaught on this issue that we have seen addressed to other areas of social policy like racism or anti-Semitism, as in the hundreds of Holocaust films. Truly, never have so many powerful people done so little to make an impact on an issue about which they feel so desperately. The question is, "Why?"

For answers, we will consider some of the industry's most recent attempts to address abortion rights in cinema and on television. What do these projects have to say to us? Have there been any kind of similar pro-life forays on the screen? Should there be?

Making Abortion Movies

Most entertainment projects stumble and are reworked in the production process because of ideological or creative differences among the writers, directors, actors, networks, and studios. But a survey of the few existing abortion films shows that they had the blessing of the industry establishment, were eagerly campaigned for by top talent, and were assured from the outset of grave, but enthusiastic reviews from the film press.

Because these projects have come out of a creative community that is so stunningly single-minded about abortion, they represent an unmediated platform from which pro-choice advocates can make their case. No "checks and balances" exist. In these films, pro-choice advocates can say whatever they want, limited only by the broad conventions of cinema storytelling to get and hold a viewer's attention.

Skilled filmmakers know that the best way to reveal character is to reveal what a character notices. A good film will reveal that a woman wants to have a child, by bringing her into a busy train station and having her notice the one baby carriage amidst the chaos. In the same way, abortion films reveal the pro-choice movement's preoccupations with abortion. They aim to be mirrors, revealing the women who choose abortion, the supporters of abortion rights, and most particularly, the pro-life movement to itself and to the broader audience. Their relative failure to get us right should not stop us from reflecting on their perception of us. Watching these films is a school of what the pro-choice movement, and probably about half of America, hears us saying (as opposed to what we think we are saying), which of our arguments have landed (and should be developed), and which fall on completely deaf ears (and should be abandoned).

> "Could you help me? Could you throw away your morals for once, and could you help me?"
> (*If These Walls Could Talk*, HBO)

If These Walls Could Talk, originally aired 10/13/96 on HBO Directed by Nancy Savoca, Cher; Teleplays by Nancy Savoca,

Susan Nanus, and I. Marlene King; Stories by Pamela Wallace and Earl Wallace, Nancy Savoca, and I. Marlene King

Daily Variety's review of this Emmy-winning HBO movie raved, "The cast is terrific! Watching two dozen of the most interesting actresses in American cinema is rewarding in its own right." Indeed. This film is hard for pro-lifers to watch mainly because of the sense of devastating futility that arises in seeing the panoply of talent in it. Even if the pro-life movement had $100 million to spend on a movie, we couldn't marshal these names. Along with Academy Award-winning actresses Cher and Sissy Spacek, the cast boasts a whole "we're standing up to be counted" roster of other stars including Demi Moore, Anne Heche, Rita Wilson, Craig T. Nelson, Eileen Brennan, CCH Pounder, Jada Pinkett Smith, Shirley Knight, Joanna Gleason, and Catherine Keener.

The film unfolds as three unwanted-pregnancy vignettes from different decades that all take place in the same house. The concept is to help the viewer realize how far women have come in being freed from the tyranny of pregnancy, and yet how far women still have to go to be freed from the fanatical and even murderous designs of some pro-life activists.

The first story, set in 1952, concerns a widowed nurse named Claire, played very well by Demi Moore. In a moment of apparently conscience-numbing grief, Claire had a quickie with her dead husband's younger brother, and is now pregnant with his child. Unwilling to expose him and herself to her Irish-Catholic in-laws, Claire sets out to find an underground abortionist to evacuate her womb. There are two really revolting scenes meant to make the viewer quake with horror at the things women used to go through before the days of legal abortion. In one scene we get to watch Claire trying to end her pregnancy with a knitting needle. The episode culminates with a dastardly "back alley abortionist" leaving Claire bloody and nearly dead on the floor of her kitchen.

Set in 1974, the second episode finds Barbara, a mother of four, played by Sissy Spacek, finally able to pursue her own dreams by going to college. Just as she starts to distinguish herself as a brilliant scholar with tremendous potential, she discovers she is pregnant. She doesn't want any more children, and so begins her own investigation of whether abortion would be a good choice for her. She reads important works like *Our Bodies Our Selves* and has heart-to-heart talks with her cool feminist daughter, and her clueless and definitely uncool working-class husband. In the end, Barbara decides to have the unwanted child and end all her chances of curing cancer or solving the problem of nuclear fission. Sigh.

The third vignette introduces us to bright young college student, Christine, played by Anne Heche, who has been impregnated and dumped by one of her professors. Her roommate, Patti, played by Jada Pinket Smith, reminds her that she has always been pro-life, but Chris now realizes that until a woman faces an unplanned pregnancy, she has no right to make value judgments about other women's choices. Chris visits her local abortion clinic, where she encounters a group of polyester-clad pro-lifers praying outside the clinic, led by a really creepy Eileen Brennan. Once she gets inside, there is a strange scene in which she is actually counseled against the abortion by a caring and earnest counselor. Apparently, this clinic is much more of a ministry than a business.

Eventually, Chris returns to the clinic where her womb is tenderly sucked empty by a gentle and compassionate abortionist, named Dr. Thompson, played by Cher. In a bizarre moment meant to contrast with the horror of the Demi Moore episode, Cher's abortionist talks Christine through the procedure, over the macabre rumbling of the suction machine in the background. Just as the abortion is over, the door is smashed in, and a wild-eyed young pro-life activist shoots Dr. Thompson in the chest. Chris scoops the dying abortionist into her arms and weeps for herself, and presumably for all women.

"Decisions can be painful, after all." (*The Cider House Rules*)

The Cider House Rules (Miramax)
Directed by Lasse Hallstrom
Screenplay written by John Irving, based on his book

A lot of good people liked this movie. I heard the case made several times that the film was a sensitive, coming-of-age story, and that abortion was just a sideline in the background. No, as John Irving described it in his Academy Award acceptance speech, *The Cider House Rules* is really one thing: "a movie about abortion." It tells the story of one young man who learns to reject his natural repulsion towards abortion, and becomes an abortionist himself. All the other stuff is window dressing.

The story begins in a quaint orphanage in Maine, run by a kindly Dr. Wilbur Larch, played by Michael Caine, a role for which he received an Academy Award. Except for being addicted to ether, Dr. Larch is fundamentally a wise and loving man, who, in the era before legal abortion, courageously provides the procedure whenever a woman really seems to need one. His young apprentice, Homer, played by Toby Maguire, opens a bucket one day after an abortion and winces at the contents. The viewers are not shown what he sees, but whatever it is, it convinces Homer that performing abortions is not something he wants to do.

Homer's repulsion for abortion leads to tension between him and his mentor, and Homer eventually leaves the orphanage in the company of some new friends, a young couple who have just had Dr. Larch abort their child. There follows a long, meandering storyline in which Homer purportedly finds maturity by having an affair with the female half of the young couple. The story climaxes when a young girl, whose father has sexually molested her, presents herself before Homer, and in a flush of new insight, he finds the compassion to perform an abortion on her. The film ends with Homer returning to the orphanage to replace the now-dead Dr. Larch. Whether Homer also becomes an ether addict is not alluded to in the script.

This film is difficult to watch mainly because it drags on endlessly and has very little story movement. It would not have registered a bleep with audiences if it hadn't championed abortion with the vigorous support of the industry.

> "There's a certain American spirit that says, "Fuck it . . . let's laugh at anything."
>
> (Writer/Director Payne on his film, Citizen Ruth – http://www.film-vault.com/filmvault/alibi/c/citizenruth_.html)

Citizen Ruth (Miramax)
Directed by Alexander Payne; Written by Alexander Payne and Jim Tayler

Conceived as a dark comedy, but ultimately much more bizarre than funny, *Citizen Ruth* styles itself as a view from outside the abortion controversy. This movie is much less about abortion and much more about the filmmakers' view of the kinds of people who line up passionately on both sides of the issue. And yet, as with most of the industry's attempts to be balanced on this question, the tie always goes to abortion rights. There are a few humorous lobs thrown at the pro-choice advocates in the film, but the pro-lifers are served up with scathing sneers. The film is hard to watch because it does nail how some of the members of the pro-life community look and sound. I know the people the film is caricaturing, and it is hurtful to see them flayed so brutally on the screen principally because of the way they dress, or because they are so cluelessly un-hip, or because of the simple way they express themselves.

The film tells the story of a woman named Ruth, who is home-less and filthy, a social drop-out, an absentee mother, a liar, a sub-stance abuser, and a thief. In a skilled performance by the talented Laura Dern, Ruth comes off not so much as being evil but as being just a complete dunderhead. She has no goals, no good qualities, and not a single conviction that she won't bargain away to indulge her addiction to paint fumes.

Arrested for vagrancy, it is discovered that the hapless Ruth is pregnant. She is ordered by a frustrated judge to end the pregnan-cy or face a long term in prison. Immediately, Ruth finds herself at the center of the national debate on abortion with both sides using her pregnancy as a platform to trumpet their cause. First spirited away by Bible-quoting pro-lifers, Ruth is soon rescued by a couple of Wiccan lesbians who are determined to help Ruth terminate her pregnancy . . . if that's the choice she really wants to make . . . of course. In the end, Ruth miscarries her baby and evades a crowd of the furious and fundamentally absurd adversaries who are so busy fighting over her that they don't even notice as she slips away through their midst.

The most insidious thing about *Citizen Ruth* is not its scathing portrayal of pro-lifers, but rather its insinuation that the real enemy in society are people who feel passionately about political issues. The movie validates viewers who would rather not have to think about complex social problems. One Internet reviewer describes the experience of watching the film as being overtaken by the "overwhelming desire to leave this no-win debate." (Christopher Null, http://www.eclectica.org/v1n7/null_reviews.html).

> "Mr. Chairman, I find the term 'propensity for abortion' misrepresentative of my position. I have a propensity for a woman's right to choose."
> (from *The Contender*)

The Contender
Directed and written by Rod Lurie
The Contender is not a film about abortion as much as it is an elaborate defense of Bill Clinton's ability to be a judicious statesman in his public life, while being a misogynist asshole in his private life. However, in the end, the issue here that separates the hypocrites from the heroes is abortion rights. And of course, we're not the heroes.

Except for the nauseatingly long, left-wing apologias at the end, *The Contender* is a well-produced, well-written, and very well-acted drama. Joan Allen was nominated for an Academy Award for her convincing portrayal of Senator Laine Hanson, the president's pick to replace a vice president who has died in office. Brilliant, principled, beautiful, witty, a loving mother, and a savvy politician, Sen. Hanson is a shoo-in for the office until an accusation arises that once in her college days she was a wild and willing participant in a fraternity sex orgy. Citing her deeply held conviction that her personal life is nobody's business but her own, the Senator refuses to confirm or deny the accusation, thereby jeopardizing her nomination.

With the scent of blood in his dastardly Republican nostrils, the Congressional committee chairman plots her demise, principally for her pro-choice views. His wife comes to the beleaguered

Senator Hanson at night, and reveals that she herself has had an abortion, and that her husband is a hypocrite for working to deprive other women of the same possibility.

The film ends with what for liberals must be a very stirring diatribe against the new McCarthyism (of holding politicians to a higher standard) by an incensed president, played by Jeff Bridges. In an ultimately unfeminist ending, Sen. Hanson is saved and raised to glory by the intercession of the white male president.

The Arguments

In the small canon of abortion movies, *If These Walls Could Talk* is regarded by pro-choice advocates as an extremely fair and balanced consideration of the abortion issue. Most critics cough slightly over the portrayal of some of the pro-lifers in the film, but basically give the production raves for its earnest and heartfelt exploration. This is interesting because the film stops short of giving any thoughtful pro-life argument a forum.

In the first vignette, when Claire finally reveals her problem to her pregnant – with too many kids already! – sister-in-law, the other woman withdraws in horror without furnishing a single reason why abortion might be a bad choice. In the second episode, the only person who seems to have angst about abortion is Barbara's husband. But he ultimately can give her no reason to keep the baby, except for drearily shrugging something like, "we'll make it through somehow." In the third episode, Patti, the pro-life roommate, who eventually escorts her best friend to the abortion clinic, makes the case to Christine that, "I know you. If you do make this choice, you will be haunted by it." She never says why, and the idea is left hanging in the air that Chris's Catholic upbringing is probably the reason.

The abortion films universally work very hard to establish that the main reason to have abortion is basically because some women need them. To their credit, contemporary abortion stories in both feature films and TV shows avoid presenting the extreme pregnancy situations – abortion, rape, incest, or life of the mother – that we have heard trumpeted *ad nauseam* by so many cowering "personally against abortion, but" politicians. (It is only the movie written, produced, and directed by men, *The Cider House Rules,* that falls back on incest against a minor female as the ultimate case for abortion.) These movies are all about abortion as a civil right, as basic self-determination and autonomy for women. The screaming of the pro-lifers in the background about the life of the fetus doesn't even register as a real argument. That pro-lifers hold fetuses sacred holds the same weight for pro-choicers as that people in India hold cows sacred. "That's fine if that's what they want to think, but how dare the Indians ever try to stop Americans from eating hamburger!"

If anything comes through in screening all the abortion films, it's that we can't keep shouting "Baby!" while the other side shouts back "Woman!" They don't see it, anymore than I would see it if a bunch of hysterical Hindus accosted me at McDonalds and pointing at my hamburger, shouted, "Murderer!" All I could say to them would be, "I'm sorry that you think so. I don't."

They know we think it's a baby. We can stop shouting that now. We should try to make a case based on their own main argument, namely that abortion is a civil right. Can we make the case that civil rights don't exist in a vacuum? What is it that qualifies even basic civil rights?

Each film eventually makes the point that their position is not pro-abortion but rather pro-choice. We have to give them this. We who like to call ourselves pro-life are actually very much anti-abortion, but those on the other side of the issue are not pro-abortion in the sense of favoring abortion over giving birth. We should take them at their word that they really don't care what a woman does with her pregnancy, as long as she has all her options open. Calling them pro-abortion is a real source of rage for them. It suggests that they are hypocritical in the one area that makes abortion so necessary in their view of life: personal freedom. In the end, calling them pro-abortion amounts to silly name-calling that only gets in the way of any real dialogue.

Another strong theme in the films is that as long as men are basically, well, pigs, abortion will be a sad but necessary part of human life. Pretty nearly all of the white men in the abortion movies come off very badly. They tend to prey on women and patronize women and then abandon women to face unplanned pregnancies alone. One of the most effective lines in *If These Walls Could Talk* comes when Chris, the college student, cries out from her chair in the abortion clinic against the man who used and then dumped her. "It isn't fair! Why doesn't he have to be here too!" The line resonates because she's right. It isn't fair that men don't have to go through unplanned pregnancies. We can try to make the case that all men are not pigs, but in the end our most effective answer will be to raise a new generation of sons who are respectful of women and able to take responsibility for the pregnancies they cause. This one is a long-term fix.

A New Kind of Hero

One of the weirdest aspects of the abortion movies is their attempt to recast the role of the movie hero into the radical providers and protectors of abortion rights. It's a hard sell because traditionally in movies, heroes are those who do the right thing, not those who do a regrettable thing.

Universally, the pro-choice hero characters are presented as ambivalent about the difficult choice involved in having an abortion, and their very heroism is couched in their ability to swallow their ambivalence to help women in need. In *The Cider House Rules*, Dr. Larch cannot do what he does without a daily dose of mind-numbing ether. We catch Cher's abortionist in *Walls* in a private tearful moment, before she roles up her sleeves and exchanges her bulletproof vest for a white coat and suction hose. She is challenged by pregnant Chris with the question, "Why do you still do this?" With painful earnestness, Dr. Thompson expresses the driving force behind her career choice as, "When a woman comes to me and says she doesn't know what she would have done without my help, I know I am doing the right thing."

In *The Cider House Rules*, the climactic moment for the main character, gentle young Homer, comes when he sets aside his own pro-life instincts to perform an abortion. He is a hero, the film suggests, because he doesn't let his conscience stop him from doing the right thing. How weird is that vision of conscience and human moral choices?

Also presented as heroic are the pregnant women who push ahead, trying to make their best choice, even if it causes them anguish. Interestingly, the only ones who don't show any ambivalence about abortion are the post-abortive women. The pro-choice dogma here is that all of a woman's angst comes before the procedure. Once the fetus is terminated, however, so are the doubts and struggles. As one post-abortive woman shrugs in *If These Walls Could Talk*, "You know, people told me I would feel depressed and guilty. But, honestly, all I felt was relief."

We know the filmmakers are being dishonest here because everywhere in America, churches and counselors, family and friends are finding themselves called on to help women pick up the pieces after their abortions. I know. I was there one long evening with a suicidal college junior who had aborted her four and a half month fetus that day. She had been enthusiastically escorted to the clinic by volunteers from the campus women's center, and then dropped off summarily afterward back at the dorm. The girl was crying at that point and one of the women's center volunteers proposed that she get drunk and then forget about it. I'll never forget her laying in a heap on the floor of her dorm room, smelling of alcohol and pleading with me to tell her that her baby hadn't felt any pain.

This is a strong case for us because it is all about the women. We need to present much more clearly and consistently that the real struggle with abortion comes afterward for most women. The argument is ours to make that abortion haunts women much more because of their own nature than because they have been trained by social convention.

Overall the movies reveal that pro-choice America cannot evade its own ambivalence. They know that championing abortion feels icky. They are trying to convince themselves that the abolitionists and suffragettes and social reformers must have felt icky too, but deep down inside, they sense that the opposite is true.

Certainty about moral convictions is very often the only consolation for long-suffering social heroes.

This ambivalence explains why abortion is not ubiquitous in the movies. They'll say the issue is too touchy to be entertaining, but so is racism and anti-Semitism, and the industry doesn't shy away from these. We need to keep the focus on the source of ambivalence here. What is it that makes abortion such a hard choice for women? Why should it be "safe and *rare*"?

Who Do They Say That We Are?

More than any other art form, movies make characters become real people to audiences. The trick in creating a hero is to get viewers in mass numbers to cleave to the unarticulated worldview of a character by playing out the ramifications of that worldview in the character's life. So, if I want people to be atheists, I create a character who is able to achieve balance, wit, and a sense of stability without ever referencing anything transcendent. *The Contenders*'s Sen. Hanson is an example. She makes a dismissive reference to the immature and embarrassing faith of her grandson, and suggests that religion is basically a coping device.

Let's face it: Pro-lifers don't live and work in Hollywood. As a result, they are largely absent from this creative community. This allows our movement to be defined from the outside, by those who don't get us, or worse, by those who see us as part of what's wrong with the world. The entertainment industry depicts us as loud-mouthed, intrusive, unintelligent, poorly dressed religious fanatics. And guess what? Most Americans don't want to be that.

Even *If These Walls Could Talk*, which was touted as a fair and balanced film, couldn't resist the opportunity to ridicule and ultimately vilify pro-life America. As one critic who otherwise lauded the film wrote about the film's third vignette,

> The protestors are portrayed a bit over the top throughout the short and while one could argue that an abortion protestor might say "You'll still be a mother, the mother of a dead baby," I find dialogue like "I'm here to represent the young women

of this country! God forgive us for taking roles that aren't ours to take. May he break the curse of independence in women's hearts!" a tad unlikely . . .[1]

Unfortunately, many pro-lifers are loud-mouthed, intrusive, unintelligent, poorly dressed religious fanatics. Ours is a visual culture that is moved by and responds to perceptions. It doesn't matter whether that is right or wrong; it's just the way it is. If we are going to win people to our ranks, we have to create the appearance of a cool momentum. We have to present ourselves as suave, stylish, funny and yes, even detached about whether people accept our arguments or not. The frantic urgency has to be replaced by calm conviction.

The abortion films clearly convey that people are pro-life because of their religious beliefs. This fact allows them to define and dismiss us, again, the way most people define and dismiss the anti–meat-eating principles of Hindus. Our repeated references to God only reinforce the idea that our conviction is a religious one, and therefore something that should not be imposed on those outside our religion. We should pray that God will intervene in bringing abortion to an end. But He can hear those prayers from our homes, and from our churches. Prayer outside clinics seems to be more political statement than prayer. Perhaps we should consider surrendering the clinic battlegrounds to the tensions that will naturally and inevitably arise within the clinics themselves because of the atrocities taking place there.

Should We Make Pro-life Movies?

The sad fact is that in thirty years, there hasn't been a single mainstream feature film that has articulated what we believe about abortion. The pro-life movement has not responded in the popular culture to the powerful popularization of the abortion mentality that comes through weekly on *Law and Order*, or *ER*, or just about any prime-time drama except *Touched by an Angel*. Our whole focus in this issue has been legal and political, and like Aesop's fox staring at the grapes, popular culture has proved too difficult a battlefield for us, so we have branded it as beneath our efforts. In so doing, we have surrendered the most pervasive and powerful pulpit from which to make our case.

We need to reverse this defeatist trend, but we have to know what we are doing before we launch into the business of crafting visual parables to support our point of view.

I read a script not long ago from a group of Christians who told me it was a "pro-life *Cider House Rules*." I winced at this moniker, not because of the pro-life part, but because *The Cider House Rules* was basically a tedious, unentertaining, propaganda film. Sure enough, their script equaled that of *The Cider House Rules* and was basically tedious, unentertaining propaganda. Why would we want to do that?

One of the writers challenged me: "It isn't propaganda if it's true." He was wrong. Propaganda is anything that manipulates emotions to induce a certain kind of behavior. By definition, propaganda is a violation of human freedom. We don't get to do that.

Movies are a bad forum for making precise legal or moral arguments the way the parables would be bad as a source from which to derive principles of Canon Law. The Holocaust and racism films work insofar as they are hero accounts, not treatises on public policy.

The Cider House Rules would have been a more interesting and honest film if Homer had held to his pro-life instincts even when a supremely difficult case was brought before him. But because it was abortion propaganda ("a movie about abortion"), Homer simply abandoned his pro-life notions in a way that felt artificial, and ultimately made the viewer feel trapped and even annoyed. The film never deals with what Homer saw in the bucket. It just presumes that viewers will see the sense in abortion for a poor girl raped by her father.

My sense of pro-choice films is that they principally serve to delight and affirm pro-choice America. It might be nice to be able to reward some of our pro-life heroes up there on the big screen, but chances are, if we had that power, we would also succumb to the sinful urge to vilify and caricature our opponents. And we would be twice as culpable because we have been on the other side.

A Long-Term Strategy

This doesn't mean that we can abandon popular entertainment. To say that we should not produce propaganda films is not to discourage us from making art that reflects the truth about abortion. Parables are a powerful means of helping people grow. It's just a matter of knowing what makes a good parable and maximizing its potential.

Movies don't sell arguments; they sell the ramifications of arguments, or worldviews. Hollywood simply doesn't need to make a lot of abortion movies because the abortion worldview is a given there and has also largely been adopted by the viewing public. It is the worldview of primetime sit-coms and romantic comedies which, in the end, are much more insidious than all the abortion films put together. The worldview of the most successful shows, like *Friends* and *Sex in the City* and *Will and Grace,* is one in which sex is pure recreation and without any moral component. It includes the conviction that looks and possessions make life worthwhile. It excludes any moral compass other than one's own needs. It holds that the worst thing that can happen to a human being is suffering, and that a life without limits is the goal. A society with this worldview will not tolerate legislation against abortion.

Challenging this worldview will require some rethinking on our part. In particular, we must rethink the importance of the arts in keeping a society whole and good. The absence of the pro-life crowd – indeed, the absence of many people who love God and virtue – from the entertainment arena for the last fifty years has been devastating to society. We need a new generation of deeply committed, skilled artists who can offer a richer (and truer) view of human life than what is now on the screen.

And yes, critical to those efforts will be movie-making and images showing the advantages of embracing the Gospel of Life.

We need to tell stories, including stories about the cost of abortion to American women and their families. We need visual stories that confirm in viewers that no matter how wounded it gets, or how small it is, a human being is special in all of creation because it is a vessel of love. Love is poured in, and love spills out on those around it; human value resides secure in this distinct potential.

Abortion movies do not fail as entertainment because of bad production, flawed writing, incompetent directing, or uneven per-formances. They fail because you can't sell a lie. There will never be a pro-choice *To Kill a Mocking Bird*, because *Mockingbird* speaks the truth about racism. Pro-life filmmakers have the truth on their side. They just need to come up with parables that bring that truth to light.

We have a long road ahead. We must be willing to plant seeds that will be tended by future generations and will bear fruit in the decades, and maybe centuries, to come. I once visited a cathedral in Orvieto, Italy, that took 700 years to build. Our tour guide shook his head with wonder, saying, "The architect who started the project knew he would never see its end. He knew his son wouldn't even see its end." Nowadays, we have no concept of beginning a venture that has a resolution hundreds of years in the future. It requires a tremendous spirit of hope.

Barbara R. Nicolosi is a screenwriter living in Los Angeles. She has an M.A. in Television and Film from Northwestern University, and fre-quently lectures on screenwriting and culture.

Endnotes
1   *If These Walls Could Talk* Review, Yvonne Tresnan, DVD Talk, posted May 14, 2000, http://www.rottentomatoes.com/click/movie-1073021/reviews.php?critic=all&sortby=default&page=1&rid=2208 66

Sex-on-Demand, Abortion-on-Demand

Judith A. Reisman, Ph.D.

Why does the work and life of Alfred C. Kinsey, the notorious Indiana University "sex researcher," matter to today's pro-life movement?

Simply put, legitimizing sexual promiscuity means legitimizing child abuse and abortion. While this year marks the thirty anniversary of legalized abortion-on-demand, the tragedy of abortion cannot be understood apart from our crisis of sexual morality, whose latest manifestation is the sexual abuse of children – both in the church and in society at large.[1]

A deliberate conspiracy to legitimize Alfred Kinsey's fraudulent research, more than any other single factor, can be said to have caused the collapse of traditional sexual ethics in our country. For although "Europeans" like Drs. Freud, Jung, and "The Frankfurt School" preceded Kinsey, an *American* sexual revolution required a trusted, midwestern American academician portrayed as a "conservative" husband and father. The acceptance of Kinsey's books normalized promiscuity and deviance. These, in turn, would normalize adultery, divorce, illegitimacy, venereal disease, abortion, obscenity, and child abuse. In sum, we are now living the legacy of what the National Research Council called "The Kinsey Era,"[2] with sex-on-demand producing abortion-on-demand as a necessary by-product.

Background and "Findings"

In 1948, Kinsey et al., shocked the world with the publication of *Sexual Behavior in the Human Male*, which claimed to show that most American men (including fathers) were sex offenders if not sexual deviants.[3] The Kinsey team falsely claimed that they had conducted 21,000 personal interviews, finding 69 percent of white males frequenting prostitutes, 50 percent committing adultery, 85 percent fornicating, and up to 37 percent acting out homosexually.[4]

In 1953, Kinsey's hand-picked homosexual and bisexual male team published similar "findings" for women in *Sexual Behavior in the Human Female*.[5] They claimed that 50 percent of white wives had fornicated and 26 percent had committed adultery (with 50 percent wanting to do so). They claimed that 87 percent of pregnant, single, white women had had abortions (a crime at the time), as did 25 percent of married women.[6] Not only did Kinsey find no ill consequences associated with abortion, he claimed that those who had had abortions had better marriages, becoming "separated, divorced, or widowed slightly less often than those who hadn't."[7] Kinsey also contended that 85 percent of family doctors performed abortions (though "doctors" included men without a medical license).[8]

Of children, Kinsey said 100 percent were erotic and able to have orgasms from the time of birth.[9] Therefore, he argued, children could benefit from sex with each other and with adults, including incest. He further contended that children needed early and explicit sex education with exposure to homosexual acts and masturbation.[10]

The Fantastic Fraud

Incredibly enough, few inquired about the pool of Kinsey's research subjects and *not one critic* asked how he would have access to infants and children to test for the capacity for sexual orgasm. As it happened, 86 to 87 percent of Kinsey's "normal" men were either convicted criminals (including pederasts) and/or homosexuals, as well as 667 molested boys.[11] Because much of the "research" was carried out from 1941 to 1945, most American men were World War

II soldiers, leaving a skewed domestic male sample for Kinsey's "study." Similarly, Kinsey redefined "married woman" as any female who had lived with a man for a year or more, which included prostitutes.[12] Most reprehensibly, Kinsey's child "orgasm" data were obtained with the collaboration of pedophiles, both in the U.S. and abroad, making the Kinsey team accomplices to crimes of the worst kind: sex offenses against children.[13]

Why did no one question such unbelievable findings, and how could the American public fall for such falsehoods?

Sexual Behavior in the Human Male was fully funded and aggressively promoted by the Rockefeller Foundation.[14] Its release was publicized in headlines everywhere, screaming the canned news that Kinsey's data proved Americans were hypocrites, our sex laws were "puritanical," and that promiscuity was not only harmless but healthy.[15] Indeed, Kinsey asserted that *all* sexual impulses were "normal" and should be indulged frequently to insure emotional and physical health. Calling them "sexual outlets, " he intended to legitimize fornication, autoeroticism, sodomy, adultery, bestiality, pedophilia, sadism, etc. Pre-Kinsey, most psychiatrists viewed these activities as mental disorders. Kinseyan psychiatrists, however, would soon teach sexual deviants to wallow in their perversions.

For example, citing to Kinsey, in 1976 the American Psychiatric Association (APA) decided to remove homosexuality as a disorder in its Diagnostic and Statistical Manual (DSM IV). And in 1995, the APA also attempted to remove pedophilia from the "disordered" classification, claiming that neither the desire to have sex with children nor the commission of sex acts with children was abnormal, unless associated with feelings of guilt. A public outcry ensued in 2000, leading to the clarification that one is a pedophile if one has "acted on these sexual urges" with a child *under the age of 13.*[16]

Ideology and Legal Reforms

Thus, behind the veneer of detached "science" was a comprehensive sex philosophy at war with Judeo-Christian teachings and wholly at odds with American practices, but supported by the big money of committed and elitist ideologues. Rockefeller's backing allowed Kinsey to tour the nation and advise state commissions. Those commissions then submitted "reports" to legislative committees, claiming that sex "science" findings required the liberalization of sex laws.

In 1949, for example, Kinsey derailed California's plan for harsher punishments for pedophiles by testifying (falsely) that his team had proven children are unharmed by sex with adults.[17] Instead of tougher sentences, the legislature moved to lighten sex crime penalties and to parole the most heinous of child molesters. Kinsey & Co. also guided sham sex-crime committees in New Jersey, New York, Minnesota, Illinois, and other key states, with similar results. Kentucky researcher, Dr. Linda Jeffrey, located scores of citations to Kinsey's role in changing sex laws, such as the 1953 Report of the Illinois Commission on Sex Offenders to the 68th General Assembly:

> The cultural tendency to overprotect women and children [is often] . . . more detrimental to the . . . victim than the offense itself. . . . the Kinsey findings . . . permeate all present thinking on this subject.[18]

Knowing he could not advocate complete freedom for violent abusers, Kinsey lobbied for treatment and parole as an alternative to prison for sex criminals.[19] He also supported psychiatrists in the new sex field, who would train experts to "treat" and "cure" sex criminals.

The problem, to Kinsey and others like him, is never the sex crime itself, but a sexually repressive environment. Kinsey biographer James Jones summed up the party line, both then and now, with this quote from the father of the sexual revolution:

> *Sexual activities in themselves rarely do physical damage*, but disagreements over the significance of sexual behavior may result in . . . imprisonment, disgrace, and the loss of life itself.[20]

To support this position, Kinsey's two books simply report no data on the deleterious health and societal effects of sexual license (increased venereal disease, rape, child abuse, incest, impotence, etc.). In *Sexuality in the Human Female*, Kinsey states that a mere 6 percent of nearly 8,000 "normal" women had illegitimate babies, despite his reported high rates of fornication.[21] In Kinsey's contrived world, frequent and indiscriminate sex is simply free of risks and consequences. Women can healthfully separate commitment from sex, and sex from children. In a Kinseyan world, criminality is always due to *sexual repression*, which a "Kinsey culture" would cure.

To this day, well-financed (and often government-subsidized) pro-sexual-promiscuity organizations claim that sexual repression is the problem and that many sex offenses – such as statutory rape – are actually "normal," healthy acts.[22] Kinsey's own Institute at Indiana University, for example, still operates to advance his ideas (and it still receives state funds), as do other similar groups, such as the Sexual Information and Education Council (SIECUS), Planned Parenthood Federation of America and its research arm, the Alan Guttmacher Institute (AGI), and the American Civil Liberties Union (ACLU), to name just a few. From the earliest days, Kinsey and his colleagues worked for this type of legal reform. Morris Ernst, ACLU lawyer for Kinsey and Planned Parenthood, for example, worked to defeat laws prohibiting obscenity, abortion, adultery, seduction, rape, and statutory rape.

Setting the Stage for Legal Abortion

Morris Ernst also played a key role in the 1965 U.S. Supreme Court case, *Griswold v. Connecticut*, which struck down Connecticut's ban against contraception. Clearly, by then, the prep work for legal abortion was well underway. By the time Kinsey's book was released in 1948, he had established a secret collaboration with the framers of the Rockefeller-funded American Law Institute's Model Penal Code (ALI-MPC).[23] His ideas and his "sex science data" were incorporated wholesale into the "sex offenses" section of the 1955 ALI-MPC (on the normality of fornication, adultery, and general promiscuity). By 1965, the year of *Griswold*, Samuel Kling published *Sexual Behavior & the Law*, which celebrated Kinsey's data as built-into the ALI-MPC:

The Kinsey Institute reported that between one-fifth and one-fourth of the white married American women interviewed in their sample had had at least one induced abortion. Three-fourths of them reported no unfavorable consequences. Most did not regret the experience.[24]

Kinsey's unsubstantiated high numbers of illegal abortions were (and remain) central tenets of pro-abortion advocacy. The Kinsey Institute had already brazenly cooked up abortion data of this sort. Despite his reported low figure of 6 percent illegitimacy rate in the 1953 *Sexuality in the Human Female*, Kinsey claimed at a 1955 Planned Parenthood conference that abortion was common and harmless, suggesting that support for legalization was obvious.[25] No one asked how Kinsey knew about the percentages of abortions, since abortion and birth control for the unmarried were still illegal, and therefore hard public health data were rare (including data on abortion-related injury and death). The phony Kinsey claims were simply accepted, and repeated, becoming a mantra for the abortion movement.[26]

By 1973, United States Supreme Court Justice Blackmun, writing for the majority in *Roe v. Wade*, explained that most states based their liberalized views of abortion on the ALI-MPC,[27] which cited the faulty claims of Planned Parenthood Medical Director Mary Calderone, who relied on Kinsey's hoax that *"90 to 95 percent of premarital pregnancies are aborted."*[28] Indeed, those within the pro-abortion movement readily acknowledge Kinsey as indispensable, as is evidenced by the 1998 collection of leftist essays, titled *Abortion Wars*. The first entry in its chronology is a tribute to him:

> 1953: Alfred Kinsey's *Sexual Behavior in the Human Female* reports that 9 out of 10 premarital pregnancies end in abortion and 22 percent of married women have had an abortion while married.[29]

Almost Found Out: The Reece Commission

The Rockefeller-funded Kinsey revolution was not entirely without resistance. In 1954, the Reece Committee of the 83rd Congress, headed by the popular Republican World War II hero, Congressman J. Carroll Reece, launched an inquiry into the special interest funding of key philanthropies, including the Rockefeller, Ford, and Carnegie Foundations, triggered by allegations that certain foundations were subverting American principles through the education system.[30] This Reece Committee actually "found" that an "elite of gigantic financial strength was working outside our democratic processes to undermine the country's Judeo-Christian foundations."[31] While examining Rockefeller's philanthropic funding, the committee happened upon Kinsey's sex "data" and endeavored to study them. In his highly laudatory biography of Kinsey, James Jones reveals Kinsey's fear of the Reece Committee and the concomitant risk of public exposure.[32]

According to the committee's legal counsel, René Wormser, Congressman Reece was then effectively blackmailed. Reece was told that if *the Kinsey research was examined, his congressional investigation would be terminated.*[33] Wormser reports that the risk of losing funding for the whole inquiry resulted in "the entire Kinsey file" being locked up, *never to be seen again.*[34]

Thus, the Reece Committee's *official finding*[35] says nothing specific about Kinsey, though it explains how the Rockefellers and other monied philanthropies used American tax money to undermine our traditions:

[S]ome of the great foundations which have done so much for us in some fields have acted tragically against the public interest in others. . . . When they do harm, it can be immense harm – there is virtually no counterforce to oppose them.[36]

There are no absolutes, that everything is indeterminate, that no standards of conduct, morals, ethics, and government are to be deemed inviolate, that everything, including basic moral law, is subject to change, and that it is the part of the social scientists to take no principle for granted as a premise in social or juridical reasoning, however fundamental it may hereto have been deemed to be under our Judeo-Christian moral system.[37]

How did Kinsey alone manage to escape detection? One could argue that Kinsey's activities – crimes against infants and children, as well as fraud – were so serious that the whole enterprise had to be covered up. Also, exposing his work as a sham jeopardized the entire sexual revolution the Rockefellers and others had supported for so long.

Kinsey had fled the country, allegedly to collect sexual artifacts.[38] Assured that he would not have to testify before the commission,[39] Kinsey returned to the Indiana University campus and continued his sex work until his death in 1956. His fully indoctrinated cadre of lawyers, psychiatrists, and legislators then carried on in his stead, charting the necessary future steps to the sexual revolution. As Louis Schwartz, a colleague and American Law Institute lawyer, put it:

> Sexual penal reforms can . . . eventually . . . [be] eased into the written law . . . presenting the changes . . . [as] merely technical improvements. . . . [People resist] when smaller numbers of articulate opinion-makers launch an open attack on the old . . . traditional faith . . . [I am] in favor of the individual visionaries who are willing to pay the personal cost to challenge the old moral order.[40]

Kinsey and the Catholic Church

The current child abuse scandal in the Catholic Church has a direct link to Kinsey. The U.S. Bishops have long been advised by doctors and "sex experts" of the Kinsey school. Yet, these sexperts are *on record* as advocating the normalcy of bi/homosexuality, fornication, sodomy, autoeroticism, pedophilia, and pederasty.[41]

Dr. Fred Berlin, for example, is still a consultant to Cardinal Bernard Law, according to the United States Catholic Conference of Catholic Bishops. Dr. Berlin co-founded a well-known sexual treatment center at Baltimore's John Hopkins University with Dr. John Money, his "mentor." John Money is a dedicated disciple of Alfred Kinsey, and was also mentor to the Kinsey Institute's third Director,

June Reinisch. Money is also revered by the Institute's current director, John Bancroft.

Money has stated in interviews that pedophilia is not only normal but beneficial.[42] His hope for the Johns Hopkins sex clinic was to offer "leeway for judges" to free active, convicted child abusers. He is now also known for his barbaric role in a tragic sex-change operation on "a baby boy whom doctors changed into a girl," almost destroying the boy's life.[43]

The Catholic Church continues to use the St. Luke Institute in Maryland to counsel and treat its seminarians struggling with sexual disorders. Yet the founder of St. Luke's was Rev. Michael R. Peterson, M.D., a disciple of both John Money and Fred Berlin. Peterson, who died of AIDS in the late 1990s, urged the Church to rely on their sexual expertise.

But Kinsey's theories enjoy acceptance throughout the entire American educational system – as well as the entire religious and secular culture – not just within Catholic seminaries and treatment centers. Indeed, "sex ed" throughout most American schools today is traceable to Kinsey, since there was no field of human sexuality before his work. Acceptance at the University level is obvious with the proliferation of "sexologists" and sex institutes. In addition to Johns Hopkins and Indiana University, the Advanced Study of Human Sexuality in San Francisco is the most notorious academic cover for normalizing sexual perversion. Their pornography film festival ("Sexual Attitude Restructuring," or "SAR") has allegedly been used in seminary training nationwide.[44]

Virtually all "accredited" beliefs about sex today are based on the Kinsey model, since its people became the Western world's "human sexuality educators." Their reach extended beyond education to influence law, public policy, government, the media, Hollywood – everything. In brief, our nation has been following a "sexuality" model designed by sexual deviants to normalize sexual deviance. We should not be surprised, therefore, by the massive increases in sexual deviance. The scandal of the Catholic Church is just a glimpse of what will soon be recognized as the pandemic scandal of our nation.

Kinsey's Legacy: A Playboy Culture with Contempt for Women and Children

On the evidence, legitimizing promiscuity legitimizes child abuse and abortion – two sides of one coin. By labeling children "erotic," sexual beings from birth, Kinsey robbed children of their inalienable right to innocence, which society and the state should secure. Today, children are daily coarsened and injured mentally, spiritually, and mortally by violence, sexual abuse, venereal disease, pornography repackaged as "sex education," prostitution, and abortion.

Before Kinsey, motherhood was also sacred. While the patriarchal culture was indeed quite unfair to women in some ways, our sex laws went a long way to favor and protect women, since self-control, not birth control, was expected of young men.[45] Abortion was illegal, and illegitimacy, rape and other forms of sexual exploitation of women and children were condemned, controlled and penalized.[4] Indeed, Hugh Hefner, founder of *Playboy*, complained that the media culture in 1953 was dominated by woman-friendly imagery promoting family and decency.[47]

All that changed with Kinsey. Hefner, having read Kinsey's claims about wanton moms and the "girls next door," advertised himself as Kinsey's "pamphleteer"[48] and vowed to popularize Kinsey's sexual ideology both in conduct and in law. Hefner succeeded. As Mom and "the girl next door" came to be perceived as sexually promiscuous, male fear, revenge, and contempt exploded. Once birth control became legalized and venereal disease treatable, girls and women found they were expected to engage in sexual gymnastics before they got a marriage proposal. With abortion, pregnancy within or outside of marriage, once due to "his" unbridled lust, became "her" fault. Sex and abortion were – and continue to be – marketed as entitlements and freedom; they are, in fact, the infrastructure of a Kinsey-*Playboy* culture.

That Kinsey threatened women and children was most apparent in the field of psychiatry, which proved ready to accept future sexuality "professions" and "specialties." For example, Ralph

Slovenko, a leading psychiatric criminologist for the Group for the Advancement of Psychiatry (GAP) echoed Kinsey's concepts in an official GAP Statement on sexual responsibility, attempting to legitimize pedophilia. "Full responsibility for sexuality," he argued, should begin at the "age of 7."[49] Slovenko continued:

> *Even at the age of four or five, [her] seductiveness may be so power-* *ful* as to *overwhelm the adult* into committing the offense. . . . The *affair* is therefore not always the result of the adult's aggression; often the young female is the initiator and seducer.[50]

With seduction, fornication, adultery, and other woman and child-favoring laws trivialized, eventually rape and statutory rape also lost their criminal status. If consensual fornication is common, how could one know if a girl was raped rather than consensually fornicating? By 1973, Vernon's Annotated Missouri Statutes, 2000 reports:

> The label "rapist" . . . should *not* ordinarily be used in the *statutory non-consent* cases. The Code reserves that term for the most heinous sexual offender...[not for sex with a] *fully con-senting . . . social companion . . . of 12 years of age.* [51]

Thus, the law rejects calling a child rapist a rapist.

In 1990 the American Bar Association reported that 80 percent of *convicted* child molesters are paroled and serve no prison time. Instead, the predator receives tax paid treatment for his "sexual orientation to children." [52]

While women and children are the first to suffer in a culture of sexual deviance, disorder for all quickly follows. From 1976 to 1999 alone, the incidence of violent crime (including forcible rape and murder), child sex abuse, illegitimacy, sexually transmitted diseases and abortion has risen to unprecedented levels. In 1999 alone,[53] 67 percent of sex abuse victims are children under 18 years of age; 64 percent of under-12 forced sodomy victims are boys; 4,200 "in school" rapes and sexual assaults are reported in 1999 (although this could be as high as 19,000[54]); 350,000–400,000 child prostitutes[55] are reported; and suicide, drug, alcohol abuse, AIDS, and pornography addictions are no longer rare among our youth.[56]

Conclusion

Kinsey's sex-on-demand "science" spawned our abortion-on-demand law. To this day, sexual promiscuity and abortion reinforce one another.

If America is to survive this "Brave New World," it must revive the Judeo-Christian laws and traditions of sexual morality that Kinsey & Co. sabotaged. Human sexuality must be restored to its special and sacred status, connected *only* to marriage and family. Though imperfectly observed, this traditional sexual ethic spared our nation the degradations and injuries catalogued above. It also inspired stable marriages and therefore a safe, sane and stable society, protective of our children.

A culture of life? Or a culture of Kinsey? The choice is ours.

Judith Reisman, Ph.D., is President of the Institute for Media Education and is the author of several publications concerning crime, pornography, and Alfred Kinsey, and the threats they pose to children. Her works include a 1989 Juvenile Justice Study for the U.S. Department of Justice, and the 1998 book, Kinsey, Crimes & Consequences. She has served as a consultant to the U.S. Departments of Justice as well as Education and Health and Human Services, and is also a news commentator for WorldNetDaily.com.

Endnotes

1   "The abuse of the young is a grave symptom of a crisis affecting not only the church, but society as a whole. It is a deep-seated crisis of sexual morality." Statement, Pope John Paul II, April 23, 2002.

2   Charles. F. Turner, et al., Eds., *AIDS, Sexual Behavior and Intravenous Drug Use* (Washington, D.C.: National Research Council, National Academy Press. 1989), p. 79.

3   Alfred C. Kinsey, Wardell B. Pomeroy, and Clyde E. Martin, *Sexual Behavior in the Human Male* (Philadelphia: W.B. Saunders Company, 1948).

4   *Id.*, 650–51; see full discussion in Judith Reisman, *Kinsey, Crimes & Consequences*, 2nd edition (Crestwood, Ky: The Institute for Media Education, 2000), p. 87

5   Alfred C. Kinsey, Wardell B. Pomeroy, Clyde E. Martin, and Paul H. Gerhard, *Sexual Behavior in the Human Female* (Philadelphia: W.B. Saunders Company, 1953).

6   Samuel Kling, *Sexual Behavior & the Law* (Random House, New York, 1965), p. 9. The percentage claimed of married women who aborted has been somewhat fluid, appearing as 22 percent to 26 percent in various citations.

7   Paul Gebhard, Wardell Pomeroy, Clyde Martin, and Cornelia Christenson, *Pregnancy, Birth and Abortion* (Harper & Brothers Publishers, New York, 1958), p. 213; in Reisman, *Kinsey, Crimes & Consequences*, p. 251.

8   *Id.*, Gebhard, p. 212.

9   Kinsey, Male volume, Chapter 5, especially pp. 148–49 and Tables 30–34; see also Reisman, Chapter 7, "The Child Experiments."

10   *Id.*; see full discussion in Reisman, Chapter 7.

11   Gebhard and Johnson, *The Kinsey Data: Marginal Tabulations of the 1938–1963 Interviews Conducted by the Institute for Sex Research* (Philadelphia: W.B. Saunders, Co., 1979), pp. 3–6 and 29. For discussion of "cleaned" data, see Reisman, Chapter 6.

12   Gebhard, Pomeroy, Martin, Christenson, *Pregnancy, Birth and Abortion*, the "Science Editions" (New York: John Wiley & Sons, Inc., 1958), p. 3.

13   See especially Britain's Yorkshire Television documentary, "Kinsey's Paedophiles," broadcast August 10, 1998.

14   See Reisman, *Kinsey, Crimes & Consequences*, pp. 35–40.

15   See enthusiastic cover stories in *Time* (August 24, 1953), *Colliers* (September 4, 1953), *Look* (May 8, 1951). Almost every major magazine and newspaper lauds Kinsey post 1948.

16   The 1995 American Psychiatric Association (APA) DSM IV *(Diagnostic and Statistical Manual IV)*. Should a nineteen-year-old have "ongoing" sex with a twelve-year-old, the APA still finds that normal – if the offender is not distressed. See the 2000 DSM IV TR, at p. 572.

17   Preliminary Report of *The Subcommittee on Sex Crimes of the Assembly Interim Committee on Judicial System and Judicial Process*, California Legislative Assembly, 1949 (Created by HR 232 and HR 43), pp. 103, 105, 117.

18   Report of the "Illinois Commission on Sex Offenders" to the 68th
        General Assembly of the State of Illinois, Springfield, Illinois, March
        15, 1953, pp. 8, 9, 36, 11.

19   *Id.*, page 17, Preliminary Report.

20   James Jones, "Dr. Yes," *The New Yorker* (September 1, 1997), p. 103
        (emphasis added).

21   Because abortion was still illegal and contraception sales were tight-
        ly controlled, this figure is highly implausible. Judith Reisman,
        Kinsey, Crimes & Consequences (Crestwood Ky.: First Principles Press,
        1998, 2000), p. 108.

22   See Ralph Slovenko statement, infra note "Psychosexuality and the
        Criminal Law," *Vanderbilt Law Review*, 15 (1962), p. 809.

23   See Reisman, "Kinsey's Impact on American Law" (199–267). Note:
        "In 1952, Herbert Wechsler wrote "The Challenge of a Model Penal
        Code," for the *Harvard Law Review* and was "gratified" that
        Rockefeller had funded the ALI "project." Wechsler knew long
        before 1950 that the Rockefeller Foundation would give the money
        "for the undertaking to proceed."

24   Kling, at p. 9; see also Reisman, *Id.*, at p. 227.

25   Robert Marshall, Charles Donovan, *Blessed are the Barren* (San
        Francisco: Ignatius Press, 1991), p. 260. The Planned Parenthood con-
        ference was sponsored by the National Committee on Maternal
        Health at the New York Academy of Medicine.

26   Reisman, p. 180. See my "female" and law chapters for more details
        on Kinsey and abortion.

27   *Roe v. Wade*, 410 U.S. 113 (1973), footnote 37. The ALI Model Penal
        Code cites to Calderone for statistics, and Calderone, in turn, cites
        Kinsey.

28   Kinsey co-author Paul Gebhard and Calderone were very influential
        authorities in the *Roe v. Wade* decision, which includes a footnote
        citation to the MPC Draft No. 9 (May 8, 1959), which states that:
        "Major sources of Information on abortion include two sources:
        Calderone, *Abortion in the United States* (1958); Gebhard and others,
        Pregnancy, Birth and Abortion, chap. 8 (1958)." See also Reisman, p.
        230.

29   Rickie Solinger, ed., *Abortion Wars* (Berkeley: University of California
        Press, 1998), pp. ix, 228.

30   The Reece Committee continued hearings originally started by the
        Cox committee. For more information on this topic, see Michael
        Loyd Chadwick, *The Freeman Digest*, "Tax-Exempt Foundations:

Their Impact on the World." Published by the Freemen Institute, Salt Lake City, UT, June 1978 issue, p. 1.

31   Reisman, *Id.*, p. 270.

32   James Jones, *Alfred C. Kinsey: A Public / Private Life* (New York: W.W. Norton, 1997). Jones also reveals many of Kinsey's own psychosexual disorders along with his fears of the Reece Committee.

33   René A. Wormser, *Foundations: Their Power and their Influence* (Sevierville, Tenn.: Covenant house Books: 1958,1993), p. 351.

34   *Id.*

35   *Id.*, "Report of Counsel to the Committee on the Proposed Objectives and Methods of Investigation: House Committee on Tax Exempt Foundations," October 23, 1953, pp. 384–99.

36   *Id.*, Wormser (back book jacket quote).

37   See also, Ronald D. Ray, "Kinsey's Legal Legacy," *The New American* (January 19, 1998), pp. 31–32.

38   Kinsey was allegedly recovering from "orchitis." "inflammation of a testis . . . usually due to gonorrhea, syphilis, filarial disease, or tuberculosis . . ." *Dorland's Illustrated Medical Dictionary* (Philadelphia: W.B. Saunders Co., 1981), p.933.

39   James Jones, *Alfred C. Kinsey.* Jones documents a broad spectrum of Kinsey's illegal, pathological, and what are still widely viewed as immoral behaviors within mainstream American society. See pp. 604–5, 669, 689, and 775.

40   Schwartz, L. B. 1948, *Sexual Behavior in the Human Male* (book review), *University of Pennsylvania Law Review*, 96 (1947–48). Also, see *Columbia Law Review* article by Schwartz (1963), reprinted in "Morals Offenses and the Model Penal Code," Wasserstrom, R. A. (ed.), *Morality and the Law* (Belmont, Calif.: Wadsworth Publishing, 1971), pp. 90, 91.

41   Interview: John Money in *Paidika: Journal of Paedophilia* (Spring, 1991), pp. 2–13; See also *Paidika* "Statement of Purpose," Amsterdam, The Netherlands (September 1987), Vol. 1, at pp. 2–3, identifying "The Editors" as "paedophiles."

42   *Id.* After stating that sex between men and boys of any age is legitimate "erotic pair bonding," to the interview question, "So you would attack the whole basis from which age-of-consent laws are constructed, in other words," John Money replies, "I certainly think that's where we have to begin," p. 13.

43   John Colapinto, *As Nature Made Him* (New York: HarperCollins Publishers, 2000).

44   Michael Rose, *Goodbye! Good Men* (Cincinnati: Aquinas Publishing Ltd, 2002), pp. 284–85.
45   Statement by Eunice Van Winkle Ray of RSVP America, June 10, 2002.
46   Although wife-beating was legal throughout the world, by 1871 Alabama and Massachusetts led the nation by declaring that battery of one's wife, "is not now acknowledged by our law." William Brennan, "Female Objects of Semantic Dehumanization and Violence," 2000, http://www.fnsa.org/v1n3/brennan1.html.
47   See Judith Reisman, *"Soft" Porn Plays Hard Ball* (Lafayette, La.: Huntington House, 1990).
48   Documentary, "Kinsey's Paedophiles," supra note 13.
49   *Psychiatrically Deviated Sex Offenders, Report No. 9*, Committee on Forensic Psychiatry of the Group for the Advancement of Psychiatry, February, 1950.
50   Ralph Slovenko and C. Phillips, "Psychosexuality and the Criminal Law," *Vanderbilt Law Review*, 15 (1962), p. 809. (Emphasis added)
51   *Vernon's Annotated Missouri Statutes*, 2000, 544.040, Comment to 1973 Proposed Code. 1973 Missouri Symposium, p. 382. (Emphasis added)
52   American Bar Association. The Probation Response to Child Sexual Abuse Offenders: How Is It Working? Executive Summary. State Justice Institute, Grant No. SJI-88-11J-E-0115. 1990, at p. 7.
53   Judith Reisman, *How the FBI & DOJ Minimize Child Sexual Abuse Reporting: A Working Paper*, The Institute For Media Education, Sacramento, California, 2002, especially pages 11 and 24: A *5.1 percent increase in the child population* does not explain these developments (1951–1997) 993 percent and (1960–1999): 396 percent more violent crime as well as 70 percent more murder; 418 percent more "forcible" rape (*excludes* data on child rape) and (1976–1999) 15,185 percent more reported Child *Sex* Abuse. Also, the data from the US Department of Commerce Census Bureau and the Statistical Abstracts of the United States, 1997 find from the 1950s to late 1990s at least 215 percent more illegitimate teen moms; 200 percent more STD's (HPV, chlamydia, syphilis, etc.) and 450 percent more abortions, illegitimacy among young girls.
54   Correspondence: "Dear Dr. Reisman: According to our data, there were approximately 12,000 rapes in or around schools in 1994. In 1999 (the most recent data that we have), there were over 19,000 rapes that occurred in or around schools."Criminal Victimization in the United States, 1994," http://www.ojp.usDOJ.gov

/bjs/pub/pdf/cvius94.pdf. Table 63. For the 1999 data, you can take a look at "Criminal Victimization in the United States, 1999 Statistical Tables," National Crime Victimization Survey, January 2001at http://www.ojp.usDOJ.gov/bjs/pub/pdf/cvus99.pdf. Table 63. These are all age 12 and over only data. You can access them from our Web site at http://virlib.ncjrs.org/juv.asp?category=47&subcategory=185. If you have any further questions, please feel free to write back and thanks for using AskNCJRS. Ken M, Information Specialist, NCJRS," received 7/23/2001.

55   Dr. Richard Estes, *The Commercial Sexual Exploitation of Children in the U. S., Canada and Mexico*, U.S. Department of Justice/National Institute of Justice), addressed in more detail in Judith Reisman, *How the FBI and DOJ Have Minimized Child Sexual Abuse* Reporting, IME (July 2002), available on drjudithreisman.org.

56   U.S. Department of Justice/National Institute of Justice; See also Reisman, FBI Report, IME, 2002. See also http://www.faithchristianmin.org/articles/teb.htm.

Crisis of Life? Crisis of Love!
Mary Hasson and Miki Hill

We are not U.S. Senators, Supreme Court Justices, or state legisla-tors. We do not stroll the halls of Congress, lobbying lawmakers. Nor do we create "respect life" ads, argue the pro-life message on talk shows, or seek corporate funds for crisis pregnancy centers. Our personal political clout is nil and our financial influence mini-mal. But changing the hearts and minds of Americans on abortion depends on hundreds of thousands of women just like us.

We are moms.

You've heard it said that the pro-life movement will win even-tually because sooner or later we'll outnumber the opposition. After all, we are the ones having babies. In the minds of some, "having babies" is what a mother's contribution to the pro-life cause is all about. More broadly, pro-life leaders honor mothers for their testimony that children are a blessing, a gift worth cherishing rather than a burden to be eliminated. But this is only part of the picture.

The role mothers have played – and will play – in the pro-life movement is critical not simply as a matter of out-populating the other side or testifying to the value of children. Rather, our role is crucial because it is mothers of today who will form and raise the adults of tomorrow. For abortion to end and, even more so, for our society to embrace a true culture of life, the next generation must truly live the pro-life attitudes they profess. At the same time, they must combat the countervailing attitudes which undergird the culture of death.

What, you may ask, does the fight to save unborn babies from a violent death have to do with "attitudes"? Why bother with "attitudes" and "forming the next generation" when there are lives to be saved right now? Besides, don't the polls show that Americans are moving our way on abortion?

The pro-life cause has indeed gained momentum legislatively and in the public square, building a consensus in favor of restricting late-term abortions. At the same time, however, our culture reflects an increasing prevalence of attitudes more consonant with the culture of death than with the culture of life, even among those who explicitly oppose abortion. These attitudes are insidious, their effects underestimated. They render the culture of death palatable, even while poisoning the hearts and souls of mothers, fathers, and children alike, leaving them inhospitable towards life that is burdensome or inconvenient. As a result, we are losing ground rapidly in the overall war against the culture of death.

The work of mothers, then, is ever-more pressing if the culture of life is to overtake the culture of death. We must effect change in ourselves, our families, our culture, and our institutions – a change of attitudes.

The Value of Life? It Depends . . .

The most damaging attitude we must fight assigns a relative value to life. It answers, "It depends" when asked whether life has value. Two generations ago, mothers and fathers would stand appalled at the thought of a life not worth living, or a baby who never should have been born. Today, lawsuits proliferate over botched abortions or inaccurate prenatal screenings, alleging that the children (or at least the parents of those children) would have been better off if the child had been aborted. The "it depends" mentality denies life's intrinsic value.

Paradoxically, many within the pro-life movement have nevertheless embraced the "it depends" mentality. Even happily pregnant mothers reflect this relativism when they answer the query, "Do you want a boy or a girl?" with the usual reply, "It doesn't matter – as long as it's healthy." The qualifier has become so standard many probably say it without thinking. But it contributes to the cultural mindset that a less than perfect child is a disaster.

Not surprisingly, materialism bolsters this relativistic view of life, measuring a person's dignity and worth by his physical perfection or his usefulness. Consequently, things, animals, or even careers can be worth just as much as a person. For some, raising children becomes a lifestyle preference of no greater moral significance than the choice to breed spaniels. For others, the decision to have children becomes merely a consumer choice subject to a hard-nosed cost-benefit analysis.

Consider the experience of one young couple: They agreed to postpone having children until both the husband and wife finished their graduate degrees. Four years later, newly graduated, they announced the wife's pregnancy to their relatives. After a perfunctory "Congratulations," the young woman's father (known for his anti-abortion convictions) shook his head ruefully, saying, "You know this was a bad economic decision." His focus on the financial and career impact of having a child recast the newly conceived life as a marginal gift at best.

When materialism influences a couple's decision to have children, this attitude persists even after children arrive. A recent *Working Mother* magazine article applauded a mother's decision to FedEx her breast milk back home to her infant daughter each day for a week while the mother traveled on business. The mother proudly noted that her innovative use of FedEx allowed her to conduct business while simultaneously "caring" for her infant. Only a world where the value of motherhood has been reduced to physical care would embrace virtual nursing. Breast milk delivered by 10 A.M. the next business day is no substitute for mom, or for love.

So what's a pro-life mother to do? We must help our fellow moms – and our children – embrace the truth that all life is good, even when it is difficult and painful. We must be deeply committed to the idea that all people have dignity simply because they are created in the image and likeness of God, regardless of age or physical or mental condition. Our conversations, our decisions about having children, our attitudes towards elderly relatives – in reality, everything we do – must present a coherent vision of the intrinsic value of life to our friends, co-workers, and children. We must rid ourselves of the "it depends" mentality because human dignity doesn't "depend" on anything. Ever.

"It's All About Me"

The second attitude dominating our culture and undermining the pro-life effort measures right and wrong solely from the perspective of personal fulfillment; maximizing personal fulfillment becomes the primary criterion for evaluating morality. "It's all about me" sums up our cultural self-absorption. As a result, decision-making is detached from the general context of "the common good," or even from a realistic consideration of another's needs and dependencies. In all cases, the dispositive question is, "Do I think this will make *me* happy?"

Abortion is only the most obvious manifestation of this mindset. The divorce revolution encourages countless bored spouses to jettison existing commitments in search of greater personal fulfillment elsewhere. Brushing aside the pain and confusion of trusting spouses and abandoned children, these departing spouses rationalize, "I'm entitled to my happiness, right?"

In other contexts as well, self-absorption easily masquerades as a virtuous use of talents. A twenty-something married woman, proudly childless by choice, explained her decision to a group of friends. "Oh, I couldn't have children. I'm too selfish. There are just too many things I want to do with my life." She continued on, describing her interests and goals. A half-dozen women nodded sympathetically and one murmured approvingly, "You have so many talents. You have to do what makes you happy." Is this a heart prepared to make room for the needs of an unborn child, a disabled spouse, or an elderly parent?

The "me" attitude first surfaces in smaller ways, less significant than the life or death choice of abortion. But those hundreds of smaller decisions build a trajectory for the major decisions that come later. One mother who postponed children for thirteen years so she could travel around the world with her husband and pursue professional success, finally decided she would not be happy without children. Her two sons were born two years apart, prompting her to take unpaid leave until the youngest was two. At that juncture, she resumed full-time work, explaining, "I've given them each two years of my life. That's enough. It's time for me again." Her carefully measured doses of generosity were all used up. Such pinching of emotional pennies destroys authentic love, which requires giving of ourselves without counting the cost.

Self-absorption rejects self-sacrifice and has one singularly predictable effect: It closes the hearts of mothers and fathers to the good of a new life. One pro-life mother, volunteering in her church nursery, was asked, in front of her children, if she planned on having more children. Her reply was direct. "No way. I've sacrificed enough." Such limits on sacrifice are in fact limits on love. But true love is generous, self-giving, and always sacrificial, *and it is central to the pro-life cause:* If we want others' hearts to be open to life, we must first open our own.

For others, the criterion of personal fulfillment poses different questions. "Should we have children at all?" "Our life is just perfect . . . why mess it up by having another child?" "If this child has Down's Syndrome, how can I ever be happy?" "What about Mom and Dad in their old age? Do I really want to spend our retirement money on their medical bills? I can't travel or be free to leave them. Isn't it better to let them (or help them) go?" All of these issues boil down to the same theme: " It's all about me."

Again, what's a pro-life mother to do? We must live and teach the paradox that true happiness lies in self-giving, not self-getting. The current culture of death sees the child as an adversary, competing for a woman's body, her time and energy. The culture of life must refuse to define the mother and child in opposition to each other. As a practical result, human relationships – especially the mother-child relationship – will be primary in a true culture of life.

People, even the very youngest of people, will matter more than money, influence, or career trajectories.

We can foster the same attitude in our children by teaching them how to sacrifice for others out of love, a profoundly counter-cultural idea. It's much more fashionable to sacrifice yourself for yourself. One young Olympic champion (recently featured on a Wheaties box) when asked who her greatest inspiration was in her pursuit of the gold medal, answered, "I am." Is this loving sacrifice, or narcissism?

We can expect better from, and for, our children. They will learn from our example that self-giving is fulfilling and self-absorption is not. Moreover, family life provides an excellent training ground for the small daily sacrifices that gradually expand the heart. A high-school-aged son who leaves his homework to help a distraught sibling learns more than just how to soothe a crying child. He learns a lesson for life: How to put his own agenda aside in order to meet another's needs. His ability to sacrifice and serve others will affect his marriage, his choice of career, and his ability to make society better. But only if we mothers do our jobs well and form our children in this attitude of sacrificial love. Do we indulge our children's natural reluctance to do difficult things? Or do we teach them not to complain or feel put upon because others need them, even when no thanks is forthcoming?

And what about our own attitudes? All the anti-abortion rhetoric in the world docs little good if our daily attitude views a child as an interloper, or an unwelcome spoiler in marriage, or an inconvenience. When the next baby must compete with next year's vacation, or a bigger house, the culture of death has taken root.

"It's Just Sex . . ."

These two attitudes – "It depends," and "It's all about me," combine with a third attitude to fuel the growing culture of death. "It's just sex," the cultural voices assert. "What's love got to do with it?"

Everything. Absolutely everything. Real sex is joyous, exuberant, and unreserved intimacy. Real sex, in other words, *is* mutual self-giving. Not surprisingly, then, it thrives only in an atmosphere of unconditional, irrevocable love – that is, in a marriage. Of course, lesser, unworthy things happen all the time and try to pass themselves off as real sex. They're not. The post-coital glow is obviously custom-made for expressions of forever love, not for vaguely anxious banalities like "So, how was it?"

The culture, however, insists that sex is just about pleasure. And sometimes it's not even about that. According to *The Washington Post*, twelve- and thirteen-year-old girls in the Washington, D.C. area have found that the ticket to popularity in their middle schools is oral sex. One eighth-grade girl spoke of performing oral sex on a boy she barely knew and didn't like. "It was no big deal," she confided. But her casual attitude belied a deeper, built-in desire. In the words of one of her male companions, sex "turned out to mean a lot more to them than to us. The guys hooked up with the girls because the girls were hot. The girls wanted to have a relationship."[1]

No surprises here. Most women experience promiscuous, casual sex as shallow and unfulfilling, and ultimately degrading. And it often has real-life consequences: pregnancy. In such a culture, it is not surprising that the majority of abortions are still performed on unmarried teens and women. Careless sex is careless about everybody – yourself, your so-called partner, and the life you may be conceiving.

How do we correct the attitudes that have paved the way for the culture of death? By insisting that sex has something to do with love. And love, by its nature, is found in self-giving. Only then will men and women know the deeper experience of the mystery and reality of sexual love.

A Fight for Love and Life

All of us who abhor abortion must do more than work to overturn *Roe v. Wade*. We must embrace the attitudes that support the culture of life and reject those which feed the culture of death. As we form our children, we will affect the hearts and minds of our peers, helping them to do the same. The battle will be won mother by mother, child by child, family by family.

Why mothers? Because the crisis in our culture is a crisis of love. And we mothers are the "love experts." We know above all that life's not really about becoming wealthy or maximizing personal potential. We know also that the real secret to great sex is the same as the real secret to a great life – self-giving love. As men and women created in the image and likeness of God, we have been created for love – seeking to love and to be loved. And it is this desire that gives us a glimpse of God in our hearts. And, like God, we experience authentic love only in the gift of ourselves. Such a gift is designed to be permanent, to speak the language of forever love.

Our greatest contribution to the culture of life will be in teaching our children how to love, and helping each other reject the superficial substitutes for love which capture our energies and attention but ultimately fail to satisfy.

In the end, our fight is not just for life, but for authentic love.

Mary Hasson is the mother of seven children and author of Catholic Education: Homeward Bound, *a popular book on home education. Miki Hill is a mother of nine children and is a frequent speaker at family conferences*

Endnote
1   "Parents are Alarmed by an Unsettling New Fad in Middle Schools: Oral Sex," *The Washington Post* (July 8, 1999), pp. A1 and A16.

Part VI
The Future

Two Traditions in Tension
John M. Haas

Bioethics has emerged as one of the most influential, and some would say, notorious, new scholarly disciplines in our day. There can be little doubt that we have moved as a society into a so-called "bio-tech" age. The first presidential address of George W. Bush to the American people was on a bioethical question – the federal funding of embryonic stem-cell research (ESCR). Shortly thereafter, the American people were faced with an act of bio-terrorism – the release of deadly anthrax bacteria in letters to targeted individuals on the East Coast.

Bioethics, however, is not really that new. The discipline used to be known as medical ethics, and "think-tanks," such as the Hastings Center and The National Catholic Bioethics Center (formerly the Pope John XXIII Medical Moral Research and Education Center), were founded in the early 1970s to tackle the moral questions arising in medicine and science. But ethical reflection on medical practices dates from even before Christ, in ancient Greece, and has continued with the Judeo-Christian philosophical tradition. There is no question, however, that recent developments in the life sciences and in bio-technology have catapulted the discipline of bioethics into greater national prominence, as the country looks to "bio-ethicists" to assist in forging policies which can serve public health while avoiding violations to the human person.

But many observers look upon bioethics with great reservation, if not alarm, because they believe that it actually facilitates and rationalizes violations of innocent human beings in research and health care. Many "bioethicists" support, for example, euthanasia, physician-assisted suicide, abortion, and destructive embryonic stem-cell research. The problem, though, is not bioethics as such, but rather the "moral methodology" or "ethical system" used by the bioethicist, or the bioethics center.

The Western Moral Tradition and the Hippocratic Oath

Undoubtedly, the ethical system most commonly used in medical schools, universities and bioethics centers today is the one known as utilitarianism. But the approach which dominated western medicine for most of our history could be referred to as the natural moral law.

What are the fundamental differences between these two approaches?

The natural moral law approach, or the "ethic of the good" (or virtue ethics), is rooted in both our Greco-Roman and Judeo-Christian past. It protects the individual patient. In the pagan tradition, it is associated with the Oath of Hippocrates, the Greek physician who lived five hundred years before Christ. It recognizes the supernatural order, since the physician would take the oath before Apollo and Asclepius. But, fundamentally, it observes and respects the natural order by appealing to human nature and to the rights and duties which human beings have toward one another. Anyone, of any moral tradition, should be able to grasp and follow the basic tenets of the natural moral law, since they are, as the Christian writer Paul of Tarsus wrote, "written on the hearts of men."[1]

The Hippocratic Oath stated: "I will apply . . . measures for the benefit of the sick according to my ability and judgment; I will keep them from harm and injustice. I will neither give a deadly drug to anyone who asks for it, nor will I make a suggestion to this effect. Similarly, I will not give to a woman an abortive remedy. In purity and holiness I will guard my life and my art."

In the Platonic dialogue *Euthyphro*, Socrates asks if certain actions are wrong because the gods have forbidden them, or whether the gods have forbidden certain actions because they are wrong. The western tradition of natural law insists that certain actions have been forbidden because they are intrinsically wrong (i.e., wrong in and of themselves), and therefore can serve no good purpose. As Aristotle says in his *Nicomachean Ethics*, certain actions simply violate human nature: Adultery is not a question of the right woman at the right time; it is always wrong.

Within this same tradition, the Hippocratic Oath states quite simply and without explanation that physician-assisted suicide and abortion are acts of harm and injustice to a patient. There is no "right time" or good way to violate a patient. However, the 1973 U.S. Supreme Court decision which legalized abortion led medical schools to remove the oath from graduation ceremonies. A two-thousand-year-old ethical code, the foundation of western medical ethics, was simply dropped.

The Modern Moral Approach: Utilitarianism

The moral approach which has since come to dominate in our medical schools and bioethics centers is utilitarianism. This approach is associated with the names of the nineteenth-century English thinkers John Stuart Mill and Jeremy Bentham.[2] In the United States, it is associated with the name of William James of Harvard and is usually referred to as pragmatism. This approach generally denies that any human action is in and of itself wrong, and therefore ought never be committed. The rightness or wrongness of an action is judged by its social utility, which is defined as the greatest good for the greatest number. The greatest good, in turn, is defined as whatever maximizes pleasure and minimizes pain.

Joseph Fletcher was an Episcopalian theologian who cast this approach in a Christian guise and developed his system of "situation ethics."[3] In this system, no absolute moral rules exist - only guidelines, or "rules of thumb." Any "loving" act could be performed, since God is love. However, when pressed to define "a loving act," we were again told of the greatest good for the greatest number, which is to say, whatever maximizes pleasure or mini-mizes pain. This approach dominates bioethical thinking to this day.

The most commonly used medical ethics book in our medical schools today is *Principles of Biomedical Ethics*, by James Childress and Thomas L. Beauchamp. It is utilitarian in approach, and argues for both physician-assisted suicide and abortion, actions quite explicitly denounced by the Hippocratic Oath.

The Embryonic Stem-Cell Research (ESCR) Debate: Two Traditions at Odds

During the intense debate over federal funding for embryonic stem-cell research, which reached its peak in the spring and sum-mer of 2001, virtually all arguments in favor of funding were utili-tarian. Stem cells are undeveloped cells which differentiate as the embryo develops and eventually become nerve cells, muscle cells, bone cells, etc. In the adult human body one also finds stem cells. They are more highly differentiated than embryonic stem cells, but not yet fully developed. For example, blood stem cells are found in bone marrow and will further differentiate into red or white blood corpuscles. The most undeveloped and undifferentiated cells are derived from the human embryo and are called "embryonic stem cells."

Many believe that these embryonic stem cells can yield "cell lines," or future generations of cells, which could then be devel-oped into virtually any cell type in the body for remarkable thera-peutic purposes. Healthy brain tissue could be "grown" to treat neurological disorders such as Parkinson's Disease or Alzheimers, for example; or healthy pancreatic tissue could be grown to treat even inherited diseases such as diabetes. There is even the hope that organs could be grown from these cells, which could be used for organ transplantation and decrease the need for organ donors.

Opponents of embryonic stem-cell research objected that the research entailed the destruction of embryos, a class of human beings protected from harm in research by federal guidelines. But supporters pointed out that the targeted embryos were merely those "left over" from in-vitro fertilization ("IVF," where embryos are engendered in a petri dish for infertile couples) and already frozen in liquid nitrogen. Supporters emphasized that they would not be creating new life simply to destroy it, but only using embryos that would be discarded anyway.

Supporters also argued that only small numbers of these embryos would have to be destroyed in order to benefit millions of human beings in our own day and into the future. Suffering would be diminished and more pleasurable lives ensured. This was clearly a case of the greatest good for the greatest number resulting from the destruction of these frozen embryos.

This debate illustrated clearly the difference in approach to a bioethical question. Those who argued from the natural moral law tradition pointed to the fact that embryos were human beings and insisted that it is never morally licit to violate an innocent human being. Indeed, there were federal guidelines protecting human subjects, including human embryos. The utilitarian approach looked, instead, to the potential social utility of ESCR. Again, the problem is not the discipline of bioethics, but rather the methodology used to decide what ought or ought not be done.

The utilitarian approach appears suited to a democratic society because it seems to ensure fairness and seems to respect the majority in the social order. However, it ought to be obvious that this approach threatens society's weak and vulnerable, as well as those in minority positions. If maltreatment of a small class of citizens would benefit the majority, utilitarianism provides no principled way to protect that class. Also, the moral rules of utilitarianism change as social thinking changes. "Time makes ancient truths uncouth," the poet James Russell Lowell wrote in 1845. The utilitarian approach, frankly, creates as it goes along, so that there are no absolutes, not even the prohibition against the direct killing of innocents. It would all depend on (changing) circumstances – and changing definitions, including definitions of who is, and is not, a human being.

Verbal Engineering

Remarkably, utilitarians not only change rules as they go, but change language to accommodate what some see as a changing reality. They actually try to mold reality itself to their way of social thinking. "Verbal engineering precedes social engineering," as the saying goes. For example, because the moral status of human life is now debated, especially at its early and very late stages, utilitarians have sometimes made up terms to suit their purposes.

This was very much on display during the ESCR debate, for example. Since there have been societal protections for the human embryo, it became necessary to devise ways to remove the human being at the earliest stages of development from this protected category.[4] In 1979, an article appeared in *Scientific American* on "External Human Fertilization" by an amphibian embryologist by the name of Clifford Grobstein.[5] The article addressed some public policy questions raised by in-vitro fertilization. In this article, Grobstein introduced the notion and term of the "pre-embryo" or "pre-implantation embryo." There was, and is, no scientific basis for such a designation of the early embryo, and it is not used in standard texts on embryology.

But utilitarians needed this new category to argue for the acceptability of research on the human embryo at its earliest stage of development. A new category helped them remove the early embryo from the protected class of "human persons." Grobstein states in one of his articles, "since the criteria for personhood have not yet appeared (prior to 8 weeks) existing persons have not been manipulated and the rights of persons are not being violated."[6] In truth, Grobstein simply wishes to treat the embryonic human being as less than a person, and so creates a category for the human embryo which he deems sub-human ("not yet existing persons.")

In the text *Human Embryology and Teratology* by Ronan O'Rahilly and Fabiola Mueller, one does read reference to the term, but it is not favorable: "The ill-defined and inaccurate term pre-embryo, which includes the embryonic disc, is said either to end with the appearance of the primitive streak or . . . to include neurulation. The term is not used in this book."[7]

Lee M. Silver, Professor of Molecular Biology at Princeton University, is even more explicit: "I'll let you in on a secret. The term pre-embryo has been embraced wholeheartedly by IVF practitioners for reasons that are political, not scientific. The new term is used to provide the illusion that there is something profoundly different between what we non-medical biologists still call a six-day-old embryo and what we and everyone else call a sixteen-day-old embryo." At least Professor Silver is honest about the scientific facts. [8]

Human Life as an Intrinsic Good

Princeton professor Robert George, however, uses a moral methodology more consistent with the "received tradition" and insists that human life must not ever be directly violated from the moment of its conception until its natural death. He, too, looks to the scientific evidence: "The scientific evidence establishes the fact that each of us was, from conception, a human being. Science, not religion, vindicates this crucial premise of the pro-life claim. From it, there is no avoiding the conclusion that deliberate feticide is a form of homicide. The only real questions remaining are moral and political, not scientific . . ." [9]

Having established the scientific fact that the human embryo is a human being, Professor George's moral judgments about its inviolability follow from our shared Western tradition – from Hippocrates to the Judeo-Christian ethic – that human life is intrinsically good: "In short," writes George, "secularism rejects the proposition central to the Judeo-Christian tradition of thought about issues of life and death: that human life is intrinsically, and not merely instrumentally, good and therefore morally inviolable." [10] In the final analysis, violations of "the good" are both unreasonable and "un-human." The proper human response is to desire, relish, protect, and nurture what is good. This is why it is simply against our nature to kill innocent human beings, to abort our children, to kill our elderly and our sick.

Bioethics must work to protect the dignity of the human person in medicine, health care, and the life sciences in accordance with this tradition. There is always the danger that an individual may actually be tempted to violate one good in pursuit of another perceived good. A researcher may be tempted to be less than honest about her data because she is so convinced of the truth of her theory, and she is convinced that the sooner it is applied to those who are ill and in need, the sooner she will make a real contribution to society. A physician may think a continued pregnancy harmful for a young woman with a chronic heart condition, and contemplate killing the child by abortion. But just as the researcher who sacrifices honesty and integrity will cast in doubt all her research in the future, so too will the physician who sacrifices an innocent human life call into question his care for human beings in the future.

America's Conscience Is Still Alive

Ultimately the human conscience cannot be quieted, for the moral law is written on our hearts. Bio-ethicists who make judgments based on the social utility of certain lives cannot, therefore, carry the day. That there has even been a debate in the United States over embryonic stem cell research is very positive: Abortion has been legal in the United States for thirty years, and yet citizens care about the destruction of the microscopic human being. We care because we have a troubled national conscience about the taking of innocent human life – still.

Even the attempt to disguise the human reality of embryos through the unscientific term "pre-embryo" is a positive indication that the conscience is still alive and unsettled. Pope John Paul II actually identified this attempt to quiet the conscience in our day. Even though the abortion mentality is deeply ensconced in contemporary societies and there are great pressures for physician-assisted suicide and euthanasia, the Pope points out that "conscience does not cease to point to [innocent human life] as a sacred and inviolable value, as is evident in the tendency to disguise certain crimes against life in its early or final stages by using innocuous medical terms which distract attention from the fact that what is involved is the right to life of an actual human person."[11]

The French statesman Georges Clemenceau is said to have stated: "War is too serious a business to be left to soldiers."[12] We might say as well that bio-medical research is too serious a business to be left to physicians and researchers. These life and death decisions, so crucial to our shared future, must be made with contributions from all sectors of society, but especially from those who insist on the inviolability of human beings. For only they will protect the weak and vulnerable in our midst, and hold those in medicine and bio-medical research to moral standards worthy of those noble professions.

John M. Haas, Ph.D., S.T.L., is the President of The National Catholic Bioethics Center.

Endnotes

1   See Romans 1:18 to 21.

2   J. Bentham, *An Introduction to the Principles of Morals and Legislation* (London:, 1823), J.S. Mill, *Utilitarianism* (London, 1863).

3   Joseph Fletcher, *Situation Ethics* (London: SCM, 1966).

4   C. Ward Kischer, "The Big Lie in Human Embryology: The Case of the Preembryo" *Linacre Quarterly* (November 1997): 53–61.

5   Clifford Grobstein, "External Human Fertilization", *Scientific American*, 240 (1979):57-67.

6   Clifford Grobstein, "The Status and Uses of Early Human Developmental Stages", in *Ethical Issues in Research*, ed. Darwin Cheney, (Frederick, Md.: The University Publishing Group, Inc., 1993).

7   Ronan O'Rahilly and Fabiola Mueller, *Human Embryology and Teratology* (New York: Wiley-Liss, 1992), p. 55.

8   Lee M. Silver, *Remaking Eden: Cloning and Beyond in a Brave New World* (New York: Avon Books, 1997), p. 39. Professor Silver still accepts as ethical the engendering of children through in vitro fertilization and their subsequent destruction, either in the IVF procedure itself or in later research and experimentation. Thus, awareness of scientific facts does not guarantee correct ethical decision-making, which is of a higher order.

9   Robert P. George, *The Clash of Orthodoxies* (Wilmington, Del.: ISI Books, 2001), p. 73.

10   Ibid., p. 4.

11   John Paul II, *Evangelium vitae* (March 25, 1995), #57.

12   B.H. Liddell Hart, *History of the Second World War* (New York: G.P. Putnam's Sons, 1970), p. 22.

Learning from Our Adversaries
Charles A. Donovan, Sr.

If the pro-life movement wants to accomplish in the next thirty years what it has failed to accomplish in the previous thirty, change within it must be overwhelming. In the year 2002, the pro-life cause is seen in the United States as partisan, sectarian, single-minded, disorganized, and discouraged. Those images of the pro-life cause are false in varying degrees, but the extent to which they are true, and some of them are highly accurate, damages a great social movement. These images are not, however, the primary factor that is preventing that movement from achieving success.

The pro-life movement is in deep trouble, above all, because of the "vision thing." As the twenty-first century dawned, we who have articulated the moral and ethical principles that underlie the right to life creed have an overriding responsibility both to think in longer perspective and to act with greater intensity now. We can do this because of the fact that, as weak as we are and as ill conceived as some of our strategies have been, our opponents, with all their material success, have built a house of cards.

Margaret Sanger and the American Birth Control League (Planned Parenthood)

The mansion of choice, as Planned Parenthood and its allies conceive it, glitters on the exterior. Its allure is that it speaks of every man, woman, and child as a monarch, royal in his person, subject to no other's rule, free to take on and abandon the most intimate of relationships without fear of consequence. "No Gods, no Masters!" Margaret Sanger emblazoned on her magazine *The Birth Control Review*. With revolutionary fervor, she and her colleagues, first the radical left, then industrialists, then religious leaders, stormed the heights of society and politics, dressing a survival-of-the-fittest code in the raiment of egalitarianism.

Armed with personal defiance and a global vision, Sanger opened her first birth-control clinic in Brownsville, New York, in 1916. Pro-life pregnancy centers today are challenged every now and then by aggressive public officials, like Sen. Ron Wyden of Oregon or Attorney General Eliot Spitzer of New York. Sanger was challenged in much more direct and efficient ways, confronted by political and religious leaders, and arrested by New York, police who led her away to jail and closed down her operation.

Sanger persisted and established the American Birth Control League, the forerunner of Planned Parenthood. Within decades, the movement she sparked had established hundreds of centers and a worldwide presence. By 1940, three decades before the first U.S. pregnancy-care center opened, there were seventy-four affiliates of the Planned Parenthood Federation of America. By 1954, nearly two decades before *Roe v. Wade*, the International Planned Parenthood Federation, Western Hemisphere, was established. In 1970, within days of passage of a liberal law in New York, Planned Parenthood of Syracuse opened an abortion facility.

Today nearly 100 of these centers perform 200,000 abortions yearly, about one of every seven done in the United States. The enterprise that Sanger founded is an entity with more than $670 million in annual income, more than $300 million in net profits during the last five years, and standing as the fourteenth largest charity in the United States as ranked by the *Non-Profit Times*. Planned Parenthood can no longer spend all the money it receives, as its contraceptive client base in the United States has stagnated for nearly a decade. Still, governments at all levels maintain their habit of pumping money into the institution, providing almost 40 percent of its budget and as much as 70 percent of the budget of new facilities.

A Long-Term Civil-Rights Struggle

The right-to-life movement has much to learn from this history, and many applications that it has yet to make in earnest. First of all, it must recognize that the ideology it fights is neither a single issue nor a single strategy. The ethic of abortion on demand is embedded within a comprehensive philosophy of sexuality, marriage, family, and the relationship of government to all that is non-governmental. It is a philosophy that is pervasive and radical in its implications, contrary in its deepest spirit to the philosophy of the American founding, with its conviction of limited government and a virtuous people who draw unalienable rights from their status as creatures of a providential God.

Second, advocates of life must realize that the groundwork for the tragedy of *Roe v. Wade* was laid half a century before the ruling was announced. The institutions that resisted *Roe* were slow to realize the threat and even slower to build new institutional responses that were capable of addressing the communications and other material advantages possessed by abortion advocates. To this day, many members of the pro-life movement regard themselves as engaged in a project from which they may yet one day retire and return to their daily lives. That is a tribute to the local and grass-roots character of the families, students, and homemakers who constitute the life cause. But it is also a self-defeating characteristic.

The conflict over abortion is over a basic civil right. Just as the civil rights of black Americans were disputed long before 1861 and well after 1865, so too are the rights at stake in this debate subject matter for conflicts that will span decades and centuries. This realization does not lessen the importance of the debate nor should it lessen the devotion of those who engage in it, but it must inform them in their reaction to both advances and setbacks. This caution is not the same as the counsel of those who suggest that advocates of the right to life must dedicate themselves to cultural change and only secondarily to legal change. It has more to do with how leaders prepare those who follow them for the successes and defeats that lie ahead, in *both* the cultural and legal spheres.

A Vision to Counter the Imperial Self

Finally, the right-to-life movement must, for the first time in its history, establish a vision that is broad enough to overshadow its opponents' ethic of the imperial self. It must couple to this an action plan that is inspiring enough to capture the instincts for life that animate today's youth, who are the survivors of the random violence of the abortion culture.

This type of vision is not new. It was the vision, as historian Marvin Olasky has so carefully demonstrated, that generated an explosion of personal charity in the nineteenth and early twentieth centuries. Across America, as the Industrial Revolution gathered momentum and cities teemed with both opportunity and exploitation, a wave of religiously motivated men and women founded institutions to aid orphaned children and women pregnant out-of-wedlock. Similarly motivated religious orders founded hospitals and shelters, putting selfless service to others at the core of rescuing individuals, families, and communities.

In the 1970s, a Florida Planned Parenthood official described her organization as the "charity that makes other charities unnecessary." Three decades after *Roe*, the inaccuracy of that statement could not be clearer. Charities that address family breakdown, counsel the divorced, treat post-abortion complications and depression, detect and treat sexually transmitted disease, and counter child abuse and neglect have burgeoning caseloads. Educational achievement continues to lag behind the levels of a generation ago. Personal and corporate morality is notoriously low, prompting persistent majorities of Americans to decry the nation's ethical climate.

Planned Parenthood's Empire Today

Still, 2002 is not 1892. The empire that Planned Parenthood has built is not challenged today by a similarly aggressive and visionary pro-life movement of commensurate sophistication. Under Planned Parenthood's umbrella in the United States is a network of 128 affiliates, 875 dispensaries, nearly 100 abortion providers, and a caseload of 1.8 million women per year for contraceptives and abortifacients. More important, under that umbrella is a network of lobbying affiliates, foundations and endowments, a research institute, a database development corporation, an internal insurance company, an overseas education and distribution arm, a get-out-the-vote fund, a political action committee, and, very soon, a full-fledged media company.

These affiliates work together with remarkable consistency in message development, legislative strategy, professional training, reporting and medical standards, and liaison with government funding sources. Through these efforts, they have succeeded in identifying their private programs with government objectives and taken full advantage of the conservative domination of the pro-life cause to isolate and alienate many right-to-life advocates from their own government and its institutions.

Disunity and alienation in the right to life cause have been among its features for a political generation. In late 2001, at the behest of the Gerard Health Foundation of Massachusetts, I undertook a study of the relative organizational strengths and business strategies of the pro-abortion and pro-life movements. The results, by any objective standard, are riveting. Against Planned Parenthood's tightly knit array of services, advocacy, and research, the pro-life cause throws some forty scattered organizations with various elements of Planned Parenthood's mission. These groups occasionally operate in coalitions, but they lack nearly all the synergy in communications, advocacy, research, fund-raising, and, above all, world view, that makes their opponents so powerful.

The combined income of these organizations in a recent period hovered around $100 million per year, a fraction of Planned Parenthood's. While Planned Parenthood has generated cash reserves in excess of $300 million in the past five years to plan and organize expansion, the right-to-life cause generates about $4 million per year more than it spends. No major move toward inter-organization cooperation and mission re-evaluation has occurred in the movement for decades, despite the fact that the current model no longer delivers the kind of results that would energize donors and volunteers.

Pregnancy-Help Centers

One exception to this trend exists with tremendous potential. The pregnancy-center movement in the United States continues to develop in strength and to make steps toward enhanced unity and cooperation. Several years ago the Family Research Council conducted market research for pregnancy care centers that disclosed a remarkable fact: Despite the sustained efforts of Planned Parenthood and NARAL to deride these centers as examples of propaganda and zealotry, the vast majority of American women – including women who self-describe as "pro-choice" – view these centers and their work positively. Many of these women have had beneficial experiences, either for themselves or a friend, with a center in their community.

The centers themselves, which operate under various national networks, including CareNet, Heartbeat International, Birthright, and the National Institute of Family and Life Advocates, are just beginning to realize the strength they enjoy in tandem. For years, pro-life media spokesmen have touted, with good reason, the wonderful work done by "3,000 or more" of these centers nationwide. The truth is, no one really knows how many centers are operating, how many women they have assisted, how many abortions they have averted, how many layettes and homes and jobs they have provided to women in need.

Planned Parenthood, in contrast, has published for years effective public-relations materials that combine their "service" results nationwide and worldwide. Planned Parenthood uses its reports to garner additional public support, satisfy donors, and intimidate political opponents. The organization has realized that it is in a global clash of visions that requires excellence in long-term planning, communications, and political fieldwork. The right-to-life cause has seen itself as a dogged and dedicated rear guard that struggles to compete against this juggernaut and to hold back a future it dreads.

The Future

This is the essence of what must change, and, fortunately, may indeed be changing. The failure of the legal, research, lobbying, legislative, and service arms of the pro-life cause to work together is more than a mere disappointment. It is more than a remnant of what were once principled differences over philosophy and approach. It is a crisis and a scandal. While each of the forty organizations examined in the survey conducted for the Gerard Health Foundation does some worthy work and carries out admirable projects, the fragmentation, duplication, and lack of communication among them are obvious and striking.

Rather than just curse the darkness, let me suggest several crucial steps that could offer the pro-life cause a brighter future.

A new Federation for Life is urgently needed. The case for alternatives to abortion, the practice of abstinence, and the promotion of marriage and fidelity is overwhelming from a personal and public health standpoint. Moreover, the population collapse evident in developed countries today is a harbinger of severe dislocations in those nations' social systems. The pro-life cause must master the data that proves these points and muster that data for use in debate and public policy. A Federation for Life that brings together public policy, research, and service arms with the seriousness of purpose evident in the Planned Parenthood Federation of America is long overdue. That organization has had a fifty-year head start. Fair enough. It is time we catch up.

The right-to-life movement must assure that every American school child sees ultrasound imagery of the unborn time and again. Today's mothers and fathers now take baby's first picture in the form of a printout from the ultrasound scanner. Every woman who conceives a child in the United States should be offered the opportunity to view her own child *in utero*. Every abortion center should be required to offer women this opportunity. As of this writing, no major pro-life web site carries ultrasound imagery of the quality available in the latest General Electric advertising and on such sites as www.3dsono.net. This is a curious omission. Ultrasound imagery will not stop abortion by itself, but it is inherently enthralling and convincing. Its message must be taken outside the doctor's offices and brought to television, to schools, to malls, to street fairs, and to any other of life's intersections where basic beliefs are formed.

The right-to-life movement must find a way to restore its nonpartisan stature. When I first lobbied the Congress for the pro-life cause in the 1970s, more Republicans than Democrats were pro-life, but the margin was not overwhelming. The pro-life cause included liberals like Tom Eagleton, moderates like Mark Hatfield, and conservatives in both parties like Democrat Harold Volkmer and Republican Henry Hyde. Today, the pro-life cause is being maneuvered into a mirror image of black Americans in the Democratic Party. An assured fraction of one party's coalition, it has little leverage to effect change and none to make its issues a priority. The 2002 elections are likely to leave fewer than two dozen pro-life Democrats in the House of Representatives.

This, too, is a crisis and a scandal.

This challenge will not be easy to solve, but efforts must begin in earnest to do so. If the right to life has any transcendent meaning, and our cause has no meaning if it does not, it can and must appeal to the members and leaders of all parties. The timber of liberal and conservative concern for women and the unborn will always be different, but it can be complementary. A new federation of pro-life entities built around service to women and families, and bolstered with research and public policy advocacy, might appeal especially strongly to Democrats who conceive of government as a voice for the powerless and the medically neglected.

International outreach. Remarkable progress has been made at the United Nations as the Bush Administration, the Catholic Family and Human Rights Institute, the Family Research Council, and a coalition of ambassadors from countries with pro-life laws has been increasingly able to stymie radical feminist activism. Even so, international pro-life service groups, most notably the Canada-based MaterCare International, continue to gasp for support. The delivery of compassionate and effective maternity care to all the world's women should be an announced and aggressively pursued goal of the pro-life movement.

Here, Planned Parenthood's head start is even longer. Last year its leaders ratified a twenty-five-year plan for the universality of casual sex and abortion on demand. Our plan has yet to be written, but all good things begin with recognition of a need and a seed of hope. That hope is in the heart of every mother and father for a better life for themselves and their children. Our cause exists because we believe that to sacrifice any child in a vain attempt to achieve that better life is, as Mother Teresa said, the "greatest poverty."

Planned Parenthood and its allies have spread that poverty around the globe. Women – and nations – deserve better. A vision sufficient to the tasks at hand can begin with that seed.

Charles A. Donovan is an author, speaker and activist who has represented the pro-life cause in Washington, D.C. since 1978. He is co-author of Blessed Are the Barren *(Ignatius Press, 1991), a history of Planned Parenthood.*

Dangerous Mischief at the United Nations
Abortion as the Law of the World
Austin Ruse

Just as U.S. abortion proponents did an end run to the courts and around the democratic process, international abortion proponents have attempted the same thing, this time using international documents drafted through negotiations at the United Nations (UN) and its attendant agencies, conferences, and commissions. Just as we understand that the courts are the part of government furthest removed from the people, how much further removed is the typical citizen from the always arcane and mostly unknown international organs that operate in New York, Geneva, Vienna, and elsewhere? Yet these are the bodies which seek to remove all limits to abortion in roughly 191 countries. Clustered around these quasi-governmental entities is a network of international and national activist groups – scholars, lawyers, journalists – which applies significant legal and financial muscle to bring the whole world into line with abortion-on-demand, that is, abortion without the necessity of a reason. This chapter will show the state of abortion in national laws around the world and how generally non-binding UN instruments are used to change those laws.

An Overview

The tide of abortion runs high around the world. We know this chiefly from two studies, one from the Center for Reproductive Law and Policy,[1] a New York-based legal and policy think tank that promotes abortion-on-demand internationally, and the other from the generally unbiased Population Division of the UN's Department of Economic and Social Affairs,[2] the chief UN statisticians. Each study examines the laws in 191 countries and categorizes them according to their abortion policies. The laws run the spectrum from allowing abortion only to save the mother's life to abortion-on-demand, with most countries (124 out of 191) falling somewhere in between. These 124 countries represent 66 percent of the world's population.[3] Abortion laws in the middle group of 67 countries, representing 34 percent of the world's population, run the fairly narrow range of familiar reasons: the mother's physical health, mental health, and socioeconomic grounds.[4] Most countries also allow abortion because of rape and incest.[5]

The seventy-four countries, representing 26 percent of the world's population, with the most pro-life laws on abortion (allowing abortion only to save the mother's life) are mostly from the developing world (Latin America, Africa, the Near and Far East).[6] They include: Bangladesh, Benin, Chile, Congo, Egypt, Guatemala, Lebanon, Mexico, Myanmar, Syria, Uganda, Yemen, and others. Three European countries are included in this group: Ireland, Andorra, and Malta.[7]

Thirty-three nations, with 9.9 percent of the world's population, allow abortion to save the mother's physical health and her life. They include: Argentina, Jordan, Kuwait, Morocco, Qatar, Peru, Rwanda, Saudi Arabia and Zimbabwe. Two European nations fall within this group: Poland and Liechtenstein.[8]

Twenty nations, representing 2.6 percent of the world's population, allow abortion for reasons of mental health, as well as to save the mother's physical health or life. They include Algeria, Bahrain, Gambia, Israel, New Zealand, Spain, Portugal, and Switzerland.[9]

Fourteen nations, representing 20.7 percent of the world's population, allow abortion on socioeconomic grounds, as well as to protect the mother's physical health, mental heath or life. This group is more economically advanced and includes Nordic countries which tend to lead the way in pressuring smaller states to allow abortion-on-demand. It group includes: Australia, Finland, Iceland, India, Japan, Luxembourg, and the United Kingdom.[10]

The last category includes those countries with the most expansive abortion laws – that is, laws without restriction as to reason. This group includes fifty nations representing 40.8 percent of the world's population. Among others they are: Albania, Austria, Belgium, Bulgaria, China, Czech Republic, France, Germany, Greece, Italy, Netherlands, Norway, Russian Federation, Turkey, and the United States.[11]

A closer look at this last category shows that, with the possible exception of China, it is the U.S. that has the most unlimited abortion. Even with measures such as parental notification, the U.S. abortion regime is abortion-on-demand up to the moment of delivery and beyond.[12] While a number of nations fall within the category of "on demand," one still finds limits in other countries that do not exist in the U.S. The most obvious is the "gestational restriction," which sets a time limit beyond which a woman may not get an abortion. Many European nations, including France, Germany, Greece, Norway and others, have legal gestational limits to abortion of between twelve and fourteen weeks.[13]

The Real Story

Of course, this survey of the international situation hides the frequently meaningless nature of many of these laws. Going even one step beyond the "life of the mother" allowance can result in *de facto* abortion on demand. In the United States, for instance, the Supreme Court decided the abortion case *Doe* v. *Bolton* the same day it decided *Roe*.[14] *Doe* established the legality of abortions for the mental health of the mother, and thus allowed abortion-on-demand. Such "mental health of the mother" loopholes exist in other countries' laws as well. Even when a "gestational limit" is part of the law, in practice it is frequently ignored.

Abortion was officially condemned in French law from 1920 to 1975. The 1975 law allowed abortion up to the tenth week of pregnancy, but this was expanded to twelve weeks in 2001. Abortions are also allowed in the later stages of pregnancy to save the mother's life, or because of a lethal disease of the child. Parental authorization had also been required for girls under the age of eighteen, but this was struck down in 2001. Moreover, every woman seeking an abortion is supposed to be counseled by Planned Parenthood about the procedure and its consequences.[15]

Germany, too, has a legal "gestational limit" of fourteen weeks, and German women also must have pre-abortion counseling and then be "certified" for an abortion. However, according to Thomas Friedl, staff member for the German Parliament, "this is most ineffective; 98 percent of abortions proceed after these counseling sessions."[16]

At the other end of the spectrum, according to both CRLP and the UN Population Division, Argentina upholds its abortion laws most vigorously.[17] An Argentine woman may seek an abortion after a counseling session with a doctor, who may then determine that her life depends on having an abortion. The decision rests with a medical professional, who, at least for now, is unlikely to expand access according to vague or unverifiable "health" claims.

Thus, the availability of abortion depends upon both a country's abortion laws and the willingness of the country's medical professionals to ensure the laws are not flouted.

All countries in the world have come under pressure to change their laws to allow for abortion.[18] This is true even in the nearly unrestricted United States. Most of this pressure comes from the international abortion lobby working from the United States and the European Union. True to their anti-democratic record, they work from the top down, using international instruments negotiated at the United Nations and the European Parliament. A wide array of international organizations is involved, including rich foundations (Ford, Gates), lending institutions (the World Bank and the International Monetary Fund), and UN agencies (UN Children's Fund, UN Population Fund, and the World Health Organization).

The Latest Ruse: Abortion as a universal "human right"

In recent years abortion has become something of an obsession at the UN and increasingly within the EU. Formally, the idea is to create what is called "customary international law." Customary international law is created either through the near unanimous, nation-by-nation ratification of certain laws, the single-stroke acceptance of an international treaty, or the repetitious use or acceptance of certain phrases and ideas in international documents.

On the question of abortion, proponents have never attempted a straightforward treaty on this subject alone, and they certainly will not try anytime soon. They simply do not have the support of world opinion, and they know it. Abortion is hardly ever mentioned by name in UN documents precisely because it is so contentious. Instead, code words are used, like "reproductive health." They have attempted mostly to change abortion laws country-by-country – sometimes through the legislative process, often through national courts.

What is fairly new, however, is the attempt to establish customary international law through the repetitious use of undefined or ill-defined terms that actually mean abortion. This strategy was in play in numerous international meetings and is now easily recognizable in many of the outcome documents of those meetings: the Cairo Programme of Action (1994), the Beijing Platform for Action (1995), and many others.

The phrase used most frequently to mean abortion is "reproductive health," although "reproductive rights" and "reproductive services" are also used. "Reproductive health" has been defined as including abortion only once in a governmentally negotiated UN document, in the Cairo Programme of Action.[19] Never in any other governmentally negotiated document has "reproductive health" been so defined. "Reproductive health," however, is officially defined by the World Health Organization as including abortion. (The WHO definition is a two-step process that says "reproductive health" includes "fertility regulation," which includes termination of pregnancy.[20]) It should be noted that the definition from an agency such as WHO does not carry the same weight as a definition negotiated and agreed to by the member states of the UN

Though vaguely defined by member states just once at Cairo, abortion proponents prefer to leave the term "reproductive health" undefined. They know the Cairo definition was a once-in-a-lifetime event, probably never to be repeated, and so they have come to rely on this implicit definition of "reproductive health" as including abortion. "Reproductive health" is therefore something of an empty glass that policy makers can fill anyway they see fit.

The phrase "reproductive health" is used dozens of times in UN resolutions and reports. It is used in documents related to women (Beijing[21] and Beijing +5[22]), housing (Habitat[23]), and the environment (Rio's Agenda 21[24] and the Earth Summit +5).[25] It is also used regularly in less formal documents produced by the myriad UN commissions, for instance, the Commission on the Status of Women, and the Commission on Population and Development.

The phrase is used frequently in UN reports. In its annual report for 2000, the United Nations Population Fund (UNFPA) used the phrase a total of 186 times (the report mentioned clean water and safe sanitation only once each).[26]

It is clear from the documentary evidence that "reproductive health," which is understood to include abortion, is among the highest priorities of the UN system. The purpose is to pressure governments to change their national laws, which is accomplished in two ways: first, in the documents individually and in the UN committees that many of the documents establish; second, the accumulation of all these documents bolsters the claim that abortion is a new international norm, or part of customary international law.

The best example of the first approach is the Convention on the Elimination of All Forms of Discrimination Against Women (CEDAW), a treaty now ratified by more than 150 nations (though not by the U.S., as of this writing in September 2002). CEDAW created a committee to which nations ("States parties") must report at least every four years on their progress in CEDAW implementation. Though the framers of CEDAW did not include abortion in the document, they did include "family planning," another notoriously ill-defined UN phrase, and based on this phrase they have pressured a number of "States parties" to legalize abortion, including Ireland, Mexico, and Peru. It should be emphasized that while the U.S. can effectively ignore pressure tactics coming from UN committees, many smaller states cannot. In fact, negative reports from UN committees can create large political disturbances for smaller states.

It is the second tactic, however, that most concerns international abortion opponents – that is, the accumulation of "reproductive health" language into customary international law. Abortion opponents have long feared that the repetitious use of the phrase "reproductive health" in UN documents could be used to argue for a new international norm – a universal right to abortion. Proponents will say that the norm has been established precisely because so many governments have so often agreed to the phrase, that the right to abortion is understood.

Abortion proponents had not admitted this tactic publicly until a lawsuit filed against the Bush Administration in the year 2001.[27] Filed by the New York-based Center for Reproductive Law and Policy (CRLP), the suit concerns the "Mexico City" policy, a Reagan-era prohibition on U.S. taxpayer money going to any non-governmental organization that supports or performs abortions overseas. The policy was maintained during the first Bush Administration but struck down by President Clinton on his first day in office. It was reinstated on the first day of the George W. Bush presidency. In the suit, CRLP claimed the policy violated their First Amendment right to free speech. But the most interesting part of their suit was the claim that abortion was a universal human right that had been established as such in non-binding UN resolutions.

According to the CRLP suit, "Customary international law is embodied, *inter alia*, in treaties (even if not ratified by the United States), the writings of international law jurists, and documents produced by United Nations international conferences."[28] CRLP goes on to say that even if *Roe v. Wade* were struck down by the U.S. Supreme Court, because of the establishment of a customary right, abortion would still be the law of our land, indeed, that abortion is the law of the world. It should also be emphasized that the CRLP claim is based at least partially on treaties the U.S. has never ratified and upon UN resolutions that possess no force in law. Though the suit was dismissed for lack of standing, it clearly reveals the intent and tactics of abortion proponents at the international level.

At this point, abortion opponents at the UN can claim a limited victory because abortion proponents have tried to make abortion a universally recognized human right in UN documents, but they have failed. They have succeeded only insofar as they have been able to obfuscate the meaning of words (specifically, "reproductive health") for their own purposes.

The Future

The greatest concern on the horizon is the International Criminal Court, ostensibly a war-crimes tribunal that came into force in the summer of 2002. One draft document on the Court included the term "forced pregnancy," which could have been used to attack pro-life laws as "crime(s) against humanity." Abortion proponents have long advocated what they call a "rights-based approach" to "reproductive health." The International Criminal Court will probably be used to advance this approach.

The good news on the international front is the increasing close contact and collaboration between pro-life movements across the globe. It is now typical that pro-life leaders, including governmental leaders, work closely together to thwart the advance of abortion-on-demand. A growing governmental and non-governmental coalition at the international level, which fights the dangerous mischief of the abortion lobby at the UN and the European Parliament, may undo the damage of recent years and pave the way for advances in the cause of life.

Austin Ruse is President of the New York-based Catholic Family and Human Rights Institute (C-FAM), an international non-governmental organization focusing exclusively on UN matters. Mr. Ruse is also founder and President of the International Organizations Research Group.

Endnotes

1 Center for Reproductive Law and Policy (CRLP), "The World's Abortion Laws," 1999 (hereafter, "CRLP").
2 United Nations Population Division, Department of Economic and Social Affairs, *Abortion Policies, A Global Review*, 2001 (hereafter, "Population Division").
3 CRLP.
4 *Ibid.*
5 Population Division.
6 *Id.*
7 *Id.*
8 CRLP.
9 *Ibid.*
10 Population Division.
11 CRLP.
12 Population Division.
13 *Ibid.*
14 *Doe v. Bolton*, 410 U.S. 179 (1973).
15 Jean-Frederic Poisson, Chief of Staff of Christine Boutin, Member of French National Assembly, interview with author.
16 Interview with the Catholic Family and Human Rights Institute (C-FAM), August 1, 2002.
17 See, for instance, CRLP report prepared for the Committee on the Elimination of All Forms of Discrimination Against Women (CEDAW), "Supplementary information on Argentina," August 2002.
18 See the CRLP website, www.crlp.org.
19 International Conference on Population and Development, Programme of Action, paragraph 7.6.
20 See World Health Organization web page, www.who.int.
21 Fourth World Conference on Women, *Platform for Action*, paragraph 94.
22 Beijing +5, Women 2000: Gender, Equality, Development and Peace for the 21st Century, paragraph 12.
23 Habitat, paragraph 136–f.
24 Agenda 21, United Nations Sustainable Development, paragraph 6.26.
25 Earth Summit +5, Special Session of the General Assembly to Review and Approve the Implementation of Agenda 21, paragraph 30.
26 UNFPA, *State of the World Population*, 2000.

27   *The Center for Reproductive Law and Policy vs. George W. Bush, Colin Powell and Andrew Natsios,* United States District Court, Southern District of New York.
28   *Id.*